Voices from the Second Republic of South Vietnam (1967-1975)

Cornell University

K. W. Taylor, editor

Voices From the Second Republic of South Vietnam (1967-1975)

SOUTHEAST ASIA PROGRAM PUBLICATIONS
Southeast Asia Program
Cornell University
Ithaca, New York
2014

Cornell Southeast Asia Program Publications
640 Stewart Avenue, Ithaca, NY 14850-3857

Studies on Southeast Asia Series No. 65

Printed in the United States of America

ISBN: hc 9780877277958
ISBN: pb 9780877277651

Cover: designed by Kat Dalton

TABLE OF CONTENTS

ACKNOWLEDGMENTS

We are grateful to all of the contributors in this volume for participating with their remembrances of the Second Republic of South Vietnam. We are especially grateful to Phan Cong Tam for his initiative and practical assistance. He provided the initial inspiration for this project and his good advice has kept it alive to the point of completion. We are indebted to Deborah Homsher, Fred Conner, and Sarah Elizabeth Mary Grossman of Cornell University Southeast Asia Publications for their professional work in preparing the publication of this book.

VOICES FROM THE SOUTH

K. W. Taylor

It is common to think of the Republic of (South) Vietnam as a unified entity throughout the two decades (1955–75) during which the United States was its main ally. However, the domestic politics in South Vietnam at that time went through a dynamic wartime trajectory from authoritarianism to chaos to a relatively stable experiment in parliamentary democracy. The stereotype of South Vietnam that appears in most writings, both academic and popular, focuses on the first two periods to portray a caricature of a corrupt, unstable dictatorship. There has been little effort to evaluate what was achieved during the last eight years.

The essays in this book were written by men who strove to build a constitutional system of representative government amidst a desperate war for survival with a totalitarian state. They did this within the framework of the Second Republic (1967–75). Those committed to realizing a non-communist Vietnamese future placed their hopes in the Second Republic, fought for it, and worked for its success. This book aims to be a step in making their story known, for the positive achievements of that time were far from negligible.

During the third quarter of the twentieth century, the transitions experienced by various peoples from colonial rule to national states varied from country to country. The Vietnamese experience was especially complex and prolonged because divergent Vietnamese opinions about postcolonial futures became entangled in ideological differences related to competition among global superpowers. In this introduction, I suggest a historical context for the Second Republic that indicates Vietnamese agency as well as the policies of great powers. I also examine salient issues arising from efforts to evaluate the Second Republic and suggest an analysis from Vietnamese perspectives.

The inhabitants of what were the French colonial territories of Indochina, which included the contemporary countries of Cambodia, Laos, and Vietnam, lived in the shadows of war for half a century, from 1940 to 1990. The first phase of wartime experience was as part of the Japanese empire during what is variously called the Pacific War or the Second World War in Asia.

After the fall of France to Germany in 1940, Japan arranged with the pro-German Vichy government of France to occupy Indochina and to mobilize economy and infrastructure in support of Japan's military operations in southeastern Asia and the

Pacific Ocean. The French administration remained in place as a convenience for the Japanese, allowing Tokyo to focus its attention on distant battlefields in Burma and on the islands of Southeast Asia and the Pacific.

Japan's most significant contribution to modern Vietnamese history was to intern the French and to take over the administration of Indochina in March 1945. This was a defensive measure by the Japanese against the prospect of the French colonial army turning against them as Allied forces drew near. This event marked the climax of rising tensions between the Japanese and the French; both armies stockpiled rice, which contributed to widespread famine in northern Vietnam during the winter of 1944–45. The Japanese disarming the French was the end of the French colonial regime. It meant that the French had either to accept that their dominion over Indochina was finished or that they had to fight their way back in; they chose to try the latter.

When Japan surrendered in August 1945, the next phase of war commenced as the French endeavored to reestablish their prewar position in Indochina. The French were resisted by Vietnamese forces that increasingly came under the leadership of Communists in the North gathered around Ho Chi Minh, who managed to eliminate or disable their Nationalist rivals. This war, which lasted until 1954, has been called the French War, the Franco–Vietnamese War, and the First Indochina War. When Chinese Communists gained control of China and by early 1950 began to assist the Vietnamese Communists, the conflict expanded into an aspect of the global competition between Communists and Anticommunists, a political divide that had been alive among Vietnamese since the 1930s.

Nationalist Anticommunist Vietnamese either rallied behind a Vietnamese government formed under French supervision with the ex-emperor Bao Dai as its titular head, or they withdrew from politics, waiting for a chance to establish a government that was neither Communist nor under French control. The most prominent of these "waiters" was Ngo Dinh Diem, to whom Bao Dai eventually entrusted his government in 1954. It was at this time that the French began to withdraw from Vietnamese affairs as part of an international agreement giving independence to the three Indochinese countries but leaving Vietnam in the care of two antagonistic governments. The Communists under Ho Chi Minh gained possession of North Vietnam while South Vietnam came under the control of Ngo Dinh Diem and his nationalist followers.

One issue that has exercised scholars and journalists is a problem of terminology. Since nationalism was such a potent force in the era we think of as modern history, and since for several decades many afforded to nationalism a respect and sense of legitimacy above any other ideological inclination, the question of whether or not the Vietnamese Communists should be allowed to claim sole proprietorship over the term Nationalist has been a fundamental issue in efforts to interpret modern Vietnamese history. Of course, from a Vietnamese perspective, this issue is not so difficult, since Vietnamese Communists after 1945 were allied with an international movement that claimed to consider class identity as a higher priority than national identity. Consequently, Anticommunist Vietnamese have considered themselves to be the true Nationalists who prioritized a national identity above formulations of class struggle. This view is eloquently expressed in Nguyen Cong Luan's memoir, *Nationalist in the Viet Nam Wars*.[1] Since a purpose of this volume is to present the voices of those who

---

[1] Nguyen Cong Luan, *Nationalist in the Viet Nam Wars: Memoirs of a Victim Turned Soldier* (Bloomington and Indianapolis, IN: Indiana University Press, 2012).

worked for the success of the Second Republic as a vehicle for Vietnamese Nationalism, as distinct from Vietnamese Communism, and who endeavored to expand the possibility of a modern Vietnam that could supercede outdated traditions without violent revolution, I find no compelling objection to using the terminology of those who invested the energy of their youth in this endeavor.

When the Chinese Communists began to assist the Vietnamese Communists in 1950, the United States began to support French and Nationalist Vietnamese forces. After 1954, the United States pursued a policy of supporting the Nationalists in the South, while the Soviet Union and the Peoples Republic of China supported the Communists in the North. This became the context for the next war, variously called the Second Indochina War, the American War, and the Vietnam War, which broke out in the late 1950s and lasted until 1975.

Events transpiring during the two decades between the end of the French war and the unification of North and South Vietnam under the Communists are generally treated as a single war. However, from a southern perspective, during that time there were three phases of warfare, politics, and government. During the First Republic (1955–63), under Ngo Dinh Diem, a relatively stable government was established in Saigon during the late 1950s. However, the government in Hanoi initiated a policy to overthrow the South using political agitation, terror, and guerrilla operations. At the same time, American policymakers grew increasingly critical of Ngo Dinh Diem because of his reluctance to expand the political base of his government beyond family members and trusted associates. For his part, Ngo Dinh Diem grew distrustful of the Americans because of their Laotian policy, which gave North Vietnam access to South Vietnam's border with southern Laos, and because of the dramatic escalation of American military personnel in South Vietnam under the Kennedy administration, which threatened to overwhelm Diem's government and to discredit his nationalist credentials.

Furthermore, Ngo Dinh Diem and the Americans did not agree about how best to respond to the northern threat. Ngo Dinh Diem believed military and security matters needed to be addressed before opening the political system to broader participation, while many Americans believed it should be the other way around. Amidst this incipient impasse, unanticipated events produced a crisis. In 1963, Ngo Dinh Diem's elder brother, the Roman Catholic Archbishop of Hue, provoked Buddhist leaders in Hue to resist the Saigon government. Hue was the precolonial royal capital of Vietnam and the center of a nationalist movement led by Buddhist monks inclined to be politically active. Public demonstrations against Ngo Dinh Diem's government led by Buddhist monks spread to the major cities of South Vietnam in the summer of 1963, causing American leaders to lose confidence in him. The First Republic ended with the murder of Ngo Dinh Diem by military officers encouraged by the US government to mount a coup d'état.

During the ensuing four years (1963–67), called the Interregnum Period, the southern government was led by military officers with the collaboration of civilian administrators. At this time, the fire of war spread as increasing numbers of North Vietnamese and American soldiers entered the country. At the same time, until 1966, there was much domestic turmoil and many changes of government; public disorders arose from shifting relationships among the military officers, from the activities of politicized Buddhist monks who had played a role in bringing down the First Republic, and from efforts by other religious and political groups to promote or oppose change.

In 1967, a new constitution was promulgated and implemented, bringing into existence the Second Republic (1967–75), which, under the presidency of Nguyen Van Thieu, stabilized politics and increasingly took responsibility for its own existence as US troops withdrew and, in 1973, departed for good. During these years, ordinary citizens, educators, journalists, politicians, businessmen, administrators, lawyers, judges, military leaders, and diplomats endeavored to establish a constitutional government based on relatively open elections with an executive, a legislature, and a judiciary. Having recently emerged from a colonial regime and from the struggles of a tumultuous decolonizing process, without traditions of constitutionalism or of democracy, with a neighboring state intent upon destroying the experiment, and with an ally in the process of abandoning the effort, the country nevertheless persevered and achieved many successes.

The Second Republic's record of accomplishments has been ignored by nearly all who have written about the last years of the war; it is an embarrassment to Americans because one of the main ideas propagated by the anti-war position, which eventually came to dominate American academic and political thought, was that the government in Saigon was an unredeemable dictatorship that did not deserve American assistance, or that in any case it was doomed to fail. This idea gave moral comfort to Americans who might otherwise have been troubled by turning away from a threatened ally in time of need; it was an idea that reflected American frustration rather than what was happening among the Vietnamese. The voices in this volume reflect the aspirations and efforts of men who were dedicated to the future of the Second Republic.

At least four major achievements were made during the Second Republic. First, from a military point of view, the South Vietnamese army (Army of the Republic of Viet Nam, hereafter ARVN) took over battlefield duty. While the Tet Offensive of 1968 turned American public opinion against the war, it had a very different effect in South Vietnam. The losses suffered by the Communists enabled the government to regain control of most of the countryside and to implement policies supported by the rural population. Furthermore, by bringing war into the cities, the Communists rallied urban populations against the Communists themselves; large numbers of people understood that they now had something worth fighting for: the Second Republic. With the ensuing withdrawal of American forces, Vietnamese assumed increasing responsibility for their own country.

In 1970 and 1971, ARVN, in cooperation with or with the logistical support of US forces, launched major cross-border operations in Cambodia and Laos in efforts to reduce the North Vietnamese ability to use those countries as bases for attacks against South Vietnam. These operations were costly and controversial, but they also developed ARVN's capabilities and experience while keeping North Vietnamese forces at bay. During the Spring Offensive of 1972, when nearly all American ground troops had redeployed out of the country, ARVN, with US logistical support, repelled an all-out, three-front invasion from North Vietnam. Nevertheless, three years later, without the material and moral support of an ally, the Second Republic was overwhelmed.

Second, in the wake of the Tet Offensive, security was sufficiently restored in the countryside for a land reform program to be implemented that revolutionized the economy, the society, and the politics of most rural areas. Although largely ignored by foreign observers, it made possible a more equitable relationship between urban and rural areas and the building up of the country's agricultural potential as the basis for future economic development. Furthermore, that this land reform was implemented peacefully and with the support of the rural population was in stark contrast to the homicidal land reforms in China and North Vietnam, offering a clear rationale for fighting the war.

Third, major achievements in rice production and distribution, market management, oil exploration, and fiscal policy positioned the country for eventual economic independence as US aid declined. A new generation of administrators, many of them trained at American universities and with strong nationalist aspirations, brought reformist, pragmatic, and activist attitudes to an entrenched government bureaucracy inherited from the colonial past. In the face of serious, even desperate, problems facing the country, the administration of the Second Republic revealed a capacity for bold initiatives despite the draining away of resources as the American ally faded into the distance.

Fourth, large strides were made toward a constitutional system of government with multi-party elections for a bicameral legislature and with a relatively independent judiciary that strengthened legal procedures for protecting individual rights and democratic norms of politics. American critics tended to evaluate Vietnamese constitutional progress by making comparisons with what they considered to be the achievements of their own system of government, which was nearly two centuries old. But if measured against the recent Vietnamese past of colonial domination and war, the Second Republic displayed many progressive features.

These achievements do not mean that there were no flaws in the Second Republic. Many postcolonial states, including both of the Vietnamese states, were excessively dependent upon resources provided by larger powers. In contrast to North Vietnam, the most serious flaw in the Second Republic was its dependence on an unreliable ally. The leaders of the Second Republic tended to take the American alliance for granted and did not find a way to preserve it or to replace it when US policy shifted away.

The Second Republic was defeated in a propaganda contest among Americans in which it suffered from being conflated with the faults of the First Republic and the Interregnum. Of course, as can be done with any country, and especially a struggling new country with formidable enemies, a critical eye can find flaws. But critical Americans, in their great-power hubris, went even further to question the legitimacy of the Second Republic as a sovereign state. Furthermore, the peace agreement that the US government negotiated with North Vietnam reflected this attitude by compromising the constitution and the sovereignty of the Second Republic.

Just as France presumed to negotiate on behalf of (and to the detriment of) nationalist Vietnamese with the Geneva accords of 1954, so did the United States with the Paris Agreement of 1973. Ngo Dinh Diem considered the Geneva accords to have been negotiated over his head by the French with his enemies, and Nguyen Van Thieu considered the Paris Agreement to have been negotiated over his head by the Americans with his enemies. Both the accords and the agreement contained provisions that either potentially or in fact handicapped nationalist Vietnamese.

One reason the Geneva accords have been controversial is that France adhered to an international agreement that ostensibly acknowledged the Vietnamese communist claim to represent a sovereign state, meanwhile neglecting to ratify the treaty granting independence that had been negotiated with the nationalist Vietnamese represented by Bao Dai. This conceit of retaining sovereignty in the South was the initial basis of French designs to retain the direction of affairs in Saigon until the expected unification "elections" to be held after two years, as mentioned in the accords.

Ngo Dinh Diem rejected this design as a continuation of the French colonial presumption to make decisions about the future of the Vietnamese. The election held in

October 1955 by Ngo Dinh Diem to discard Bao Dai and thereby to open the way to proclaim the First Republic was, in effect, a nationalist declaration of Vietnamese independence from France. This was possible because the Nationalists found an ally in the United States. However, when the Americans eventually made a deal with the Communists that enabled the United States to disengage from Vietnamese affairs, the Nationalists found nowhere else to turn.

Perhaps there was no way to overcome this fundamental flaw of lacking reliable allies when the enemy's allies remained engaged to the end. And maybe there was no way to overcome the handicap of being associated in the minds of Americans with the failures of the First Republic and the Interregnum Period. But it can be argued, as some of the authors in this volume do, that the Second Republic could have increased its effectiveness in managing its alliance with the United States by more actively participating in the arena of American public opinion in order to prolong and maximize US commitment to its survival, however daunting that may have been considering the domestic turmoil that was absorbing American attention.

There is no question but that the Second Republic struggled with serious problems; most, if not all, of these problems were in some way related to the fading away of external assistance and the need to build internal strength to withstand the pressure of an enemy that retained the support of powerful patrons. The essays in this volume by Tran Quang Minh and Nguyen Duc Cuong describe efforts to restructure the economy and to plan for self-sufficiency. Ho van Ky-Thoai describes how, in 1974, US naval ships watched from afar as Chinese communist forces took over the Paracel Islands, unwilling even to rescue South Vietnamese sailors from a ship sunk by the Chinese. This indication of US military disengagement should perhaps have alerted Saigon that no further American help could be expected in time of need; the failure to be disabused about any expectation of further US assistance and to plan accordingly may have been the most fundamental failure of the Second Republic, yet there was apparently no plausible alternative to the American alliance.

Strategic and tactical battlefield decisions made by Nguyen Van Thieu during the fighting of spring 1975 are easy to criticize, but what exactly could have been done to obtain a better result in the end is not at all obvious. Since the final departure of American military forces in 1973, US support for the Second Republic had rapidly faded away. Meanwhile, the enemy army had been allowed by the Paris Agreement of 1973 to remain in the country to be strengthened, reinforced, resupplied, and trained for further campaigns.

It can be argued that the Second Republic's commitment to constitutional democracy was a handicap in comparison with the totalitarian regime in North Vietnam, which mobilized the entire population for war and suppressed any dissent. It is true that a diversity of opinions with a relatively free press and relatively free elections resulting in opposition politicians active in the National Assembly and a not entirely subservient judiciary precluded the kind of national mobilization that occurred in the North. But this is exactly what the war was about. To mimic the total control of culture, society, and politics that characterized communist rule in the North would have removed any good reason for the South to continue the fight.

• • •

The essays in this volume emerged from a symposium held at Cornell University in June 2012. They represent a diversity of experiences and perspectives during the

Second Republic of Vietnam, 1967–75, and reveal the aspirations and efforts of Vietnamese to build a constitutional democracy in wartime. The project of establishing a viable democracy and of implementing reforms and policies to attain that goal occupied the thoughts, the hopes, and the efforts of many Vietnamese, despite harsh wartime conditions and the distortions produced by an ally that at first overwhelmed national interests and then disappeared. I want to express gratitude for the courage of these authors. After decades of writings by Americans that have denigrated the Second Republic, these men have retained their voices, and they now write with the knowledge of their experience and with the integrity of their thought.

Bui Diem's essay is based on his experience of Vietnamese politics since the 1940s and of several years serving as a diplomat in the middle of the Saigon–Washington relationship. He offers a thoughtful retrospective on the long-term struggle between Vietnamese Communists and Vietnamese Nationalists that predated and postdated American involvement; in his view, the manner of US involvement and of the subsequent US disengagement handicapped the Nationalists in a way that the Communists were not handicapped by their foreign allies.

Phan Cong Tam served in the Central Intelligence Organization (CIO), which was similar to the CIA (Central Intelligence Agency) in the United States. His account provides information about the formation, organization, and development of the CIO, and about his experiences working on a variety of international issues, including the Paris Peace Talks, the 1970 turmoil in Cambodia, and diplomacy with the leader of an African country.

Nguyen Ngoc Bich narrates his efforts to represent the South Vietnamese government in the United States and other countries amidst the pro-Communist propaganda that animated the anti-war movement. His career was essentially that of an educator as he endeavored to engage and refute fashionable falsehoods about the Second Republic.

Tran Quang Minh was a professor of veterinary medicine who served in various government agencies and ministries related to agricultural production and marketing, including the 1970 Land to the Tiller land-reform program. His essay provides a lively personal account of his more than decade-long work in the agricultural sector of the economy.

Nguyen Duc Cuong served as cabinet minister in the Second Republic with responsibility for economic development. His essay provides a description of the South Vietnamese economy during the years of rising American military involvement, but particularly focuses on his efforts to adjust to the withdrawal of US aid during the last years of the war.

Phan Quang Tue provides a vivid account of his father's and his own political careers during the First and Second Republics. His father, Dr. Phan Quang Dan, was a prominent critic of the government of the First Republic, and both he and his family suffered as a result. Phan Quang Tue describes growing up with his famous father, his own career in the judiciary of the Second Republic, and his campaign for a seat in the House of Representatives during the election of 1971.

Tran Van Son narrates the events of his family during the twentieth-century wars and his own career as a naval officer, his experiences as a member of the opposition in the National Assembly after being elected to the House of Representatives in 1971, his postwar incarceration by the Communists, his escape from Vietnam by sea, and his later career in émigré politics in the United States.

Ma Xai served as an opposition member of the House of Representatives in the National Assembly throughout the Second Republic, being elected in 1967 and again in 1971. His essay provides an account of the Tan Dai Viet Party and its agenda and activities during those years.

Ho van Ky-Thoai served as rear admiral in the navy. His essay is an account of his experience as theater commander when Chinese forces seized the Paracel Islands in 1974 and of how the Vietnamese navy tried unsuccessfully to defend the islands. His account provides firsthand information about this Battle of the Paracel Islands.

Lu Lan's essay is based on his career as a general in the armed forces of the Second Republic. He served in staff and training positions, as division commander, and as inspector general. He provides a thoughtful mixture of analysis and descriptions of events.

The accounts in this volume reflect a great variety of experiences, points of view, and styles of expression. They demonstrate the diversity of aims and opinions among educated people in South Vietnamese society during the 1960s and early 1970s, when the vicissitudes of civil war and foreign intervention provoked rapid change and a succession of crises in leadership, in political organization, in military operations, in economic well-being, in social peace, and in administrative policy. This diversity reveals the most fundamental reason for the war when it is compared with the totalitarian society of North Vietnam. The pasteboard stereotype among Americans at that time and later, even to this day, of the Second Republic government as a dictatorship that deserved to be defeated is perhaps a convenient slander, but it is a slander nevertheless. The efforts of Vietnamese to create a democratic government under adversity is a story that has yet to break through the self-serving American myths that have shrouded what is probably the most reviled abandoned ally in US history. The aim in compiling this volume is not only to retrieve Vietnamese voices from the Second Republic before they are gone, but also to give Americans the option of finally, after nearly half a century, seeing more clearly the ally for whom thousands of American youth died.

CHAPTER ONE

A VIETNAMESE PERSPECTIVE ON US INVOLVEMENT IN VIETNAM

Bui Diem

On the many issues related to the Vietnam War, one can say that with the passage of time we have already in many ways tempered our judgments. However, the fact remains that the US involvement in Vietnam was devastating in terms of its political, social, and economic consequences on American society. There can be no doubt that it was a watershed in American history. In this respect, in other forums during the past decades I have expressed my view that history likely will never render a clear and final verdict as to why in the first place the United States got involved in Vietnam, this faraway land in Southeast Asia, and as to what went wrong during the war and why American and South Vietnamese forces failed to prevent North Vietnam from conquering South Vietnam. Many of those who opposed the war at that time continue to consider the US intervention wrong, even immoral, and many of those who supported the war continue to believe that it could have been won if only the United States had had the stomach to see it through to the end. The arguments on both sides probably will continue as long as there are different views and opinions, not only on Vietnam but also on larger issues such as those pertaining to the US role in the world, the use of US military forces overseas, or in general the advisability of US intervention abroad on any level or in any fashion (for example, in the cases of Afghanistan, Iraq, or Libya).

Rather than attempting to address these issues, I will focus on the modern history of Vietnam. Mine is simply a non-communist Vietnamese perspective, in general terms, on the whole episode, and I will share some of my views and experiences accumulated through a decade (from February 1965 to the end of the war in April 1975) during which I served the Second Republic of Vietnam. In fact, as a Vietnamese who happened, by the hazards of his assignments (minister in the prime minister's office in Saigon, ambassador in Washington, DC, and later a roving ambassador-at-large), to be an eyewitness of what was going on, I had the opportunity to watch American and

Vietnamese leaders in South Vietnam at work during the peak of the US involvement in the mid-sixties as well as at the end in 1975. Hopefully, these reflections of mine could, in some small way, contribute to "the quest of wisdom" that all of us are looking for, in terms of lessons from that tragic war.

FROM MERE INTEREST TO COMMITMENT AND INTERVENTION

Getting back to the very beginning of American interest (not yet involvement) in what was going on in Indochina, we know that when the war in the Pacific against Japan was nearing its end, Major Archimedes Patti from the OSS was sent to Vietnam in an attempt to establish a clandestine network along the border between North Vietnam and China. While there he helped the Viet Minh to train their first guerrilla units. This initiative lapsed after the death of President [Franklin] Roosevelt with the United States busy on a wide range of post-war activities. The establishment of the Democratic Republic of Vietnam by Ho Chi Minh in September 1945 was treated as a non-event by a Truman administration apparently trying to keep its distance from both the French colonialists and the emerging communists. The French Indochina war broke out in December 1946, but the United States remained neutral until the collapse of the US-supported Chiang Kai Shek regime and the coming to power of Mao Zedong in 1949. Concerned about the rise of the communists, the United States then decided to take sides by starting a military program of assistance to the French and pressuring the French to accept the pro-western Bao Dai solution, considered as an acceptable alternative to the Hanoi communist regime. There was then no direct US involvement as yet. The Eisenhower administration, still cautious in its ambivalent support of the French, chose not to rescue them when they were beleaguered at Dien Bien Phu in 1954. But as we can see from later events, this was simply a pause on the road toward involvement. After the war in Korea and the Geneva Accords of 1954, US involvement became quite visible with the decision to help the government of Prime Minister (later President) Ngo Dinh Diem in South Vietnam through a program of economic and military assistance, and especially with the Kennedy administration sending no fewer than twenty thousand advisors to Vietnam by 1963. Then, by way of the tragic deaths of two presidents (President Diem killed in a coup in Saigon and President Kennedy killed in Dallas by an assassin's bullet) came the very turning point of the situation involving the two countries.

By now, you know already the rest of the story of this long and uneven process of involvement. Having to face a serious deterioration of the military and political situation in Vietnam in the aftermath of the 1963 coup and for fear of a takeover by the North Vietnamese Communists, the Johnson administration intervened directly and massively in the war, right at the beginning of 1965. Here, perhaps I don't have to get into the history of the war because simply by mentioning the familiar names about the US strategy at that time, such as search and destroy operations, limited war, gradual escalation, light at the end of the tunnel, Vietnamization, etc., all of us can remember how inconclusive the war was until the days after the Tet attacks in 1968 when American public opinion forced the Johnson administration to think of finding a way out of the conflict. The era of tortuous negotiations began, but fierce fighting continued for a few more years before the Paris Agreement of January 1973, negotiated by Henry Kissinger of the Nixon administration, brought an end to the war, at least on paper. The real end came two years later with the fall of Saigon in 1975 under the indifferent watch of President Ford.

THE US INVOLVEMENT AND ITS NATURE; THE VIEWS OF A VIETNAMESE

So, as the above chronology indicates, the process of US involvement in Vietnam is a long one. It took three decades, and up to seven presidents, from Roosevelt to Ford, Democrats and Republicans, to travel the road from initial interest to commitment, involvement, and disengagement. For this extraordinarily long process, is there some cogent explanation? Quite naturally, those critics of the extreme left are very quick to respond by saying that the United States intervened because an imperialist power always tries to dominate the world. There are also those who think that in assessing its own interests the United States exaggerated the geopolitical importance of Vietnam. There are even those who choose to have an easy and convenient explanation: it was for the independence of South Vietnam and its freedom. Apart from all these explanations, in all honesty, I think that many of us can admit that the dominant and central fact of US foreign policy, beginning with the Marshall plan in Europe, had all along been anti-communism, a policy that George Kennan called containment.

Obviously, it is not up to a Vietnamese to pass judgment on how the United States defined its interests; besides, at the time of the US intervention, not many Vietnamese knew anything about Kennan or his containment doctrine. But looking back at this period, Vietnamese cannot help being impressed by the fact that, at the onset, the United States and Vietnam had nothing in common and that if it were not for the fortuitous geopolitical events and international circumstances of the post World War II era, these two peoples would never have come together. Indeed, two nationalities, quite apart in terms of geographical location, international status, civilization, culture, and conceptualization, were thrown together at a time when the Vietnamese knew almost nothing about America and Americans knew even less about Vietnam.

Personally, I still remember those days in the fifties and early sixties. The few notions that I had about the United States involved the generous Marshall plan to help Europe, the prestigious General Douglas MacArthur in the war in Korea, and especially the idealistic inaugural address of John F. Kennedy: "We shall pay any price, bear any burden, meet any hardship, support any friend, oppose any foe, in order to assure the survival and the success of liberty." South Vietnamese knowledge and understanding of the United States was limited, but the attraction to what America represented in the world was irresistible and that was the reason why, in their fight for freedom against both the French and the communists, they looked upon the Americans as their natural friends and allies. In their innocent eyes, the American military intervention was simply a logical continuation or extension of US policies in Europe (Marshall plan, Greece, Berlin airlift) and Asia (Korea) aimed at containing the expansion of combined Soviet and Chinese power. They knew that the presence of foreign troops on their side could be a psychological handicap in their fight against the communists, yet somehow they did not even question the virtue, or the right or wrong, of the American intervention.

South Vietnamese faith in America was rock-solid simply because, in the trusting and naive minds of most Vietnamese citizens, they believed that such a powerful and seemingly omnipotent nation as the United States could not be wrong. But if the faith of the South Vietnamese in American power was total, their ignorance about America's people, culture, and politics was equally profound. The great majority of Vietnamese, including the southern leadership and intellectual elites, did not have a good grasp of the American political process. Having lived too long under one authoritarian regime or another, the Vietnamese could not evaluate the influence and power of public opinion on the US Congress or on the president and his administration. South Vietnamese leaders, mostly military men, especially those who served during the years of the Second Republic, had close contact for many years only with their American military counterparts, and in many ways were influenced by the generally conservative ideas of the US military establishment. They could not believe that the United States would soon be compelled to withdraw from Vietnam. In politics, perception quite often counts more than facts. In this respect, the Vietnamese perceived the Americans as having a contingency plan for every situation and, of course, the CIA was believed to be behind everything. These misperceptions gradually led to an abdication of judgment on their part and to increased reliance on the Americans. They failed to understand the real nature of the US intervention, making erroneous assumptions about the staying power of America and, in the process, without knowing it, abdicated their own role in the war. In effect they gave to the outside world the impression that the war was purely an American war. The Americans for their part did nothing to dispel this notion. Either out of impatience or overconfidence, they came in and tried to do everything themselves, armed with the belief that there was no problem that could not be solved if Americans set their minds to do it. The mood was simply "let's do it" and they did it, with, at one time, almost half a million men in Vietnam. How could anyone say that it was not an American war?

I can best illustrate the innocence and naiveté of the South Vietnamese by my own experiences. In this respect, in 1964, as a journalist, I made an initiation trip of three months to the United States. After that trip, I wrote some articles about life in America and what I had seen in San Francisco at the Republican National Convention (with Senator Barry Goldwater selected as Republican candidate in the presidential election of that year) and later, in August, at the session of the US Congress when the Tonkin Gulf Resolution was adopted (the resolution authorized President Johnson to take military action against North Vietnam after the USS *Maddox* was attacked by torpedoes in the Gulf of Tonkin). From that time forward, I was seen by many South Vietnamese as something of an expert on American affairs. Thinking of it, I cannot help but be embarrassed because there is a mountain of difference between even the little that I know now about America, American policies and politics, and what I knew then in the 1960s.

The above-mentioned few examples illustrate what I said earlier about the lack of understanding of the South Vietnamese about America. The Americans, for their part, did not have any better understanding of Vietnam. This was bad enough with regard to their allies in the South, but it was about the enemy, too, the Hanoi communist regime in the North, and that was what turned out to be a serious flaw in the US strategy for the conduct of the war. The whole concept of gradual escalation was, in this context, a vivid example of misunderstanding. It was based on the assumption that at some point the communists would have to accept a compromise because the cost would be too high for them to go on fighting. The truth of the matter was, after having been assured publicly that their territory would never be invaded, the communists found that if they could extend the war indefinitely they could win simply by not losing. By the some token, the search and destroy operations in the South ultimately became a hide and seek game in which the communist forces controlled not only the place, but also the tempo of the fighting, when and where they were strong. When they were not strong, they could hide in their sanctuaries in North Vietnam, Laos, or Cambodia. Thus, they only had to survive and wait for America to tire of the war.

The list of errors and mistakes throughout the years by both Americans and South Vietnamese is a long one, but if I can afford a general reflection on the US involvement, I would say that what was most shocking to the South Vietnamese was the cavalier way in which the American administration and the American Congress dealt with South Vietnam during the last years of the war. Of all the successive phases of US involvement, from the intervention in 1965 to the Americanization of the war, the subsequent Vietnamization, and finally the disengagement, it is the disengagement that will linger most in the memory of the South Vietnamese. The US administration used its enormous weight to lean on us, alternating promises and threats to force us to accept the Paris Agreement, yet the US Congress failed to honor even the clauses spelled out in the agreement when in 1974 and 1975 it was no longer a matter of American blood but only a matter of resupply costing a few hundreds of million of dollars. Such abandonment of an ally was unworthy of a great power and certainly not one of America's finest hours. Fortunately, that blot on a page of the American history book was to a certain degree (here, one has to be fair) compensated for by the generosity of the American people who welcomed hundreds of thousands of Vietnamese refugees and offered them the opportunity to remake their lives and to prosper in a free society.

ONE MAN'S VIEW OF THE VIETNAM WAR

One of the many characteristics of the Vietnam War is its complex nature. The root causes of the tragedy in Vietnam are many and the US intervention was not the only one. In the first place, we must understand that even during the time of the French occupation a profound and latent disagreement, if not conflict, existed between Vietnamese nationalists and communists over the future of the country once the goal of independence would be reached. But starting by the end of World War II we have to mention the obduracy of France, which in the late forties refused to concede independence in good time to a people who hungered for it. Then there was the ideological obsession of the Vietnamese communists, who, not content to fight a dying colonialism, relentlessly sought to impose on the Vietnamese people their dogma of class warfare and proletarian dictatorship. The massive intervention by the United States came only in the mid-sixties, as part of an overall containment policy whose roots were in the Cold War itself. Of all these forces that shaped the lives of the Vietnamese during the three decades of the war, French colonialism is dead and gone, and as for communism, no one but the blind any longer argues the merits of this dying system. But American intervention is a living issue. In the wake of failure in Vietnam, and in the face of hard choices elsewhere, the questions about its correctness and wisdom still dominate American policy debates. Americans still learn the lessons on intervention, as do other small countries that cannot help but see in the fate of South Vietnam intimations of their own possible future.

It has been said that America lost its innocence and arrogance in Vietnam. As I have already written in other papers, as a Vietnamese, I would say that South Vietnam had no arrogance to lose, but instead lost its innocence and in the process also lost its existence as a free nation.

CHAPTER TWO

TESTIMONY OF A SENIOR OFFICER, SOUTH VIETNAMESE CENTRAL INTELLIGENCE ORGANIZATION

PHAN CONG TAM

My education was in public administration at the National Institute of Administration (NIA), a public college to train administrators for various government positions. I graduated in January 1962 and was assigned to work at the Central Intelligence Organization (CIO), which had been created just a few months before. I did not know anything about intelligence as a field, and the mysterious nature of the job concerned me. More surprising was the fact that of the twenty graduates from the NIA, I was the only one selected by the CIO to work in its Clandestine Operations Branch. The then-CIO Commissioner Colonel Nguyen Van Y called me in to meet with him and announced that the agency had decided to send me to operations. At the end of the short meeting, he left me with the following advice: "You are now riding on the back of a tiger. Do not try to jump off. You will break your legs, to say the least."

My father was a government employee for over forty years. Although he worked for the colonial administration, he was once arrested and mistreated by the *Sûreté* (French investigative police) because he had a sibling and many cousins with the anti-colonial resistance fighting for independence. My father did not distinguish a police or security agency from an intelligence agency. It took me several months to gather the strength to tell my father about my appointment to the first job of my life. When I finally did, he said he would shave his head and live the rest of his life as a monk.

The CIO existed in shadow during the last year and a half of the First Republic. The change of the regime in 1963 propelled the agency into action, but frequent changes of leadership, both at the national level as well as at the CIO level, delayed its growth. When the political situation of the country stabilized after the 1967 presidential election, the CIO embarked on the road to maturity.

I spent my first year and a half at the CIO mainly in training and learning on the job. When the agency launched its first domestic operations after the fall of the First Republic in 1963, I had my first experiences in operations as chief of one of the seven domestic operation units that had just been established. The CIO was reorganized in 1969, and this was the starting point of the last but most productive period in the agency's life. I was then named to head the Directorate of Operational Planning that had been created by the new reorganization. In this capacity, I assisted the commissioner in directing special operations and conducting special missions abroad. I also acted as the CIO representative in joint task groups with other intelligence and national security agencies.

In the first part of this essay I will recall the circumstances of the creation of the CIO and share my experiences with the conduct of one of the first domestic operational units of the agency. I will also discuss the 1969 reorganization and highlight the main achievements during the last years of the agency's life. In the second part, I will recall three missions that I undertook in France, Cambodia, and Central Africa.[1] I will offer some personal thoughts at the end of the paper.

THE CIO IN HISTORICAL PERSPECTIVE

The CIO in its Infancy

After successfully ejecting the French from Vietnam and establishing domestic security and order, President Ngo Dinh Diem faced a critical challenge: a war had just started in 1958 and the Republic of Vietnam (RVN) had an army with little combat experience and was short of officers. On the insurgent side, the National Liberation Front (NLF) reactivated units covertly left behind in the South after the 1954 Geneva Convention. In Saigon, political opponents of President Diem openly challenged his leadership. The United States began sending military aid and more advisors to South Vietnam.

In November 1960, a military coup caught the regime by surprise. The coup failed, but the Diem government suspected that the US embassy had encouraged the coup. US–Vietnamese relations became more difficult. It was under these circumstances that the CIO was created. President Diem signed a decree for the creation of the CIO in May 1961, but it wasn't until 1962 that the new agency put into place an organizational structure and began recruitment and training.

It is important to note that at the time of the creation of the CIO, South Vietnam had a small intelligence agency operating from the Office of the President, the Services for Political and Social Studies (SPSS). The SPSS's main mission was to conduct intelligence collection and activities for the protection of the regime. It had limited activities outside the country, mainly in neighboring Cambodia. It had no specific activities directed toward North Vietnam. Counterintelligence was not developed until the Special Task Group from Central Vietnam (STGC) uncovered a network of North Vietnamese Strategic Intelligence.

The CIO was modeled after the American CIA, which had been created in the aftermath of World War II. There were two major components in the agency's first structure: the Directorate of Research was charged with intelligence analysis and estimates and the Directorate of Operations was the clandestine operational arm of the agency. The CIO's main mission was to collect strategic information in support of the war. As SPSS continued to function, the CIO remained in shadow and proceeded to build its image as a professional and "nonpolitical" organization. This shielded US advisors from political implications while they helped to construct the agency.

---

[1] For some individuals in this section I will abbreviate their names in consideration of their privacy.

In the beginning, the CIO reached out to the NIA and the Saigon University Faculty of Law for staffing its Research Branch. Graduates from these two institutions, especially the NIA, constituted the core professional staff of the CIO in Research and Administration. With few exceptions, military officers dominated the Directorate of Operations.

The military coup of November 1, 1963, ended the First Republic with the murder of President Ngo Dinh Diem and his brother Ngo Dinh Nhu. I had the privilege of meeting Diem in his office in the Independence Palace in 1954 when he had just returned to Vietnam to assume the position of prime minister. Throughout my high school years I witnessed his successes in building South Vietnam as well as his agony in trying to defend the country.

My first exposure to communism was associated with an image of violence and war. I grew up in South Vietnam during the struggle for independence. At the age of eight I lived in constant fear, because at nightfall communist cadres went from house to house in my village, kidnapped the nationalists, tied their hands together with their legs, and threw them into the river. One of those victims was a cousin of my father. This type of execution was called *mo tom*, literally, "catching shrimp."

I believed that the Diem regime had a cause and a vision for a free Vietnam. The regime did extremely well during its first four years. Somehow it began to make mistakes thereafter. (Some critics contended that the regime had become arrogant after its successes.) The worst mistake was the handling of the Buddhist crisis, which precipitated the failure to work out a partnership agreement with the United States to fight the war. I regretted this loss of opportunity, and I deplored the killing of Diem and his brother.

The CIO in Transition

Just days after the 1963 coup, the new military regime ordered the arrest of the key leaders of the SPSS and the STGC. The new regime then hastily dismantled these two agencies because they were accused of making illegal arrests and of torture. Further, political groups pressured the new government to release "political" prisoners jailed during the First Republic. Among those released were some key figures of the North Vietnamese intelligence network that had been arrested by the STGC. The 1963 coup also brought back some military leaders from exile in Cambodia (who fled after the 1960 failed coup against the Diem Regime). Along with these officers were some agents of North Vietnamese intelligence. These actions enabled North Vietnamese intelligence to recoup and to resume activities.

With the elimination of the SPSS, the CIO emerged as the only functioning national intelligence agency. All new commissioners tried to redirect the agency into fulfilling the task left by the SPSS's demise, which was to collect information for the protection of the regime. All attempts in this direction met with a passive reception from the core staff members, who continued to believe that their agency was immune to politics. Furthermore, all these reform attempts proved to be in vain because of the political instability following the coup. Five commissioners, all military officers (four generals and one colonel), succeeded one another during a four-year period from 1963 to 1967, each one averaging a term of less than one year.

While this political disturbance continued, US advisors pushed for the launch of the first domestic operational units. By the end of 1963, when the first case officers graduated from the basic training for clandestine operations, the CIO organized its first domestic operations. Seven units, named Special Operational Corps (SOC), were set up by the Directorate of Domestic Intelligence and posted at key regional locations around the country. The SOC's mission was to infiltrate the North Vietnamese organization in the South, called the Central Office for South Vietnam (COSVN), starting at the provincial level and moving up from there. US advisors were posted at regional levels and they provided direct support to the SOCs.

Within a short period of time the SOCs became effective, producing intelligence reports that captured the attention of regional and local military and civilian agencies. While some regional and local security and military agencies welcomed the SOCs, others felt as though the SOCs were duplicating their own efforts. Bureaucracy also impeded the successes of the SOCs. Although the SOCs were undercover units, they were placed within regional divisions of the military and security organizational structure. The relationship between the SOCs and Military intelligence or National Police and Military Security was not well defined. Competitiveness and jealousy hampered success and increased the risk of the SOCs being compromised.

Another factor worth mentioning was political in nature. I headed an SOC covering the twelve provinces of the Mekong Delta from 1964 to 1966. These provinces were in the territory of the Armed Forces 4th Tactical Zone and Corps Command (IV Corps). The corps commander was Lieutenant General Dang Van Quang. It was known at the time that General Quang had an odd relationship with the prime minister, Air Marshall Nguyen Cao Ky. The prime minister wanted to remove Quang from office because he opposed the central government's policy of allowing US troops to operate in the IV Corps area.

On a quiet Sunday afternoon in 1965, I received an order to report to Quang immediately. When I walked into his office, Quang asked if I knew anything about an attempt to kidnap him. He told me that he went to Saigon by helicopter and "Ky's men" tried to force his helicopter down (but failed). He went on to say that I headed a unit that reported directly to Saigon and that I had US advisors working with me in the region.

Quang was a strong man in the region. He launched a successful program to re-arm the religious sect of Hoa Hao to supplement his fighting troops. Quang therefore viewed the coming of US troops as unnecessary and a possible threat to his reputation and power. About a year later, a campaign accusing Quang of corruption led to his departure from IV Corps. It is my understanding that CIA declassified information has indicated that these corruption charges were overblown by enemy propaganda. Quang later joined the Office of the President, and I will return to him later in this essay.

The Delta SOC earned an award from the CIO in 1965 for producing high value intelligence reports and for successful penetration of the enemy provincial committee of Ca Mau province. This was just a small step on the long road ahead. The toughest challenge in pursuing the SOC mission was to find motivation for recruitment of infiltration agents. The other problem worth mentioning was intelligence fabrication, which had become a booming market in the Mekong Delta at the time.

After I spent two years in the Delta, a large package of dynamite exploded in the alley separating my residence and a US Army Signal Company. I was not in the house at the time of the explosion and therefore escaped the drama. However, this incident led me to decide that it was about time to take a break. I returned to my roots at the NIA and claimed an award (earned five years previous as top graduate of my class) for a two-year study tour in the United States.

While I was studying in the United States, South Vietnam organized a presidential election in 1967. I was now temporarily out of the CIO and in a place where expression of political conviction was free and unhindered. I thought it was a proper moment to voice my support for a civilian candidate because I was so disappointed with the past four years of military leadership. It seemed as though South Vietnam's generals were simply busy grasping for power and left the fighting in the hands of US troops. The "young" nationalism that was built by Ngo Dinh Diem during the First Republic had evaporated. The coming of US troops was a necessity, but the military government took no action to educate the rural population about the reasons for the arrival of US troops in Vietnam. Millions of dollars were poured into the campaign to expose the atrocities of the communist regime. While this campaign seemed to work if one observed daily life in Saigon and other urban centers in South Vietnam, it was countered at night by the communist propaganda machine portraying the regime as another manifestation of "western imperialism."

It was at that point that a friend of mine, an armed forces officer who happened to be in the United States for training at Fort Leavenworth, Kansas, contacted me. He attempted to convince me to support General Nguyen Van Thieu. He warned me that a civilian regime would not survive another military coup. He then assured me that, if elected, General Thieu would appoint a civilian prime minister and would consider returning power to a civilian government when the political situation became stable.

Just a few months later, the Tet Offensive struck South Vietnam. This tragic event wiped out all political thought that went through my mind at that time. I completed my studies in the summer of 1968 and headed directly to Saigon. I reported back to the CIO. A day after my return, I was asked to take over the Directorate of Domestic Intelligence.

South Vietnam had a new government, with General Nguyen Van Thieu as president and Air Marshall Nguyen Cao Ky as vice president. I had heard that this government had made an understanding with the administration of the newly elected President Nixon by backing out of the departing President Johnson's peace initiative. Thieu strongly believed that Nixon would adopt a much tougher stance toward North Vietnam. Thieu then moved to consolidate his power. As part of this process, he named his private secretary, Lieutenant Colonel Nguyen Khac Binh, to take over the CIO. The new commissioner spent his first six months in the office drafting a plan for reorganizing the agency.

From Professional to Political: Maturation of the CIO

The reorganization plan was completed in 1968 and went into effect in 1969. This reorganization did not change the basic structure of the agency; it simply rearranged some key functional components to enable the new commissioner to keep direct control of all operations and expand the agency's scope of activity beyond the traditional enemy front to also cover friendly organizations, and that included other governmental agencies as well as civilian social and political organizations.

An important feature of the new structure was the creation of the Directorate of Operational Planning, or Section A, at the central office. Section A managed the planning and operations of the CIO. Section A also had a Special Operations unit that operated from the central office. The chief of Section A was often called to assume special missions on behalf of the agency. While special operations were long-term intelligence activities, special missions were usually one-shot events in response to a crisis, a request for assistance from another government agency, or an opportunity for initiating an intelligence operation. Section A was also in charge of joint operations with other governmental agencies and it also staffed the National Council for the Coordination of Intelligence and Security, which I will elaborate below.

Under the rubric of Section A, the commissioner took over a special unit, the A10, which was charged with the responsibility of preparing the Daily Intelligence Bulletin for the president. Somehow this bulletin included only intelligence reports received from the police on political activist groups. Because of the delicate nature of this type of activity, the commissioner put the A10 under his direct supervision.

The 1969 reorganization split the Directorate of Domestic Intelligence into three independent units, each reporting directly to the commissioner. The Intelligence Directorate continued to manage the SOCs. The two remaining units were both in counterintelligence. However, one targeted North Vietnamese intelligence organizations and the other sought to uncover enemy infiltration into friendly organizations.

Some critics have pointed to this latter assignment as a cover for political surveillance of opposition groups. I was not in a position to know the facts. However, I can state confidently that the North Vietnamese Strategic Intelligence Network's infiltration of the social, religious, and political organizations posed a serious problem at that time. I mentioned above the release of political prisoners after the 1963 coup. North Vietnamese Intelligence's infiltration into the foreign press corps was another issue. Several North Vietnamese agents worked as double agents for the foreign press corps. They were the sources and contact persons for the press corps and this was how they earned their protection. South Vietnam was at war but was under constant pressure to maintain democracy and to give privileged treatment to the foreign press corps.

External intelligence operations expanded after the reorganization thanks to a budget being provided for this purpose. In addition to the original stations in the neighboring countries of Cambodia, Laos (two stations), and Thailand, the CIO installed three new stations in Paris, Hong Kong, and Japan. The Paris station seemed to stem from the peace talks taking place there. Hong Kong could become useful, but Japan did not serve any need. The CIO should have invested its resources to build a station in the United States instead.

Highlights of Achievements

With the trust of the president, the CIO continued to gain power and influence. It also earned strong support from the US advisory group. The first landmark of success was in the area of prisoner interrogation. A presidential decree had required all government military and civilian agencies to transfer high-ranking North Vietnamese prisoners of war to the CIO for interrogation. As a result, the CIO gained substantial influence over an important area of military and security affairs and experienced tremendous improvement and success. The National Center for Interrogations (NCI) was the unit that benefited the most from this change. By having access to the high-ranking prisoners of war, the NCI became highly productive in terms of both delivering interrogation reports and developing leads for counterintelligence operations. At least three operations were launched in Europe following interrogation reports produced by the center.

I can recall one particular case of a North Vietnamese network infiltration being detected through interrogation at NCI. In a skirmish, local forces had sunk a small boat and captured some prisoners and seized a large amount of South Vietnamese currency and some military maps. The captured leader claimed that he was a high-ranking officer of a local militia. The CIO Special Operations unit (Section A) pieced together information connecting this incident to intelligence it had received six months previously regarding a message from COSVN to its central office requesting additional supplies of maps and money. A scenario was constructed and it led to the prisoner admitting that he was sent to the South via the sea to make contact with a number of cells of the Strategic Intelligence Network. His cooperation enabled the CIO to uncover a large network of North Vietnamese intelligence operatives in two government agencies, one military and one civilian.

The NCI was well equipped and staffed with highly trained interrogators and never used violent methods of interrogation. During the war, Phu Quoc Island served as the detention center for some 25,000 North Vietnamese prisoners. During one of my frequent trips to the island, I was told of a rumor among the prisoners that being taken to the CIO for interrogation was just like going to a luxury hotel. During the early 70s, the center provided leads and sources that enabled the Special Operations Unit of the A Section to launch a long-term cross-border operation.

The creation of the NCCIS, which I mentioned above, was another landmark. The NCCIS represented a smart move to connect intelligence with security. It further solidified the status of the CIO as the central focal point of the intelligence and security community. General Dang Van Quang, former commander of the Armed Forces IV Corps, then assistant to the president for military affairs, chaired the NCCIS. The NCCIS had no budget and had to be staffed by the CIO. The CIO commissioner was one of the three permanent members along with the heads of Military Security and National Police. The Section A chief headed the Council's Task Group for Joint Operations.

The CIO had a steady relationship with the CIA station in Vietnam. During the time of the SOCs, US advisors worked directly with regional units. They touched base with the central office only for appeals or interventions. The reverse trend started in 1969 when the relationship was beefed up. It was structured and functioned from the top down. There were more advisors, more support, and more cooperation.

It was in this context that the CIO refrained from putting a station in the United States. On at least two occasions, I used my access to the NCCIS to bring up the need to have a CIO station in the United States. Both times I was told it was not necessary. As the CIO maintained a good working relationship with the CIA's Vietnam station, both the president and the commissioner did not see the need to post agents in Washington, DC. This one-way communication certainly affected the CIO's ability to collect intelligence of strategic importance. In the following section on special missions, I will recall an incident in Paris that illustrates this point further.

Special Missions

Special missions were usually short and most often carried out by Section A. I have selected three missions in which I was personally involved. All three were overseas. These are meant as examples of the various activities of the CIO in support of or related to foreign affairs.

Paris 1969: Keep the Secret Talks Secret

In the summer of 1969 the CIO Station in Paris sent in an intelligence report about a secret meeting between Henry Kissinger (then national security advisor to President Nixon) and North Vietnamese representatives. "Surprise" was not really the right word to describe our reaction when this report reached the CIO. The Paris station had recently been set up and there was no way it could have produced an intelligence report of such magnitude. As the report contained information about high profile politics, the commissioner immediately reported it to the president. There was also an immediate show of interest from the US advisory side. I later heard from the commissioner that the president had called US Ambassador E. Bunker after he read the report.

Back at the CIO, the commissioner recalled Major T. V. H. (the Paris station chief) back to Saigon. He then asked me to rush to Paris. My objectives were to take control and find out what was going on. On the day that I landed in Paris I went directly to the station (which was located on the fifth floor of the General Consulate of Vietnam building) to meet with the bewildered staff, especially Army Captain N. who was the case officer of the project that had sent in this sensational report.

I began debriefing contacts with the sources that provided the information. As I have just mentioned, Captain N. ran an intelligence project with two paid informants: agent code name Ph1 operated in the Vietnamese French political circle in Paris, and agent code name Ph2 functioned inside the French intelligence and security agencies. I conducted intensive debriefings with Ph1 and Ph2. Ph2 was the main source for the intelligence report about Kissinger's secret meeting, although Ph1 had also heard about it. After a few more contacts, Ph2 finally gave me the names of the sources at the *Sûreté* from whom he had obtained the information. I then called in a number of contacts to cross-check. Thanks to a few of my old high school classmates, living and working in Paris at the time, I met "commissaire" C. of the municipal *Sûreté*. The information appeared to be accurate and I was told by one source that there was electronic evidence to back it up. I was not able to determine the motivation for the leak, if there was any. Perhaps it was just a patronizing act from an old colonial ruler. I reported the result to Saigon and also indicated that I had now taken direct control of the project.

Soon Saigon ordered the termination of Ph2. This order came as no surprise to me in light of the intensity of the interest from the advisory side. However, I still had hope that the station could continue this project and work co-operatively with our advisor on-site. As regards to the case officer who ran this project, Army Captain N., Saigon wanted him back home and it had to proceed in a way that would not allow him a chance to defect in France. This proved to me that the central office wanted the case to be closed.

I spent a few months after this in Paris trying to "reorient" the station by developing new leads. During that time I continued to hear about the secret meetings through my contacts. I did not act on this intelligence given that my direct orders were to "keep off." After a few months in France, I returned to Saigon for a brief time and then took on an assignment in Cambodia.

Cambodia

Prince Norodom Sihanouk once said that both Ho Chi Minh and Ngo Dinh Diem wanted to "swallow Cambodia." From this statement, I presumed that the prince believed a civil war in Vietnam to be somewhat beneficial to Cambodia. My next presumption was that in order to maintain this war he had to allow North Vietnam a way to get into the South. As is well known, President Ngo Dinh Diem broke off diplomatic relations with Cambodia in 1958.

In March 1970, a coup led by General Lon Nol ended Prince Sihanouk's regime. Cambodian military leaders stated that they had to stop North Vietnamese aggression. The news of the regime change in Cambodia brought a huge sense of relief in South Vietnam. However, media and intelligence reports revealed that Cambodian soldiers and civilians were attacking and killing large numbers of ethnic Vietnamese living in Cambodia. The Vietnamese media associated these violent activities against ethnic Vietnamese in Cambodia to the traditional ethnic tension between the two countries dating back to the seventeenth century. The South Vietnamese government welcomed the regime change but expressed concern about the violence against the ethnic Vietnamese. It then sent a delegation to Phnom Penh to assess the situation and work with Cambodian authorities to end the violence.

The delegation was headed by Tran Nguon Phieu, South Vietnamese Minister of Social Affairs, a physician by training and a veteran independence fighter. The armed forces as well as the CIO sent representatives to join the delegation. I arrived in the Cambodian capital city of Phnom Penh on May 18, 1970, with two objectives: to assist the delegation and to set up a field station for the CIO.

The delegation was lodged at the Hotel Royal. Our host, the Cambodian Ministry of Foreign Affairs, warned us that the situation was still dangerous and that we should not leave the hotel without a police escort. The first night at Hotel Royal I threw an antenna through the hotel room window to establish contact with Saigon and then slipped out to make contacts. On the third night, I came to a building on Ohna Peich Avenue where the South Vietnamese Embassy had previously been located. The gate was closed, but I broke in and spent the whole night looking through the dusty files still undisturbed in a dozen file cabinets.

My work for the delegation and the CIO were intertwined. My first goal was to touch base with the ethnic Vietnamese in Cambodia (over half a million strong). These people were either brought to Cambodia during the colonial era to fill jobs in administration or were attracted by other opportunities in Cambodia. Ethnic tension between the Vietnamese and Cambodians had lessened during colonial times; however, the 1970 coup seemed to reignite it.

When I arrived in the capital city of Phnom Penh, acts of violence by Cambodians against ethnic Vietnamese, including robbery and murder, were still widespread. In the capital city, most Vietnamese either hid or disguised themselves and tried to seek refuge anywhere they could. Those who could afford it paid their way to get out of the country. The remaining civilians left their homes and sought refuge in some sixteen camps throughout the city. These camps were mostly in Catholic churches or other Catholic facilities. By early May, the staff of the delegation reported that some 180,000 Vietnamese lived in these refugee camps.

Refugees occupied every inch of the churches, filling the main yards, and flocking to the churches to escape the violence. There were no toilets and the smell was awful. Refugees slept on the wet ground and were so crowded that the camp workers had to give out sponges soaked with ether to children and elderly people to prevent them from fainting. The pastor of the Catholic Parish of Russey Keo—the first Vietnamese Pastor in Phnom Penh—told me that he had come to Cambodia twenty-five years before to serve the Vietnamese Catholic community in Phnom Penh. Now he wanted to take his parishioners back to Vietnam.

In rural areas, the situation was more severe. Attacks against Vietnamese occurred even in daylight. People had no refugee camps to go to and had virtually nowhere to hide. Those who had money bought their way through several checkpoints in order to get to Phnom Penh. They said that getting to Phnom Penh increased their chance of survival by 50 percent. I had the opportunity to join a boat trip up the Mekong River to Battambang Province in order to evacuate the Vietnamese from this area. There were about a dozen boats piloted by South Vietnamese Navy men. Each boat had a member of the delegation and a Cambodian police officer. At the end of the day, on the way back to Phnom Penh, all boats were overburdened. Along the river shore, people were kneeling, crying, and begging the ships to stop to save them. We felt helpless and extremely frustrated. This and other similar situations triggered some regrettable actions by isolated and undisciplined Vietnamese military men on assignment in Cambodia at the time.

From what we could see, the Cambodian government seemed unable or unwilling to stop the violence. Instead, they urged the Vietnamese to leave Cambodia, though they did not have the means to enable them to do so. Some Cambodian leaders deplored this attitude and argued that the "deportation" of the Vietnamese out of Cambodia would hurt its economy. Kapun Khan, a former minister in the Cambodian cabinet, said that manufacturing companies in Cambodia employed some 600,000 workers of which some 80,000 were skilled Vietnamese workers.

Each day planes coming to Phnom Penh's Pochentong airport were loaded with cargo only. But when they left, they were overloaded with passengers. Every morning I would go to a refugee camp, pick up as many refugees as I could, then proceed to the airport, wait for a landing, and then load them on for their trip to safety. I put people in the space near the cockpits, in the toilets, in the aisles. Pilots always refused at first, but relented after I told them that if they did not take these people, their lives would be in danger at nightfall.

As the violence persisted, camps filled up, supplies fell short, and infectious diseases flared. Dr. Phieu fell under mounting pressure from the Cambodian government to evacuate the Vietnamese in Cambodia to Vietnam. A mass evacuation of Vietnamese from Cambodia back to Vietnam would create a multifaceted problem for South Vietnam, and the most significant one involved national security. This mass evacuation would give North Vietnamese cadres an excellent escape route from Cambodia and a "legal" means of entering South Vietnam. Dr. Phieu, the delegation chief, said that at the moment we had no choice but to "swallow the snake." After consulting with Saigon, the South Vietnamese delegation adopted a slow evacuation plan while talks with Cambodian authorities continued. The first mass evacuation occurred by boat after Cambodia allowed a South Vietnamese Navy Fleet to enter Phnom Penh in mid-May 1970. The fleet left Phnom Penh on June 2 with almost ten thousand refugees. The official list contained only about eight thousand names, but 9,400 were counted on board when the ships left.

My second objective in Cambodia, as mentioned above, was to establish a field station on site. This required me to travel back and forth from Hotel Royal and my new site office at Ohna Peich every day. My presence at the old embassy compound soon attracted ethnic Vietnamese seeking my help. The first of these said they carried a lot of money to bribe their way out of Cambodia. Every one had suffered losses of property and loved ones. They begged for a way to safety. Day by day more people came and, as I expected, some of these were, in fact, undercover North Vietnamese agents. It was a tremendous opportunity for intelligence collection and recruitment.

For eighteen years, North Vietnam had enjoyed a monopoly of action in Cambodian terrain. The North Vietnamese had indeed created a very effective party apparatus within the Vietnamese community in Cambodia, and used it to support its war in the South. Under this apparatus, various local Vietnamese organizations in Cambodia used aggressive measures to acquire supplies, collect "dues," and mobilize youth to be drafted to fight in the South or to become liaison cadres for the North Vietnamese intelligence network. Intelligence reports indicated that the recruitment of youth to be drafted to fight in the South met resistance from the community.

I began to establish contact with Cambodian intelligence and security agencies. My access to President Lon Nol's entourage was through his younger brother, Lieutenant Colonel Lon Non, director of Military Security. Lon Non was the leader of "the Group of Five." These were the five most powerful men in the security and intelligence community in Cambodia at the time. Lon Non welcomed contact with South Vietnamese intelligence and had a hobby of collecting sophisticated "espionage devices" and weapons, which he claimed were requested by his brother. I also worked closely with Ly Ngau, director general of the Cambodian National Police. Ly Ngau communicated with me in French for three months until he revealed that he was born in Vietnam. Ly Ngau was very cooperative whenever I intervened for the release of Vietnamese who were victims of mass and unjustified arrests by Cambodian Police.

In July 1970, I was the target of an ambush, which resulted in the death of one of my staff. The incident occurred when a group of youth stopped my car in front of Sisowath High School. I was not in the car. They mistook one of my staff as their target, made some kind of declaration, and then stabbed him to death. The Cambodian Police were quick to identify the Marxist Youth Group as responsible for this action.

As has been long recognized, North Vietnam used the border areas with Cambodia as safe zones for the transportation of supplies. Among the main supplies that moved through this area was rice to feed troops in the South and chemicals, among them potassium chlorate (an agent in explosives), to be used for terrorist activities in Saigon. Key to this area of activity was a small group of Chinese merchants who were rich enough to buy off Cambodian authorities and who collected millions for their import–export activities. They imported illegal and legal materials into Cambodia and then sold them for use by North Vietnamese troops and Communist organizations in South Vietnam.

One night, I managed to get invited to a lavish party at a durian plantation in central Cambodia. It was amazing to mingle with these big business men and hear them making deals that I knew would result in many deaths in my country.

For a long time, Cambodia served as a sanctuary for North Vietnam's COSVN. Cambodia also served as a transit base and safe house for North Vietnamese Strategic Intelligence networks operating in the South. Following the 1970 coup in Cambodia, North Vietnamese spy infiltration into the South by way of the sea increased because the inland road via Cambodia was more or less closed.

By the end of the summer 1970, South Vietnam established formal diplomatic relations with the new Cambodian government and the CIO station in Cambodia was already functioning.

The Daughter of President Bokassa of the Central African Republic

Jean-Bédel Bokassa served with the French Army in Saigon during the early 1950s. He met a Vietnamese woman and fathered a daughter. By the time he left Vietnam in

1953, the girl was about six months old. He remembered the young baby by a scar she had on one of her thighs as the result of a small pox vaccination. In 1971, Bokassa, now president of the Central African Republic, asked the French Embassy in Saigon to find his daughter. The French Consulate in Saigon found a half-Vietnamese, half-African young woman and sent her to Central Africa. Bokassa welcomed the girl but later declared that she was not his biological daughter. Bokassa then intensified his pressure on the South Vietnamese. He threatened to cut off diplomatic relations with South Vietnam and initiate diplomatic relations with North Vietnam if his daughter could not be found. The media in South Vietnam widely published the story and characterized it as a fairy tale. Bokassa's daughter, Nguyen Thi Martine, lived at that time in Bien Hoa, a city twenty-five kilometers east of Saigon, and earned her living by carrying bags of cement. Her uncle read the news and the family gathered enough money to travel to Saigon. They went to the Ministry of Foreign Affairs and were kicked out as a scam. Thanks to the persistence of the daily newspaper *Trang Den*, the Ministry of Foreign Affairs agreed to cross-check and verify her identity. Once this task was done, the ministry then contacted the office of the president of the Central African Republic and made plans to reunite Martine with her father.

The Ministry of Foreign Affairs prepared a delegation headed by its number three man that included Martine; her mother, Nguyen Thi Hue; and the editor of *Trang Den* newspaper. The ministry also raised the issue of safety. There was, of course, the previous failed attempt at reuniting father and daughter by the French General Consulate in Saigon, and also the potential for a significant North Vietnamese diplomatic gain if South Vietnam failed to reunite Bokassa with his daughter this time around. The plan selected an itinerary to avoid a stopover in France or any communist country. The trip had to be conducted in secrecy. At the last moment before departure, the ministry went to the president and asked that the CIO also be involved. I was asked by the CIO commissioner to join this delegation as a security officer just two and a half days before it departed. Therefore I had minimal input into the pre-departure planning.

When I came to the ministry early on the morning of January 8, 1971, to depart with the rest of the delegation, I sensed immediately a potential problem: Staff members from the ministry had Martine dressed up in a traditional Vietnamese dress (*ao dai*). Martine was tall and she looked almost totally African. To have her wear a Vietnamese dress was to draw uninvited curiosity that could lead to compromising the secret nature of the trip.

Martine and Phan Cong Tam in Nairobi, Kenya, enroute to the
Central African Republic. Photo from the author's personal collection.

On the second day of the trip, at around 3:00 AM, during an unexpected layover in
Bombay, a Japanese journalist (of the *Shizuoka Shinbun*) spotted Martine. I had to let him
take a picture of Martine in exchange for his promise to keep it secret until our final
destination. Our delegation stopped again in Nairobi without incident, but the last stop
before the final destination was somewhat hectic. When we walked out of the Kinshasa
(Congo) airport terminal, four cars rushed in and men in civilian clothes pushed us into
the car without a word. We were taken by car to a suburban location. Only at
dinnertime were we told that they were sent by the Central African government to take
care of us. The next morning we were airlifted to Bangui by President Bokassa's private
aircraft, a beach craft with a French pilot.

Once we arrived in Bangui, we were greeted by the South Vietnamese ambassador
to Central Africa and the Central African minister of protocol and taken by motorcade
to the palace where the whole cabinet and the diplomatic corps were waiting. When
Bokassa arrived, he ordered our delegation into a private room. When he walked into
the room, the first thing he did was to pull Martine's trousers down to look at her thigh
for the scar. It was there. At this magical moment, I noticed an immediate

transformation in his expression. Bokassa then hugged Martine and broke into tears. I felt a sense of relief and was also touched by what I had just seen. Before I took this trip, I had read some rather ambiguous reports about Bokassa. But this emotional reunion seemed to erase all of these negative thoughts.

After awhile, the South Vietnamese Ambassador introduced the delegation to Bokassa. In an apparent attempt to score points, the ambassador introduced me as a colonel from President Thieu's security detail. He then went on to say that because Thieu cared so much about the safe transfer of Bokassa's daughter to Bangui, he had sent his personal security officer along with the delegation. These remarks earned me special treatment during my stay in Bangui. Bokassa turned his attention to me and said that he did not owe anyone but President Thieu for the safety of his daughter. While he asked me to thank President Thieu, he seemingly forgot or omitted to do the same to the man who actually led the delegation, as well as the Vietnamese news reporter who had helped to find his daughter in the first place. Bokassa praised Thieu for keeping South Vietnam safe. He thanked Thieu for keeping his daughter alive. He went so far as stating that if ever President Thieu was overthrown by a coup, that he would be welcome in Central Africa.

After the ceremony, I was separated from the delegation and escorted by the minister of protocol to a luxury hotel (the only one in the country to lodge VIP guests). There was a half squad of honor guards in front of the hotel. The minister took me into a large suite with champagne and roses (imported from Paris, he said). Before leaving the room, the minister pointed to a picture on the wall and said: "This is the picture of President Mobutu of Congo. He stayed in this room last week."

Because I grew up in Vietnam during French colonial times and was educated in a French high school, I was able to communicate with President Bokassa in French. He enjoyed talking about his memories of Vietnam. These conversations also brought back memories from my teenage years during the French Indochina war. Bokassa served in the French Army Saigon Cholon Battalion. Sometimes he rode a motorcycle to deliver military mail. He burst into laughter when I told him that I remembered those "Motobecane" that were so slow but worked forever, the same kind he used to deliver mail. Bokassa then paused, turning serious, raising his finger and cursed in Vietnamese. He had become angry remembering an accident in which a military truck hit him one day as he drove by the central fire station in Saigon. That accident broke his finger. Bokassa enjoyed drinking. After a few drinks, he grasped a guitar and sang a Vietnamese song:

> Co Muoi Co Chin hai co may muon co nao?
> Muon dat no di dung cho Ma no hay
>
> [Miss number ten or number nine, which are you interested in?
> If you want to take her out, do not let her mother know]

In Vietnam, children are often referred to by the order of their birth instead of their first name, and families with ten children were common. This song was popular in bars frequented by French soldiers.

Bokassa did get into serious conversation sometimes. He was curious how President Thieu was protected from being overthrown by a coup. He said he likes military men and does not trust civilians. He jokingly offered to make me a general if I wanted to stay in Bangui and work for him. I had heard that Bokassa overthrew the previous president to seize power, and the South Vietnamese ambassador in Central

Africa later told me that the current president was Bokassa's uncle. His primary concern was his own safety. This explained his attitude toward me.

I had noticed a white man who always stood by Bokassa's side during official ceremonies. He introduced himself as Mr. Alexandre. The South Vietnamese ambassador later informed me that he was a Frenchman and a political counselor to Bokassa. The ambassador said that Bokassa loved to show off. One day he went to the Bangui jail, took a German prisoner out, and hit him. The ambassador said that Alexandre had once said of Bokassa: *"C'est un toqué"* (He is a madman).

At the end of the first day in Bangui the delegation was invited to a dinner party with the president. To my great surprise we were taken to a place call "Hong Ha Vietnamese Restaurant" where we were served Vietnamese–French cuisine. The owner was a half-Vietnamese and half-French man who had visited Bangui once and was subsequently invited by Bokassa to open this restaurant.

I had about a day to get to know the capital city of Bangui and meet the extremely small Vietnamese community in Central Africa. There were only four Vietnamese citizens living in Central Africa. They were Catholic nuns who came to the country as missionaries with a vow to serve for life. I met these four nuns in their convent and they informed me that there was yet another Vietnamese in the Central African Republic, a "great man" they said, not a living person but a dead man in a grave. It was the grave of a former Vietnamese emperor, Emperor Duy Tan, who was exiled by the French to Reunion Island in Africa. Emperor Duy Tan died in a plane crash on his return from a meeting with French General de Gaulle in 1946 and was buried in B'Makai, Central Africa.

The night before my scheduled flight out of Bangui, at about 11:00 PM, I answered a knock at my hotel room. The minister of protocol was at the door and he said the president wanted me to come downstairs for a dancing party. I came downstairs in the large room where about a hundred guests were dancing. They all wore a shirt that read "Papa Bokassa." There were no other members of the delegation or staff of the embassy there. I was taken to the table of honor where Bokassa looked at me with an amused smile. The minister showed me a seat next to a lady and said that her husband was a colonel and he was away on mission. After a while, I was told that I was expected to join in a hunting party the following day. I told the President that I had a ticket for a flight out of Bangui the next day, headed for Paris. He then called on an aide and said: "Close the airport tomorrow." The next day I woke up to discover that there was no hunting as previously announced. I realized by then that he may have given up on me.

I left Bangui on the fourteenth of January on an Air France flight for Paris. As the plane flew over Chad, I kept thinking about the past few days of my life in "luxury"; but I also questioned why my government cared so much for its image in a country that had no connection with the defense of South Vietnam at this critical time. I had the opportunity to live in the United States for two years and I saw the image of South Vietnam being tarnished and there was no significant activity from our government to improve it. Perhaps our leaders took the support of the United States for granted.

CONCLUSION

Despite my reluctant entry, I worked for the CIO from its inception to the end in 1975. I had discovered the high standard of this profession that called for unrewarded sacrifices. I also understood the critical importance of intelligence in the defense of the country. I was glad that I had the opportunity to serve among a highly educated core staff. My father also changed his perception of intelligence work that had been shaped during colonial times when intelligence was known to the public as nothing more than informants for the French *Sûreté*.

The CIO introduced the concept of centralized strategic intelligence and formed a new wave of young professional intelligence officers to carry it out. The CIO was perhaps the only agency in the country that had an overall staff of mostly college graduates or high-ranking military officers (over 60 percent).

The CIO also achieved modest success in intelligence collection and analysis in support of the war effort. It achieved a truly spectacular achievement in the area of protecting the political safety of the regime. Key to this was the success in securing a close relationship with the CIA's Vietnam station.

After 1975, some critics pointed out certain failings in intelligence, especially the failure to understand friends, among which the most important was the United States. If this allegation has any merit, the CIO may share part of the blame. The agency had, in some instances, used resources in the wrong direction. It also relied overmuch on the good working relationship with the CIA station to fulfill its need for strategic intelligence affecting the survival of the country. Although the US advisors acted in good faith, there were instances where information of critical interest to South Vietnam did not reach the agency in time.

In closing, let me return to the incident in Paris in 1969. After the war ended, I discovered that intelligence information regarding Kissinger's secret meetings was given to another leader in addition to the CIO. In a book written in 1985, General Tran Van Don, former defense minister, senator, and one of the leaders of the 1963 coup, revealed that by late summer of 1969 he was also made aware of a secret meeting between Kissinger and North Vietnam representative Xuan Thuy on August 4 of that year.[2]

Contrary to years of misconceptions, South Vietnam's top leaders had known about the secret talks between Kissinger and North Vietnamese representatives since 1969. The reasons why Saigon remained silent and allowed the talks to proceed can only be answered by the parties directly involved. The consequences of these actions, on the other hand, are self-evident.

List of Agencies and CIO Units in Vietnamese

Central Intelligence Organization: Phu Dac Uy Trung Uong Tinh Bao
Directorate of Research: Nha Nghien Cuu
Directorate of Operations: Nha Dieu Vu
Directorate of Intelligence: Nha Tinh Bao
Fourth Armed Forces Tactical Corps: Quan Doan IV
National Center for Interrogation: Trung Tam Quoc Gia Tham Van
National Council for the Coordination of Intelligence and Security:
    Uy ban Quoc Gia Phoi Hop An Ninh va Tinh Bao
Services for political and Social Studies: So Nghien Cuu Chanh Tri Xa Hoi
Special Task Group of Central Vietnam: Doan Cong Tac Dac Biet Mien Trung

---

[2] Tran Van Don, *Les Guerres du Vietnam* (Paris: Vertiges Publications, 1985).

CHAPTER THREE

FROM FACING ANTI-WAR CROWDS TO NATION-BUILDING

Nguyen Ngoc Bich

In May 1975 I arrived in Guam with exactly one pair of swim trunks on me and not a penny to my name. This was in stark contrast with just two weeks earlier when I came to Washington, DC, on a last trip with Gregory Nguyen Tien Hung, sent by President Nguyen Van Thieu, in a desperate attempt to avert the catastrophe of the total cutoff of American aid, which would be the final stab in the back to a near collapsing army.

Of course, Hung and I failed because "the hounds are out," as Sven Kramer, then in the National Security Council, said with tears in his eyes as he embraced me. On the 23rd of April President Thieu resigned in Saigon. Hung chose to stay in Washington, but I decided to go home to report on the failure of the mission. I arrived back in Saigon on the night of April 26, on the very last flight of Air Vietnam into the country, just in time to give my report to my superiors in government;. I then made a U-turn and got out with my wife and a party of twenty-five people.

Much nonsense has been spread in the thousands of books that have so far appeared about Vietnam and especially about the Vietnam War, even Pulitzer Prize-winning books that are found almost universally in syllabuses covering the Vietnam War. I take this opportunity to tell my experience as I lived it working for the government of the Republic of Vietnam in what is called the Second Republic (1967–75).

• • •

I was a graduate student, a doctoral candidate at Columbia University, working on my thesis in medieval Japanese literature when I was asked by Ambassador Vu Van Thai in late 1966 to join the Embassy of Vietnam in Washington, DC. I wasn't sure what prompted him to offer me the post of Second Secretary in the Information Office. I never did find out, since he left his post two weeks after I arrived, to be replaced by Ambassador Bui Diem. It could have been that he had heard about my voluntary contributions (speeches, writings, and editorial comments) to the cause of the southern republic refuting anti-war positions at the time. For instance, I debated anti-war orators at Columbia University and Professor Staughton Lynd at Yale right after he came back from a visit to North Vietnam. Or perhaps anonymous friends, whose identity I have never learned, recommended me.

At any rate, under the new ambassador I was given quite a bit of leeway. This was partly because my direct supervisor, Nguyen Dinh Hoa, was a friend of the family and knew me well. I not only had a good command of English, but I also had some skill as a public speaker. At the embassy, I took responsibility for producing a weekly English-language *Vietnam Bulletin* and a monthly Vietnamese-language *Troi Nam* (Southern Sky). The *Bulletin* was mostly news with one or two features in each issue, whereas *Troi Nam* was a much more engrossing monthly with plenty of interesting features about many aspects of Vietnamese culture, history, and civilization.

When the Paris peace talks started in 1969, the South Vietnamese delegation in Paris produced a semi-monthly called *Tin Que Huong* (News from the Homeland), which was then adapted by me for distribution in the United States with the inclusion of US-related news. These publications and my speaking engagements (which went from seventy in the first year to 110–120 in my last years at the embassy) were enough to keep me extremely busy. From time to time I was asked also to study specific aspects of the war, such as the Tet Attacks of 1968, the war policies of North Vietnam, or trends in student opinion among the Vietnamese students then studying in the United States. Some of these studies were later published by the Vietnam Council on Foreign Relations in Saigon (such as the study entitled *North Vietnam: Backtracking on Socialism*) and translated into other languages (French, Japanese, etc.).[1]

The demand for information about Vietnam was such that, besides the regular news bulletins, I had to come up with a series called Vietnam Info Series, which in the end came to about fifty-five different titles covering every aspect of my country and my people, from education to social services (e.g., medical care, orphanages) to music, art, literature, film, architecture, and land reform. I also published *An Annotated Atlas of the Republic of Vietnam*.[2]

During my four years at the Embassy of Vietnam in Washington, DC, not all my efforts were aimed at refuting the arguments of the anti-war movement. It was not unusual for me to demonstrate also against unfair criticism from the American press and even from authorities pretty high up in the US government. There was the criticism that the South Vietnamese army was not as good as the communist guerrillas facing them because the latter, we were led to believe, were fired by idealism, which is why they fought so valiantly armed with nothing more than primitive weapons such as machetes and pungi sticks or homemade grenades. So I had to demonstrate that the other side's regular outfits were already supplied with AK47s starting in 1964. The ARVN (Army of the Republic of Vietnam) did not get equipped with M16s, the equivalent of the AK47s, until four years later. When I tried to bring these unpleasant realities out on television, the hosts would try to drown me out, so it was a tough fight to reveal the truth even on supposedly friendly territory.

In late 1967, and especially during the Tet offensive launched by Hanoi in early 1968, we learned that there were Chinese troops stationed in North Vietnam from the Chinese border down to Bac Giang, north of Hanoi. When three defectors rallied to the

---

[1] Nguyen Ngoc Bich, *North Vietnam: Backtracking on Socialism* (Saigon: Vietnam Council on Foreign Relations, 1971).

[2] Nguyen Ngoc Bich, *An Annotated Atlas of the Republic of Viet-Nam* (Washington, DC: [Embassy of Vietnam], 1972).

government side with concrete information on the Chinese presence (numbering at least 100,000), I tried to broadcast this fact to the world, but the Americans immediately squashed the story, with the CIA pooh-poohing all of our information as unsupported.

I also had an argument regarding using body counts as an indication of success in war. Robert McNamara, when he was US defense secretary, relied on his World War II experience as a logistics person, thus he wanted to quantify everything as indicators of success. I disagreed with this way of looking at things for two reasons: one, it did not take into account the will of the enemy (cf. the Japanese fighting man in World War II), and two, even from a quantitative point of view, I argued that North Vietnam could go on indefinitely given how the war was being fought. This led me to write about "population, manpower, and food production in North Vietnam," showing that Hanoi could go on much longer than American strategists believed it could.

The Vietnam War was fought by the enemy as a "total war," which meant that it was fought not just in the swamps and jungles of Vietnam, it was fought also in the villages and cities of Vietnam through acts of terrorism, and it was also fought on American campuses and in Washington, DC, where the Communists correctly believed that they would win—as they did in Paris during the First Indochina War.

Thus, my life during the four years that I spent at the embassy in Washington was no piece of cake. There were innumerable encounters that were memorable but which I cannot possibly relate in this short essay. But mention could be made of the time I went to Purdue University to talk about the war and had a grenade thrown at me— fortunately, it was merely a tear gas grenade. Or the time I went to American University in Washington, DC and found myself speaking in a hall guarded by Nation of Islam fighters holding submachine guns at all the exits.

In May 1968, after Martin Luther King, Jr., was assassinated, there was rioting in the streets of Washington, DC, and whole blocks were looted and burned down on 14th Street NW, requiring the posting of National Guardsmen at many corners in downtown Washington. Some of us at the Embassy of Vietnam found ourselves in the ironic situation of going out and helping Americans get food and clothing that was being distributed at various churches around town.

In late 1971, I resigned from my post at the embassy and went back to Vietnam. The immediate reason was because my wife (Dao Thi Hoi, EdD) and I were offered the chance to go back to Saigon to build a university, Mekong University, which specialized in only two fields, Mass Communications and Management. This was because we figured that Vietnam had plenty of good professionals, but things still did not go well simply because we had poor management and were even less skillful at explaining ourselves. We saw the need for such an institution to bring the country into the modern world.

I wasn't acting chancellor of Mekong University for very long when I was asked to join the government to handle the foreign press. During those years there were between two- and three-hundred foreign reporters working in Vietnam at any one time. There were the representatives of all the major news networks (e.g., Reuters, UPI, AFP, DPA, Kyodo); of US television networks, like ABC and CBS; of international radio, like the BBC, NHK, and ABC; and, of course, of all the major newspapers and magazines in the world (e.g., *Far Eastern Economic Review, Newsweek, Time, Life, Le Monde, New York Times, Washington Post, Los Angeles Times, Wall Street Journal,* and *Christian Science Monitor*).

Besides issuing press credentials and handling reporters' many-faceted requests, including arranging for interviews and site visits in a country at war, and helping with interpretation in some cases, the Press Center was responsible for two press briefings a day, one in the morning and one in the afternoon. In most cases, my junior assistants, who spoke French and English well and had good connections in town and with the military, could handle the situations by themselves. But in sensitive cases I myself had to be involved, for instance, for major interviews with President Nguyen Van Thieu. One case in point was Oriana Fallaci's interview with the president, which eventually appeared in her book *Interview with History*.[3] Next to Thieu's interview there appeared also her interviews of Henry Kissinger and Vo Nguyen Giap. Kissinger portrayed himself as a lone ranger riding into town at high noon, whereas Giap readily admitted that he sacrificed half a million men for the folly of the Vietnam War. So in the end, Thieu came out as the much more thoughtful and responsible leader.

Then there was the story of the Tiger Cages on Con Son Island. Don Luce broke the story in *Life* with full color photos taken by Tom Harkin in 1970.[4] From the dramatic photos and Luce's accompanying article, one had the impression that these cages were underground, with the prisoners caged just like wild animals in a zoo. This was far from being the case. I later went there accompanied by a group of foreign reporters who took lots of pictures from the ground level. It turned out that the cells reserved for the more recalcitrant prisoners were quite tall—about eight feet tall—bare but clean, and well aerated, from the grid-like ceilings. Despite the demonstration of such patent falsehoods on the part of Luce and Harkin, the real story never got out—it got squashed in editorial board rooms in the United States—and the *Life* version was never retracted. Such was the prevalence of anti-war sentiments at the time that the truth was no longer honored!

During my time at the Press Center I made friends with dozens of foreign reporters, of whom some became lifelong friends. This was not only because I spoke their language(s); I understood their needs, and tried to help them accomplish their mission. I was not long at the Press Center when Information Minister Hoang Duc Nha decided to create an entirely new branch in the ministry, the Directorate of Overseas Information (Cuc Thong-tin Quoc-ngoai). This was quite a bold move, since traditionally overseas information was a function of the embassies in various countries, thereby belonging to the Ministry of Foreign Affairs. But Nha did not trust the old functionaries at the Ministry of Foreign Affairs and he had the support of President Nguyen Van Thieu. Furthermore, he believed that young specialists freshly out of colleges and universities, with good command of at least one or two foreign languages, are more likely to be aggressive and to blend in more easily with the local population wherever they go. So at first he appointed his friend and Lycée Yersin schoolmate Pham Duong Hien director of the new branch. But when Hien preferred to go to the US to head the Vietnam Information Bureau in Washington, DC, he recommended that I take his place in Saigon. That was how I came to accumulate two government jobs while at the same time continuing to run Mekong University in my private life.

As director of overseas information I oversaw a network of four overseas Vietnam Information Bureaus: one in Washington, DC (run by Hien), one in London (headed by Bui Bao Truc, previously a government spokesman), one in Paris (headed by Pham Ngoc Kha), and one in Tokyo (run by Tran Van Lam, nicknamed "the Handsome Colonel"). With a group of dynamic young people, we worked together quite effectively.

---

[3] Oriana Fallaci, *Interview with History* (Boston, MA: Houghton Mifflin, 1977).

[4] Tom Harkin, photographer, "The Tiger Cages of Con Son, *Life* Magazine (July 17, 1970): 26-29.

For example, let me take the case of Premier Phạm Van Dong of North Vietnam, who was then planning to visit Olof Palme in Sweden. As you are well aware, Sweden under Olof Palme was quite left-leaning, providing sanctuary to American draft-dodgers and welcoming the Bertrand Russell Tribunal, which condemned the United States as an aggressor and war-criminal government. What could we then do to disrupt this chummy Swedish romancing of North Vietnam? We were still at a loss as to what to do when the Communists in Vietnam mortared an elementary school in Cai Lay District, Tien Giang Province, killing twenty-three children and wounding more than forty others. Photos of the incident showed the school yard splattered with blood and the mangled bodies of the children. (But obviously, such a crime did not rate even a mention in the Western press at the time.) Nonetheless, in Vietnam it was quite a big story that outraged people's sensitivities and cried out for condemnation.

Was there a possibility that the story of Cai Lay elementary school could be relayed to Sweden in time for Pham Van Dong's visit? Upon checking, we soon found out that it would be impossible to bring in posters of that cruel massacre by air into Sweden (for they would be stopped right at the airport in Stockholm and confiscated). The only possible way to get the posters there would be by car driving from France, as there was less checking at the border with Norway. Then there was the question of language: the posters would not be very effective if the language was in English or French. Fortunately, I had a Swedish friend who was passing through Saigon at the time. I immediately drafted him and got him to write for me a slogan in big letters: "Is this COMMUNIST HUMANITARIANISM? Cai Lay Elementary School, Vietnam." Since time was of the essence, I had the National Government Printing Office print overnight a couple hundred posters of this tragedy and had them immediately put on an Air France plane going to Paris. Forewarned, our man in Paris, Phạm Ngoc Kha, was ready to receive the posters at Charles de Gaulle airport and immediately set out post-haste to drive through Belgium, Holland, Denmark, and Norway to reach Stockholm in time to greet the North Vietnamese premier. Pham Van Dong's surprise was great, and the Swedish hosts were caught totally off guard when nearly three hundred posters of the Cai Lay massacre, with writing in Swedish, "welcomed" the North Vietnamese premier as he made his way to Premier Olov Palme's office and to the Swedish Parliament. But it was too late and there was not much that they could do since the whole demonstration was totally peaceful!

It was during my tenure as director of overseas information that I was drafted to go on a rather unusual mission. In 1973, because he finally acquiesced to the signing of the Paris so-called Peace Agreement of January 23 that year, President Nixon promised to meet with President Thieu in a summit in the United States. This came to pass in April 1973. I was drafted to go with Hoang Duc Nha and Pham Duong Hien on an advance mission to prepare the detailed itinerary for President Thieu. We later came back to the United States in President Thieu's entourage, which then included Ambassador Bui Diem and Hoang Duc Nha, among others. At the end of the US tour, during which Thieu met with Nixon in San Clemente, President Thieu was a state guest of Vice President Spiro Agnew in DC and spoke at the National Press Club. The whole group then went to Germany and on to Rome, where President Thieu visited the Vatican, after which we flew to South Korea for a meeting with Park Chung-hee and to Taiwan to meet with President Chiang Kai-shek before returning home to Saigon. That was the pinnacle of President Thieu's career. I came home exhausted because of the work that I had to do during the trip, but I was also exhilarated by the experience.

Possibly because he had seen me at work, most especially through the several interviews with important foreign reporters that I had arranged for him, and also through my performance during the summit trip, President Thieu readily agreed when Hoang Duc Nha proposed that I became the new director-general of Vietnam Press, the national news agency of South Vietnam. This was, of course, quite an extensive operation, with branch offices in most major cities inside South Vietnam (Hue, Da Nang, Can Tho) and in many capitals outside Vietnam, ranging from Paris to Bangkok and Tokyo and Jakarta. Each day Vietnam Press issued a stream of news and features in four languages—English, French, and Chinese, besides Vietnamese.

It was during this short tenure that I got to know the working habits of President Thieu. He worked rather late at night and I sometimes got calls from him in the middle of the night, often after midnight or even at 1:00 AM or later. He had a mind that paid close attention to important details, sometimes drilling me at length on the background of prospective interviewers or the ideological bent (if any) of the media that asked for interviews.

The government did not interfere in my work or give me ideological guidelines. That is, I did not have to answer to a party cadre as would be the case of my successors after 1975. I would be called in for consultation from time to time, but it was usually as an equal-to-equal and not as someone summoned in for instructions. And this applied whether my boss was Hoang Duc Nha or, later on, his successors, Ho Van Cham and General Phan Hoa Hiep.

Two incidents occurred while I was at Vietnam Press that deserve retelling. One was the bombing of the presidential palace by a renegade pilot, Lieutenant Nguyen Thanh Trung, on April 8, 1975. Since my office was right across the street from the presidential palace, you can imagine how shook up we all were. But immediately after the explosions there was speculation that this was a coup mounted by Vice President Nguyen Cao Ky aimed at overthrowing President Thieu. The question for me was what to put out, as everybody, the foreign press in particular, was clamoring for some explanation. While I did not get any instruction from the palace as to how to portray the event, I got a visit almost instantly from a friend of Ky, a colonel in the Air Force, who sat in my office and refused to go until I agreed to print a denial from his boss that he had anything to do with the incident. This, of course, put me on the spot. Fortunately, word soon came that Nguyen Thanh Trung had landed in Loc Ninh, in communist-held territory. This allowed me to put out a balanced story in which I could incorporate Ky's denial without appearing as if I was on his side and working against the President. In the evening the National Liberation Front radio confirmed that Trung was their mole, which fully supported my press release during the day.

The other incident was the death by shooting of French reporter Paul Leandri shortly after the fall of Ban Me Thuot. Since this happened at police headquarters, it caused quite an uproar. Colonel Hoang Kim Quy, who many suspected was the man behind the shooting, adamantly rejected even the implication that he was involved. He put heavy pressure on me to use a police-drafted statement that was not very convincing since it left out a great many details. In the meantime, the French ambassador demanded an explanation. The police chief, General Nguyen Khac Binh, I later learned, had to go to CIA station chief Tom Polgar to concoct a version that eventually became the official one. Meantime, those were some of the most uncomfortable hours of my life as I rebelled against what I knew not to be the truth, yet there was hot air literally blown down my neck not to try to dig any further.

My work on behalf of the Second Republic seemed always to put me in the position of mediating between my country and foreigners. Although sometimes it was a difficult and even disheartening task, I was always motivated by a deep love for my country and a strong desire that foreigners be able to see my country as I did.

CHAPTER FOUR

A DECADE OF PUBLIC SERVICE: NATION-BUILDING DURING THE INTERREGNUM AND SECOND REPUBLIC (1964–75)

Tran Quang Minh

My career in agriculture and veterinary medicine was oriented toward executive planning and the implementation of programs in the service of my country, rather than as a bureaucrat concerned with writing official documents. Consequently, I have written this paper as an informal account of my experiences rather than as a formal analysis of events, which in any case is alien to my skills and experience.[1]

After the First Republic of Vietnam's land reform program in the 1950s, my mother retained about two hundred acres of rice land in Chau Doc Province that she had inherited from her father, who had been a district chief in various provinces of the Mekong Delta during the French colonial administration. Vietnamese landlords

---

[1] This essay is based on my experiences as a direct participant in the events described, on the references presented in the footnotes, and these additional sources: (1) Private communications with major participants in or architects of the programs described, such as Cao Van Than, former minister of MLRAD and simultaneously former minister of rural development; Nguyen Duc Cuong, former minister of trade and industry; Hoang Duc Nha, former minister of mass mobilization; and Tran Van Dat, former chief of MLRAD Rice Service and United Nations Food and Agriculture Organization rice expert; (2) Gerald H. Huffman, land reform consultant, USAID (Washington, DC), "Vietnam Land to the Tiller Program, Joint Evaluation Report," Saigon, November 5, 1971; (3) Chad Raymond, "'No Responsibility and No Rice': The Rise and Fall of Agricultural Collectivization in Vietnam," *Agricultural History* 28,1 (Winter 2008); (4) Randolph Barker, Cornell University professor emeritus, personal communication, June 7, 2012; (5) *Viet Nam Bulletin*, a publication of the Embassy of Viet Nam, Vol. V, No. 15 (April 12, 1971) and vol. VIII, No. 3 & 4 (March 1973); (6) William J. C. Logan, "How Deep is the Green Revolution in South Viet Nam? The Story of the Agricultural Turn-around in South Vietnam," *Asian Survey* 11,4 (April 1971), pp. 321–30; (7) Nguyen Ngoc Phach, *Land Reform Law* (Saigon: Vietnam Council on Foreign Relations, June 1970), introduction, "The Vietnamese Land Reform Law"; and (8) "Agricultural Development in Viet Nam," Vietnam Council on Foreign Relations, a report I wrote as a briefing for a US Senate Fact Finding Delegation, circa 1970.

customarily sent their eldest sons to live and work with their best and most trustworthy tenant farmers, who usually managed arrangements with the other tenants. Eldest sons would inherit most of the land, and it was thought that they should learn about rice farming first-hand as early as possible. So, when summer vacation came when I was in middle school, I was sent to learn how to grow rice. It was backbreaking on-the-job training from dawn till dusk with a few short breaks. At night, I was taught the tradition of rice farming by memorizing scores of rhythmic adages, sayings, and proverbs about rice growing.

When my mother came to visit me I begged her to let me go to high school and study to be a bureaucrat and to let my brothers inherit all the land. Consequently, I was sent to Saigon to study for the entrance exam for a French high school for boys named Lycee Jean-Jacques Rousseau. This was a place where French citizens and privileged Vietnamese children received their secondary education; graduation commonly led to college training in France. Every year the school reserved about three dozen seats for students trained in the Vietnamese educational system who had qualified via the entrance exam. I passed the exam and enrolled in 1951, graduating in 1958 with a diploma in mathematics.

I thought my mother would send me to France, but she decided to send me to America instead because the French had departed and the Americans had arrived. My mother sent me to private English lessons for three months, which enabled me to achieve a high score on the English test given by the United States Operations Mission (USOM, the precursor of USAID/Saigon) to select its first dozen Leadership Training Program candidates. Then an American official interviewed me and asked what I wanted to study. I answered "poultry farming" because my father was a poultry farmer; my father had told me that the United States was the best country in the world for poultry farming, and I wanted to help him become the biggest poultry farmer in Vietnam. Consequently, I was sent to Oklahoma State University (OSU) because of its reputation in agriculture.

I enrolled in the College of Agriculture at OSU to study Animal Husbandry with a minor in Poultry Science. I was the first Vietnamese to attend that university until Hoang Duc Nha showed up a couple of years later. My first summer there I met Nguyen Thanh Hai, who was enrolled at the University of Pennsylvania to study veterinary medicine but was sent to Oklahoma for a summer job cleaning horse stalls and cattle barns. Meanwhile, I shoveled chicken manure. Influenced by Hai, I eventually applied and was accepted to study at the OSU College of Veterinary Medicine.

Hai and I obtained our Doctor of Veterinary Medicine (DVM) degrees in 1964 and were sent back home. Hai asked me to join him in applying for a teaching job at the Superior School of Agronomy, Forestry, and Animal Science (*Truong Cao Dang Nong Lam Suc*, SSAFAS). At SSAFAS we faced discrimination at the hands of the French-trained clique that still dominated all our institutions of higher learning at that time. For example, an American DVM (Doctor of Veterinary Medicine) took at least six years to complete but was classified with less pay than a French DMV (*Docteur de Medecine Veterinaire*) that took only four years to finish. However, the French-trained faculty did not work full-time at the SSAFAS; to generate more income, they also worked at the zoo, at slaughterhouses, at laboratories, or had private practices, so they could and would not teach more than one course.

When we were given an opportunity to upgrade our curriculum and improve our instruction, Hai and I revamped the antiquated French-model three-year curriculum into a world-class four-year curriculum and created a dozen new courses that only American-trained people could teach. Hai and I ended up having to teach three courses each, controlling six votes between the two of us. So we wielded more and more power in the department. The trouble was that we wasted three precious years fighting for turf, not able to do much of anything else, just biding our time and waiting for more American-trained graduates to come home and join forces with us.

Finally, Hai and I, along with a few other American-trained faculty members, engineered the overthrow of the old French-trained clique and took over the Animal Science Department. Hai ultimately became Rector of the National Agriculture Institute (NAI, the renamed SSAFAS), and years later he became Associate Professor of Pathology at Cornell University. As for me, I was voted head of the Department of Animal Science at age twenty-eight. During my time as head, three events shaped the rest of my career.

In 1967, I was invited by the government of South Korea to attend the second presidential inauguration of Park Chung Hee with a delegation of about a dozen deans and representatives of various colleges in South Vietnam. I was chosen to represent the SSAFAS because the dean, Ton That Trinh, had been named minister of agriculture and I was a department head who spoke English fluently while others did not.

Professor Nguyen Van Bong, the rector of the National Institute of Administration (NIA) and also a well-known leader of the Progressive Party (*Dang Cap Tien*), was the head of our delegation. Since I was the youngest in the group and knew English, he asked me to be the "Benjamin" (French for "gofer") of the delegation. That put me in charge of running all the errands for the group, including staying up past midnight to draft numerous short speeches in English for Professor Bong to make at the beginning and the end of each stop on our month-long itinerary. We traveled up and down the whole country, visiting educational institutions and sites of economic development. Professor Bong liked my performance so much that he asked me several times if I wanted to be transferred to his institute to be his personal assistant. I was glad that I decided against this or else I probably would be dead with him when the communists later threw a bomb under his car and killed him and his assistant at a stop light in Saigon.

Before returning home, our delegation had an interesting audience at the Blue House with President Park Chung Hee. On that occasion, Professor Bong asked President Park why only academics from South Vietnam were invited to his inauguration. President Park replied that academics held the key to South Vietnam's economic development: to develop a country at war, you need good educators who are dedicated, committed, and patriotic people, able to produce the personnel that the country needs to build its economy from the devastation of war. So he invited us to see how the Koreans were doing things in order to give us helpful ideas. He also said that he liked President Thieu. In a way, these two presidents were quite similar: both were generals of humble origin who fought the northern communists in their divided homelands and wanted to develop an economy to benefit the growth of democracy in their countries.

When I was given a turn to talk, I asked President Park how the Koreans had managed to build refineries, fertilizer plants, power plants, and other industrial complexes three times faster and at half the cost of similar plants built in the United

States. He answered that Koreans worked on construction around the clock in three shifts even during the harsh Korean winter, and that Korean workers were not as wasteful as the Americans and their wages were relatively low. He showed us maps and charts of industrial projects at various stages of completion and explained that he followed their progress on a regular basis, making unannounced spot inspections on weekends to assure speedy and efficient construction. He said that he did not rely entirely on reports by people in charge because potential problems had to be identified and quickly resolved by the highest authority in order for things to move ahead according to plan. He emphasized three points that stayed with me for the rest of my career: you need skillful, energetic, and dedicated people to carry out development projects; you need to monitor projects regularly and on-site; and you need to know how to benefit from the knowledge of American experts while, at the same time, knowing not to argue with the stupid Americans that appear from time to time. I subsequently followed President Park's advice and achieved good results in all the programs I implemented. In all of my jobs, I had great working relationships with my American advisers, who liked to work with me because I got things done, did not care about red tape, and failure did not faze me.

The second important event for me happened when President Nguyen Van Thieu won the presidency in 1967. My college friend from OSU, Hoang Duc Nha, was President Thieu's special assistant at the time, and he asked me to organize an agricultural fair and exhibit to commemorate the inauguration because President Thieu loved agriculture, coming from a humble origin himself. I was given only one week's notice, so the best I could come up with was an exhibition in the auditorium at the college, which was located a few blocks from the presidential palace. Since there were no funds earmarked for something like this, and being such an unplanned event, I enlisted the help of my father and his livestock industry acquaintances who provided funding and exhibits. I also drafted the agribusiness private sector into this endeavor.

These connections later helped me to organize the next three annual Farmers' Day National Agricultural Fairs that grew bigger and more complex each year. President Thieu, Prime Minister Khiem, and guests including US Ambassador Bunker were fond of these events, and I was the person able and willing to organize them, because no other high-ranking official in the government was willing to live and work at the sites in various provinces for sixteen to eighteen hours a day for at least a whole month, sleeping in makeshift beds, using nature for a bathroom, and eating bad food.

At that time, I was working under Minister of Land Reform and Agriculture Development (MLRAD) Cao Van Than. In 1974, I was transferred to the Ministry of Trade and Industry (MTI) to head up the National Food Administration (NFA). In that year, Ton That Trinh, who had replaced Minister Than, cancelled the annual Farmers' Day National Agricultural Fair. I was concerned about the landmark event that I had built up being relegated to the back burner, and I was at the same time irritated that Minister Trinh publicly blamed the MTI, and specifically the NFA, for a rice supply problem that had developed at a difficult time when the NFA had just begun to function. He openly criticized the MTI for requesting that the Americans divert three shiploads of rice destined for other Southeast Asian countries to South Vietnam; he claimed that this compromised our miracle rice production effort, which was not accurate, for he was aware that this was primarily a measure for psychological effect to quell public anxiety over a feared rice shortage, and, in fact, we had to sell hardly any of that rice until the very end of our country's existence.

I vented my irritation about this by alerting my friend Hoang Duc Nha about MLRAD's decision to cancel the agricultural fair, which resulted in a last minute order from the presidential palace that the fair should, indeed, be held. This caused consternation in the MLRAD; a decent fair could not be organized in a couple of weeks, and it was the shabbiest, as well as the last, of these fairs. I mention this to show how there was friction, bickering, sniping, blaming, and animosity between the two ministries responsible for the production and marketing of food. This was especially the case whenever there was a food crisis, of which there were many over the years.

Another anecdote related to the last agricultural fair is my experience with the quail fiasco. A month prior to the event, I received a shipment of a dozen different species of domesticated quails from Marsh Quail Farms in the United States, a gift from my Oklahoma godfather because I used to love to hunt and eat quail when I was studying at OSU. I pampered these wonderful birds by raising them in my mother-in-law's living room, of all places, bless her heart of gold! At the fair, I had these quail exhibited in a prominent place. When President Thieu saw them he asked me why we should be raising quail. I made a little speech explaining the benefits of quail as a source of eggs and meat. This created quite a stir and soon lots of people began to raise quail. The price of baby quail went through the roof in a few weeks. In fact, I was able to buy an automobile with my quail business and my sister bought a house with hers. My father's feed mill had to work around the clock to supply quail feed and his hatcheries ran out of capacity for quail hatching. But, this was not quail farming. It was free enterprise at its worst. It was profiteering and black marketeering. My father said that this bubble will burst soon. My mother was scared to death about my involvement in promoting this brouhaha. As my father predicted, the quail bubble burst a few months later, and I learned the importance of avoiding unrealistic exuberance, hype, and excitement when developing an economic program.

The third important career-shaping event for me revealed the dedication of the agricultural technocrats that we trained. In 1967, USAID sent to South Vietnam five hundred breeding pigs of various stocks, such as the red Duroc, the white Yorkshire, the black Poland China, and the black and white Hampshire. The idea was to start a swine-breeding program to improve the local low-yield native breeds and to acclimate and then propagate the new high-yield breeds of pigs. Someone made two big mistakes: first, it was forgotten that Vietnam, like most other Asian countries and unlike the United States, had endemic foot-and-mouth disease (F&MD), an extremely contagious and crippling disease, and the pigs were not vaccinated for F&MD. Second, the pigs were put in the Quarantine Station, which had been built next to a slaughterhouse where thousands of animals were brought for meat processing.

All the pigs caught F&MD in a matter of a few days. Nobody in charge at the Directorate of Livestock Production and Protection (DLPP) of the Ministry of Agriculture (MoA) knew what to do, or was willing to do what was needed, especially when it involved so many precious and costly breeding animals. Do Cao Hue, a colleague of mine who was the director of the DLPP, asked me to help him deal with the situation.

I came with our fifth graduating class in Animal Science, and what a teaching and learning experience that was for our students and for the DLPP cadres! This was something I had never done before. In my American textbooks, the only treatment of F&MD was slaughtering, burning, and strict quarantine for years not only of the animals involved, but also the animals all around for miles. You could not do that in South Vietnam.

So my students and I spent a couple of weeks sleeping on army cots; eating carry-out food; playing poker at night for entertainment; bathing in the dirty river nearby; staying away from wives, kids, girlfriends, and lovers to remain at the Quarantine Station and treat five hundred crippled pigs day and night. We had to paint the feet and mouth of every pig with antiseptic iodine and healing oils every few hours and inject antibiotics three times a day, hand-feeding them twice a day. It was a monumental job, but we saved the vast majority of the pigs, having lost only a handful of them. They did not lose their hooves nor become uselessly crippled. Most importantly, having survived that debilitating disease, they obtained a solid life-long immunity against F&MD. Not only that, we saved the swine breeding program.

If we had listened to the American veterinarian who told us to kill all the pigs and burn their carcasses, our program would have been set back at least another year and would have cost millions of dollars more. I spent my entire monthly salary feeding the hungry horde of students who helped me during the crisis. It cost the government almost nothing to tackle this enormous problem. But the biggest gain I got from this strenuous experience was that I was able to identify the best individuals of the first class I taught whom I would use later in various capacities in the MLRAD and MTI programs that I implemented.

Soon after this, Do Cao Hue, a French-trained veterinarian and a part-time staff member at the SSAFAS, came to thank me for saving his pigs and to ask me on behalf of the minister of agriculture if I would like to join the MoA to take charge of the Accelerated Protein Production Program (APPP) as director of the Tan Son Nhut Livestock Experiment Station. I was interested, but did not want to give up my position as head of department in SSAFAS; I was suspicious that the French-trained faculty was trying to get rid of me, and I did not understand why the minister of agriculture did not ask me himself since he was my former dean. Hue thought that he himself was sent to ask me because the minister expected me to decline. My contact in the MoA who had helped me with the pigs said that many people wanted me to take over the APPP because it was in disarray and no one could speak English well enough to communicate with the American advisors. So I told Hue that I would do it if the minister of agriculture wrote to the minister of education to "borrow" me for the APPP, so that I could keep my place in education and my position as head of department at SSAFAS.

The following week, SSAFAS Interim Dean Bui Huy Thuc gave me my transfer paper and said that as long as I continued to teach my three courses and did not cause undue hardship to my department, I could remain as head until I finished with the APPP and could come back. I was unable to come back as a full-time staff member for the next eight years because higher authorities kept handing me bigger responsibilities and more important programs to implement. Finally, my dear colleague, Nguyen Thanh Hai, after he became rector of the NAI, called on me one day in 1972 to say that I had to make a decision because it was not fair to either the students or the institute to continue in this way. So I resigned as head of department and even gave up two of my courses. We had sent a few PhDs to the United States for postgraduate training, and they came back, which helped our staff. I still taught surgery to keep my tenure.

The agricultural graduates of SSAFAS played a vital role in the agricultural development programs. I was closely involved in training twelve classes of them from 1964 to 1975. Every year, we carefully selected the two hundred successful applicants who became the first-year students. I was always the chairman of the Entrance Exam Committee in charge of organizing the annual entrance exam for some five thousand high school graduates who applied each year. No matter what high function I held at the MLRAD or the MTI, or how busy I was, I supervised fifty-some exam halls to eliminate on the spot each year several hundred examinees who talked or copied or cheated during the day-long test in math, physics, chemistry, and biology. I had zero tolerance for cheaters and trespassers of rules of conduct.

I taught three courses—Anatomy (first year), Surgery (third year), and Animal Diseases (fourth year). No faculty members except my fellow American-trained colleague, Nguyen Thanh Hai, taught that many courses. Hai taught Histology (first year), Physiology (second year), and Pathology (third year). It was by teaching as much as we did that we were able to control the department, shape the curriculum, and escape from the French academic influence.

In the summer and during most weekends, we even took the seniors out into the countryside on field trips for on-the-job training, directly helping farmers because the college did not have a lot of animals for practice. At every lecture and in all the excursions I had with our students, I never forgot to give them also a civic lesson on love of country and service to the people. At graduation, I even made them take a solemn oath akin to the medical Hippocratic Oath of yore. As a result, the veterinary science graduates were a group of solid, dedicated, driven, purposeful, idealistic, and well-trained individuals geared up for service to their country and people. Over the years, I recruited a lot of these fellows in every program for which I became responsible, and they never let me down.

These three events—the trip to Korea, the agricultural fairs, and the sick pigs— eventually led to a sharp turn in my career to implement major development programs launched by the Ministry of Agriculture during the Second Republic of Vietnam: the Accelerated Protein Production Program, the Land to the Tiller Program, the Accelerated Miracle Rice Production Program, and the Rice Marketing Program.

I believe that the Americans in USAID exerted some pressure on Minister Ton That Trinh and/or Director Do Cao Hue, to bring about my transfer to run the Accelerated Protein Production Program. I do not think that Minister Trinh or Director Hue would have thought to entrust a young American-trained veterinarian to run such an important program in their ministry, especially someone who had just engineered the overthrow of French influence in the Department of Animal Science. Nevertheless, in the whole country, I was the only person trained in animal husbandry with a poultry science minor and with hands-on commercial farm experience in poultry production, both in the United States and in South Vietnam, in addition to which I worked in veterinary medicine. How this came about is worth relating because it reveals an aspect of rural life and how it affected my education.

• • •

My father was the number one commercial poultry farmer in Vietnam in the 1950s–60s, but the lack of modern technology prevented his business from taking off. He learned by trial and error. At that time, Vietnamese farmers raised animals at a subsistence level in their back yards as scavengers to be consumed within a five-to-six-mile radius of their farms due to the lack of transportation and the limited number of animals that could be raised. Understandably, losses from diseases and other causes were high and yield was low. These considerations occupied my thoughts when I chose to study poultry science and went to Oklahoma State University. From Oklahoma, I sent to my father any information I could find about raising poultry on a commercial scale, including poultry books and magazines. I also sent him feed supplements, medicines, vaccines, and breeding stock. Consequently, my father's business started to grow to a profitable level.

In the summer of 1963, I asked to study modern commercial poultry operations in the field to acquire hands-on knowledge. I was sent to Cobbs Broiler Farms, a big commercial operation in Concord, Massachusetts, where the poultry scientists gave me a three-month crash course in all phases of modern commercial poultry farming. Cobbs Broiler Farms even sent me, at their expense, with their scientists to the Regional Poultry Conference at the University of New Hampshire, where I sat in a lot of eye-opening seminars and presentations on modern poultry farming. I was also introduced to a lot of commercial poultry operators and representatives of supporting industries and made contacts that later helped me very much in implementing the Accelerated Protein Production Program.

Americans could raise a chicken from egg to market size in just six weeks, instead of six months as in Vietnam. American layers could lay 200–250 eggs a year instead of our 20–25 eggs a year. And they could do all that with minimal loss. My father imported Cobbs breeding stock and got great results. And Vietnamese broiler producers liked Cobbs chickens due to their fast growth. Even though my father's commercial operation was growing, his losses from disease were unacceptably high. I was the only Leadership Program trainee allowed to spend more than six years to study in the United States and to complete a doctoral (DVM) degree, which helped my career, because in Vietnam the doctor title carried much prestige, respectability, and credibility.

ACCELERATED PROTEIN PRODUCTION PROGRAM

The APPP was the first major agricultural development program of the Second Republic. There were four such programs in the nine years that I worked for the Ministry of Land Reform and Agricultural Development (MLRAD, the renamed Ministry of Agriculture after Cao Van Than became minister in September 1969) and for the Ministry of Trade and Industry (MTI, the renamed Ministry of Economy after Minister Nguyen Duc Cuong assumed the portfolio in 1973). I was involved in all of these programs, one indirectly as a trouble-shooter and monitor and three directly as implementer.

My animal husbandry and veterinary medicine training at OSU, my first-hand knowledge and hands-on experience in large commercial poultry operations at Cobbs Broiler Farms, and experience with my father's farms served me well in my tasks. I knew from day one exactly what I had to do to carry out the APPP. I learned from the quail fiasco, from my experience at Cobbs Farms, and from my USAID advisers that I had to get investors seriously involved in the program at its inception. The government bureaucracy and its intricate red tape precluded the public sector from doing any business in a timely, gainful, honest, and non-wasteful manner. Graft and corruption were always major drawbacks in anything the government did that involved dishing out favors or picking and choosing winners or losers.

The primary purpose of the APPP was to secure a reliable source of food for the major urban centers, especial the capital, where most consumers of marketed meat and poultry products were located. These areas were relatively secure, unlike many parts of the countryside where the enemy was active, so we could work without much interference from the war.

We began by mobilizing prospective entrepreneurs and investors with meetings and overseas observation trips. We explained in detail our objectives and plans for implementation. We enlisted the participation and cooperation of livestock associations, agricultural co-ops, importers, exporters, and banks. We found ways to streamline availability of credit and foreign exchange and to speed up customs and health inspections of imported breeding stock at ports of entry. We arranged financing to build the infrastructure for the livestock industry, from slaughterhouses to processing plants, to a refrigerated warehouse at the Saigon Central Market.

We organized the Directorate of Livestock Production and Protection at the Tan Son Nhut Livestock Experiment Station to provide training to both farmers and government cadres and to support the private sector in developing needed enterprises. We conducted regular training programs for farmers and for national and provincial livestock cadres in modern poultry and swine husbandry practices and commercial animal feed formulas. We imported vaccines from Thailand and organized mobile vaccination teams with American veterinarians as advisors to train livestock cadres and commercial producers of pigs and chickens in livestock protection. We sent students to study veterinary medicine at Chulalongkorn University in Thailand, and we trained artificial inseminators to serve our swine-breeding program.

We set up demonstration stations in the provinces to train farmers in commercial poultry and swine farming with breeding stock that we developed from animals imported from the United States. We obtained practical assistance and imported breeding stock from broiler farms in Thailand, the Philippines, Japan, and the United States. We acclimated imported poultry and swine breeding stock and selected those most suitable for use in our country.

An example of something we did is applying a technique for baby chick sexing in egg production operations. Unlike broiler operations, where both male and female chicks are used, egg-laying operations require only female chicks, so the sex of chicks had to be determined immediately upon hatching. In the United States, male chicks were drowned and ground up for meat meal because it is not economical to raise these birds for meat, as they were bred for egg laying. In South Vietnam, these male chicks were sold cheaply to farmers in the countryside who raised them as scavengers with native chickens. It did not cost anything to feed them and there was a good chance that they would pass on their high egg-producing genes and improve our native birds. Also, over the years, millions of such birds produced an enormous amount of meat for the farmers.

Until we had enough time to develop an adequate commercial animal feed industry using local ingredients, we imported yellow corn from the United States. We experimented and tested feed formulas using local ingredients with the assistance of American technical experts. One aspect of this was the introduction of high lysine corn, which provides a high level of protein, and sorghum, which became the most popular feed grain in South Vietnam. Sorghum had four assets: it was a perfect second crop after a miracle rice harvest when the rice field was still wet and the soil still fertile; it floats on water, making it ideal for feeding caged fish, which were being raised in increasing numbers in tributaries of the Mekong River; it produced good grain alcohol at less cost than did rice; and it increased farmers' incomes with relatively small amounts of investment and labor. Eventually, a Sorghum Production Program was developed, with my strong advocacy, as part of the Animal Feed Grains Production Program, which was an offshoot of the APPP and of the Accelerated Miracle Rice Production Program. A long-term benefit of the spread of sorghum production in South Vietnam was that after 1975, when the communist effort to collectivize agriculture resulted in a drastic decline in rice production and widespread rural hunger, people mixed sorghum with other staples to avoid starvation.

We worked to enlist the assistance of other ministries and government units in achieving our goals. The Ministry of Trade and Industry gave the new agribusiness sector top priority for scarce foreign exchange to secure production inputs. We persuaded the Ministry of Defense to defer our livestock experts from conscription and to reassign conscripted experts back to their civilian jobs. We persuaded rural banks and agricultural development banks to provide small loans to farmers, medium loans to merchants, and large loans to entrepreneurs and investors. The Institute of Bacteriology, with the help of an American scientist, increased the types of livestock vaccines from four to nine, and monthly production rose to three million doses using modern cell culture technology instead of the old incubated eggs technique, which was costly and slow. We also requested that the Pasteur Institute increase its veterinary vaccine production to satisfy increasing demand.

Funding the APPP was a perennial problem in our war economy. However, thanks to USAID special funding, we were able to overcome this problem. If the Americans saw results, they invariably were able to help. Private sector donations also helped us maintain our activities when the benefits of what we were doing became known. Furthermore, I was blessed with an abundance of free labor from my willing students, who contributed hundreds of hours to help with organizing events. I even had several students who lived with me in the program complex and stood armed guard with me to defend our facilities during the 1968 Tet Offensive, when communists invaded the station while attacking the nearby Tan Son Nhut Airport. My students and I were ready with carbines, and the invaders managed to cause some damage only to the chicken houses and swine pens. Our recovery from that damage and disruption was very fast. The surge in demand for pork, poultry, and eggs at that time stimulated production tremendously.

One problem was that we lacked a sufficient number of trained people when we most needed them. Although South Vietnam had an agriculture-based economy, it was slow to develop strong agricultural educational institutions. The faculty at the Department of Animal Science taught a curriculum that led neither to expertise in animal husbandry nor to proficiency in veterinary medicine until we eventually reformed it with assistance from the University of Florida and USAID/Saigon. It took time to remedy this problem.

Another problem was that a lot of our officials refrained from close association with the private sector or were reluctant to publicly cultivate good relations with businessmen or entrepreneurs for fear of being accused of collusion or favoritism or nepotism or cronyism. A lot of officials lost their jobs because of such perceptions. I did not have such qualms. For one thing, I came from a commercial background. For another thing, I did not depend on any job I held. If I lost my government job, I would go back to teaching, which I loved.

After three years of implementation, the APPP brought about remarkable results. One result was the development of a vibrant cottage industry of backyard livestock farming among fixed income people, such as families of soldiers and civil servants. These people raised a couple of pigs or a hundred layers or broilers at a time at their residences. This was an unintended but welcome consequence during this period of high inflation. When I was drafted into the army, I gave the drill sergeants and lieutenants coupons that they could take to my father's poultry farms to get a hundred chicks and small rural bank loans to raise chickens and develop extra income. They could easily double or triple their wages with extra business activity of that kind at home in their backyard.

This program contributed immensely to our capability to defeat the Maoist strategy of "using the countryside to encircle and strangle the cities." There was no time during the whole conflict when insecurity fomented by the enemy in the countryside ever succeeded in cutting off the urban population from its food supply because we were able to produce enough protein right there around the cities. Unlike with rice, here was no interruption of transportation between production and consumption sites that could cause supply problems.

Statistics from 1969 best indicate the success of our program. Here is some information extracted from US Ambassador Bunker's papers that appear to be indicators of success:

- There was relative stability of prices for most protein products, unlike other commodities that had to come from afar.
- There was an 11 percent annual increase in the number of swine raised. Two shipments of five hundred pigs for breeding stock imported from the United States soon produced several hundred thousand piglets that started the modern high-yield swine industry. Private commercial farms then cooperated to import needed breeding stock.
- Pork was the single major item in the Vietnamese diet that cost less in 1969 than it did in 1968.
- Five and a half million more broilers were raised than in the previous year.
- Laying flocks for commercial production rose by roughly a million hens and produced some 200 million eggs in 1969. That amounted to fifty eggs per person in Saigon.
- The number of hatcheries increased during the year from thirteen to thirty-five, with an increase in incubator capacity that made it possible to accommodate half a million breeding birds. That many birds could produce 100 million eggs for hatching.
- At this rate of progress, the APPP aim of producing 150,000 broilers and 2,500,000 eggs a week by 1971 to meet domestic demand for poultry products at reasonable prices was on track.

The APPP was one of the most successful programs initiated by USAID and implemented by our government. In a few short years it completely changed the poultry and swine businesses of South Vietnam from a subsistence level of animal husbandry to a high level of industrial production. It improved the livelihood of a sizeable portion of our population that was displaced by the war from the countryside to the fringes of secure urban areas. It also had a beneficial unintended consequence by providing a source of supplemental income to the fixed-income segment of our society at a time of escalating inflation due to the disengagement of American forces.

The APPP also made full use of the greatly increased by-products (bran, both white and brown) of the successful Accelerated Miracle Rice Production Program. It vigorously stimulated the Feed Grains (sorghum and corn) Production Programs and spawned vibrant spin-off supporting industries. But the best part was that it helped to secure the protein component of the food supply for our cities and towns.

My service with the APPP was abruptly interrupted in 1969 when I was drafted in the general mobilization following the Tet Offensive and sent to a boot camp designated for officials in the government. Every official, whether high or low, was affected by the general mobilization decree. Nguyen Duc Cuong, the future MTI minister, and Nguyen Thanh Hai, the future NAI rector, were both in my training battalion. At the end of the nine weeks of basic training, many were transferred back to their civilian jobs while others were sent to the Reserve Officer Training School. Eventually, I was honorably discharged from the army and went back to teaching and the APPP. The APPP was in good hands during my absence, thanks to my able second-in-command at the TSNLES, Mrs. Nguyen Thi Quoi.

One day in 1969, I was called to the office of Nguyen Thanh Qui, the assistant minister to the newly appointed, thirty-five-year-old minister of Land Reform and Agriculture Development (MLRAD), Cao Van Than, whom President Thieu appointed to carry out his social revolution, the Land to the Tiller Program (LTTTP), for land reform. He asked me to help implement the LTTTP as the ministry's director of cabinet. I said that I would do this if I were allowed to continue teaching at the SSAFAS. Minister Than had no problem with my request. It was a big step in my career. At twenty-nine, I was the youngest director of cabinet of a major ministry. This position was a French creation similar to but not quite the same as the job of chief of staff in American officialdom. The position ranks third in power, right below the minister and the vice-minister (if appointed by the president) or the assistant minister (if selected by the minister).

The director of cabinet assisted the minister with political and public relations, represented the ministry in negotiating aid from foreign countries, represented the ministry in inter-ministerial work, attended meetings when the minister could not go, carried out any special mission that the minister assigned, and gave his personal opinion to the minister on matters of importance concerning the ministry's operations and management to help in making decisions. I fielded complaints and requests for favors from elected politicians, trade associations, and farmers' organizations. I negotiated assistance agreements with South Korea, Taiwan, Japan, and the Philippines, and often traveled to international meetings. I helped resolve problems with other government units that required coordination. I attended meetings of province chiefs with military commanders to solve problems and to advance the ministry's programs. The MLRAD had more programs and provincial services than any other ministry, because 65 percent of our people were directly involved in agricultural activities, so I spent much time in the provinces on routine inspection of program implementation. Most of our programs were concentrated in Military Region IV, in the Mekong Delta, where the country's agriculture was concentrated. Six million of the eleven million people in this region were farmers.

The MLRAD had two directorates general: the Directorate General of Land Affairs (DGLA), which implemented the land reform program; and the Directorate General of

Agriculture (DGA), which carried out at any time up to two dozen major agricultural development programs as part of the government's Five-Year Agricultural Development Plan, as well as many other smaller projects. The DGLA had Provincial Land Affairs Service (PLAS) offices in thirty-five of the forty-four provinces; there were none in the highland provinces, where there was not enough rice land to justify the cost of setting up an office there. The DGA had nine sub-directorates covering nine sectors of agriculture and most of them had provincial or regional offices. Consequently, the ministry had an extensive network of local offices in the countryside.

In anticipation of the passage of the Land to the Tiller law by the National Assembly, Minister Cao Van Than spent nearly half a year setting up the massive organization and the intensive training plans that would be needed to carry out this revolutionary program.[2] I say massive and intensive because eventually it would involve some fifty thousand central and local, intra- and inter-ministerial people, mostly in the 2,100 villages of the country. This was more people involved in any single government civilian program than at any time in the history of our country. USAID-Saigon at the beginning had only one land reform expert. Eventually, to keep up with us, it had thirty-five of them in its land reform division alone.

LAND TO THE TILLER PROGRAM

I believe that the most important achievement of the Second Republic was land reform. This was no ordinary land distribution, but it was truly a rural social revolution. Unlike most revolutions, ours was very peaceful and equitable. Under the leadership of President Nguyen Van Thieu, we launched this rural social revolution by building an ownership society almost overnight. I was lucky to have this once-in-a-lifetime opportunity to participate in the implementation of such a historic undertaking.

The Second Republic aimed to build a rural ownership society under the gun barrels of an implacable enemy. This was an ownership society of the free-private-entrepreneurial type. It was not for the benefit of any privileged class of citizens, but for the benefit of the underprivileged and long-suffering mass of rural people. President Thieu wanted to create a rural middle class that would include the majority of our people. Land reform was part of an ambitious Five-Year Agricultural Development Plan.

Throughout most of our history, dynastic regimes claimed ownership of all the country's lands, which rulers doled out to mandarins, generals, and veterans as rewards for loyalty and meritorious service. These lands tended to become the private property of powerful families. Some land was designated as communal land, to be a source of revenue for village governments. In the nineteenth century during the Nguyen Dynasty, there were some policies to limit the amassing of privately owned land and also to reclaim wetlands for agriculture, but there were no fundamental changes in the agrarian situation.

Beginning in the 1860s, the French colonial authorities allowed their citizens and the Vietnamese who served in their administration, and who acquired French

---

[2] See Cao Van Than, *Agrarian Reform in Viet Nam* (Saigon: Viet Nam Council on Foreign Relations, 1970).

citizenship, to exploit virgin lands for cultivation of both industrial plants (hemp, jute, sugar cane, tea, coffee, and rubber trees) and rice or secondary crops (beans, peanuts). The colonial administration also used public funds to finance vast land reclamation schemes and private citizens with means could buy these lands at auctions upon completion of the project. Of course, these auctions were out of the reach of common poor people.

Consequently, newly cleared lands were usually bought exclusively by the rich, famous, influential, and powerful people in our society. South Vietnam had roughly 15,000,000 acres (6,000,000 hectares) of cultivable lands. Around 50,000 landowners with holdings of all sizes owned half of this land (7,500,000 acres, or 3,000,000 hectares), and just about 6,000 landowners possessed nearly half of that land (3,000,000 acres, or 1,200,000 hectares). In the Mekong Delta alone, 430 French citizens owned 625,000 acres (250,000 hectares).

Why was land reform not successful during the First Republic (1955–63) and the Interregnum Period (1963–67)? I will explain with the example of my own family. My mother's father, Do Van Son, and his two brothers, Do Van Diem and Do Van Kia, were French citizens who owned vast estates and served as rural administrators in the Mekong plain under the French in the late 1930s and early 1940s. They were members of the Do clan, which was very large and, in colonial times, had been active in clearing rice lands, digging canals, and building roads in the districts where they owned land and served as administrators.

During the First Republic, when I was a student, clan members gathered for ancestral worship a couple of times each year at the house of my great uncle who was the leader of the clan. On these occasions, the topic I heard continuously and vehemently discussed by at least a couple hundred relatives, who were mostly absentee landlords living in France or Saigon, was how to use all the loopholes there were in the land reform laws to keep the land in the family's possession. One of my uncles, Nguyen Van Trinh, was the Director General of Land Affairs (DGLA) and was in charge of agrarian reform programs during the First Republic and the Interregnum Period, and his son-in-law was the Provincial Land Affairs Service (PLAS) Chief in Go Cong Province; they held court explaining what to do to fight expropriation, circumvent the regulations, and evade the laws. The powerful Do clan was dead set against land reform because they thought it was unfair, illegal, and smacked of communist highhandedness and class warfare.

After the Geneva Accords of 1954, the French supposedly bought up all the rice lands owned by French citizens and gave them to the government of Chief of State Bao Dai, with Ngo Dinh Diem as his prime minister, to be distributed to landless farmers. But all my uncles and their descendants still had large holdings of rice lands. I remember that when my parents moved to Saigon in the late 1950s, they bought a unit in a new three-story, sixty-unit condo that my great uncle Do Van Kia was given by the French in exchange for giving up a part of his landholdings.

The sons-in-law and grandchildren of my great uncle Do Van Diem played some important roles in South Vietnam's history. His son-in-law Le Tan Nam held ministerial portfolios, mostly in the Ministry of Justice, in the early to mid 1950s; he was the first Vietnamese to receive the French *Licence-en-Droit* (JD) and was Tan An district chief and Saigon mayor for many years. Le Tan Nam's son, Le Tan Loc, became director general of *Viet Nam Thuong Tin* (Viet Nam Credit Bank), the big government bank. Another son-in-law of Do Van Diem was Nguyen Van Trinh, the DGLA who was in charge of implementing agrarian reform programs in the late 1950s and early 1960s. Obviously, it was a poor choice to pick a member of a big landholding family who didn't believe in agrarian reform to do land redistribution. Not much was accomplished, not to mention a lot of evasions of the law perpetrated through insider information.

That was why, when Minister Cao Van Than was entrusted by President Thieu to implement his landmark Land to the Tiller Program, and a new young Northerner from a landless rural family, Bui Huu Tien, was made director general of Land Affairs, a completely new team was put in place to vigorously carry out the hard and pressing work.

I relate these details of my family to give some insight into one of the reasons why President Diem's land reform failed and to give a probable explanation for why almost half of all the grievances filed by landlords during the Land to the Tiller Program originated in Long An, An Giang, and Chau Doc Provinces, where the Do clan was most influential. You can multiply this problem by at least three hundred, the number of similar clans in South Vietnam, to understand the magnitude of the obstacles that President Thieu and Minister Than had to overcome to implement the Second Republic's land reform program.

There were two early attempts by President Ngo Dinh Diem to control the excesses of the land tenancy system in South Vietnam by controlling rent and by giving a greater degree of land tenure to tenant farmers. Ordinance 2, promulgated on January 28, 1955, mandated that land rent be between 15–25 percent of the average harvest and be formalized with a three-year written contract to reduce evictions. Ordinance 7, promulgated on February 5, 1955, was designed to protect the rights of tenants on new and abandoned lands to encourage cultivation (squatters' rights protection). These ordinances also reduced rent payments after crop failure and gave renters first right of refusal should the owners decide to sell their holdings

A more serious effort at agrarian reform came with the promulgation of Ordinance 57 in October 1956. It put a 250-acre (100 hectare) limit on rice land ownership and gave the landlords the right to keep 37.5 acres (15 hectares) for ancestral worship. Any excess land would be expropriated and owners would be compensated. Expropriated land would then be sold to farmers in installments. Landowners received 10 percent of the land price in cash and 90 percent in government bonds redeemable in twelve years. The huge 250-acre cap left only 1,130,000 acres (452,000 hectares), which made up just 20 percent of agricultural land, available for expropriation from some 2,035 landlords. These lands were usually not prime rice lands because the landowners claimed the best lands as the 250 acres to be retained for themselves and their relatives, and their 37.5 acres of ancestral worship land. The expropriated lands were usually not near rivers, canals, and rural roads, but were abandoned plots in remote areas, cultivated lands in communist-controlled areas from which landlords could not collect rent, or lands far away from transportation networks. On the other hand, the prime land that each landowner was allowed to keep—287.5 acres—would continue to keep up to eighty tenant farmers in perpetual bondage because the average rented plot of land in the Mekong Delta was 3.5 acres (1.4 hectares).

The program had many loopholes that were easily exploited. According to Roy L. Prosterman and Jeffery M. Riedinger,[3] by the end of 1967 the Ordinances of Ngo Dinh

[3] Roy L. Prosterman and Jeffrey M. Riedinger, *Land Reform and Democratic Development* (Baltimore. MD: The Johns Hopkins University Press, 1987, p. 126.

Diem had distributed some 275,000 hectares (687,000 acres) of land to 130,000 families. This represented less than one-eighth of cultivated land in South Vietnam, with benefits going to barely one-tenth of those who were wholly or substantially dependent on tenant farming.

Because of complex centralized bureaucratic procedures, from 1957 to 1963, only 50 percent of expropriated lands were redistributed, or roughly 560,000 acres (226,000 hectares). Poor farmers had little money to buy the necessities of life much less to buy land; only around 100,000 out of approximately one million tenant farmers (almost all in the Mekong Delta) benefited from the program. In the Interregnum Period from 1963 to 1967, 127,000 acres (49,000 hectares) were distributed to thirty thousand families. The political, social, and economic impact of these land reform efforts was minimal.

Shortly after he became chief of state, President Thieu realized that to prosecute the war against the communists effectively, he had to focus on land reform a lot more than the previous administrations had done. In September 1968 he began to formulate and enunciate his own concept of land reform by giving an accurate assessment of the situation: The government was faced with a long-standing problem of social injustice, which demanded a solution if pacification was to be effective. The practice of tenant farming, which in effect made the tenant farmer a slave to the land and to a continuous cycle of poverty, prevented the development of South Vietnam's agriculture-based economy and had to be abolished once and for all.

I had first-hand knowledge of land reform under the Second Republic as the director of cabinet under Cao Van Than, the new, dynamic, hard-working minister who was a close adviser of President Thieu in agrarian reform and economic development and the architect and implementer of the Second Republic's successful land reform program.

In 1967, around 60 percent of the South Vietnamese population, or a little more than ten million people, was rural, mainly dependent upon rice farming. Three-fifths of these farmers lived in the Mekong Delta, where 80 percent of rice was produced. The remaining two-fifths lived in the narrow coastal plains of the northern provinces.

According to available statistics from UN/FAO in the early 1960s there were 1,175,000 farming households, but only 257,000 (22 percent) of these families owned all their land, mainly in the Mekong Delta. Their average acreage was roughly four acres (1.7 hectares). Another 334,000 families (28 percent) farmed an average of six acres (2.4 hectares) of rice land, with two-thirds of this rented from landlords (with families owning just one third). There were 521,000 farming families (44 percent) who farmed an average of 3.5 acres (1.4 hectares) of land that was totally rented from landlords. Therefore, 72 percent of the Delta farmers relied on both rented and owned or on totally rented lands for their livelihood.

According to the Stanford Research Institute, in the Mekong Delta, landlords supplied virtually no credit, seeds, fertilizer, or farm implements, but usually collected rents in-kind in the form of one-third or more of the harvest, which was usually fixed in advance. It did not matter whether the harvest was good or bad. If the harvest was bad due to bad weather or insect or disease damage, the tillers still were responsible for the rent. If they could not pay, interest as high as 60 percent a year would be applied to what they owed, and lead to as much as three-fourths of the harvest being collected by the landlord after the next harvest.

Most landlords lived in France or in the cities. At harvest time, landlords or their agents, who usually were village notables or military officers, would collect the rent due. The agents were entitled to a cut (15–20 percent) of what they could collect. Therefore, coercive methods were often used.

Farmers also suffered from selling their rice crops at a fixed price to local middlemen, usually the Chinese operator of the local grocery store who advanced the farmers the money or the groceries his family needed to subsist until harvest time, to hire needed labor, or to acquire agricultural inputs.

In the Central Lowlands, where agricultural land is scarce, the situation was a lot worse. There, only 190,000 families out of 695,000 (27 percent) owned an average of 1.5 acres (0.6 hectare). The majority, 403,000 farming families (58 percent), tilled two acres (0.8 ha), with half of that land rented from someone else. A minority of 74,000 farmers rented an average of one acre (0.4 hectare) of land, which they farmed. Rents in the area amounted to 50 percent of the harvest.

With this sad state of affairs in our rural society, one could easily understand why it was easy for the communists to foment revolutionary unrest. We could readily deal with aggression from the North, but having an internal insurgency in the countryside, whereby disaffected peasants sheltered and supported the guerillas with food and manpower, would make things much more difficult. For this reason, President Thieu realized that he must transform our rural society by changing it into an ownership society to give the poorest and most numerous segment of our population a chance to break out of its grinding cycle of poverty. Consequently, during the Second Republic era, from 1967 to 1975, radical, transformational, and aggressive land reform, along with vigorous, comprehensive, and accelerated agricultural development, was implemented. It was no ordinary undertaking, but a revolutionary program bold in design, grand in scope, swift in implementation, and life changing in its impact on the rural population.

The strategy was formulated in April 1969 under the leadership of President Thieu and his adviser on economic development and land reform, a former army officer, a lawyer, and a University of Pittsburgh-trained economist named Cao Van Than. The National Assembly passed the necessary legislation, with minor changes from the original draft, after heated and lengthy debates; it was signed into law as the Land to the Tiller Law and promulgated on March 26, 1970. Thereafter, this date became a national holiday known and celebrated with a lot of fanfare as Farmers' Day.

According to Charles Stuart Callison, in the book based on his dissertation about land reform in South Vietnam,[4] the provisions of this law went further than the revolutionary land reform of the Viet Cong. The Viet Cong were careful to maintain solidarity with the middle peasants and permitted small landowners (with fewer than 25 hectares) to keep their rented lands if they reduced rents and paid taxes to the communists. The LTTTP of the Second Republic sought to eliminate tenancy altogether, expropriating and redistributing all lands not directly cultivated by the owner. Furthermore, the NLF granted new ownership rights on a provisional basis only, contingent on continued, active support of their cause, whereas the LTTTP granted definitive titles to all current tillers, regardless of their legal status upon the land or of their alignment in the civil war. Unlike the Diem land reform, this law was designed to eliminate land tenancy throughout the Republic, even in the sharecropping, small-

---

[4] Charles Stuart Callison, *Land-to-the-the-Tiller in the Mekong Delta—Economic, Social, and Political Effects of Land Reform in Four Villages of South Vietnam* (Berkeley, CA: Center for South and Southeast Asia Studies, University of California–Berkeley, Monograph Series No. 23, 1973).

landlord areas of the Coastal Lowlands, areas practically untouched by previous land reforms.

For most knowledgeable South Vietnamese, the so-called Viet Cong land reform was a travesty, since there was no legal basis for it, landowners were left with nothing, and farmers had no clear legal title to the land. On the other hand, President Thieu's LTTTP created an ownership society composed of new middle-class cultivator-farmers who replaced tenant-farmers by providing the rural population with ownership of land, guidance for how to increase production, and a way to escape perpetual, grinding poverty. The political and social impacts were far-reaching.

The program provided ownership of land to tenant farmers with full compensation to native and French landlords. Ownership went to farmers who worked the land with or without contracts, a crucial feature because a lot of tenant farmers without contracts were forcefully evicted from their rented lands by landlords during the previous land reform program and tenant farmers had no recourse due to lack of legal documentation.

The LTTTP also dealt with the thorny issues of distributing cultivated communal lands to current tenant farmers with limited compensation to villages, and of distributing lands belonging to religious groups (mainly Roman Catholics) that chose to relinquish their landholdings to the government with full compensation. These two previously untouchable domains had been the source of resistance to reform because they provided revenue, influence, and power for village officials, churches, pagodas, and temples. A special prime-ministerial decree was required, but President Thieu was determined to make it work.

Landlords who tilled their own lands could keep a maximum of 37.5 acres (15 hectares) with or without hired labor. But landlords who did not till could retain only 5 hectares (12.5 acres) for ancestral worship, for their family cemeteries, or for other religious purposes (*huong-hoa, hau dien,* and *ky-dien*).

Farmers who applied for land ownership received a maximum of 7.5 acres (3 hectares) in the Mekong Delta, where 80 percent of the land subjected to this law was found, and 2.5 acres (1 hectare) elsewhere where such land was scarcer.

The elected Village Administrative Committee (VAC) determined the compensation price of each plot of land according to government guidelines, which amounted to 2.5 times the average annual paddy yield of the last five years. Notice the word elected. People that the local farmers and landowners trusted enough to represent them and who knew better than anyone else about prevailing local conditions would make the decisions to enact the law. President Thieu wanted to empower local authorities to promote democracy at the grassroots level.

The owners of expropriated land were compensated with a 20 percent payment in cash and the rest in negotiable government bonds indexed to the current price of paddy, earning 10 percent interest over eight years after which they would be redeemable. Negotiable bonds meant the landowners could use them to buy stocks of government-owned companies and treasury bonds. Indexed to the price of paddy at the time the land was expropriated and evaluated made the compensation bonds inflation-proof.

Village Land Distribution Committees (VLDC), chaired by the village chiefs, processed applications for land ownership and issued titles of ownership, which were then registered with the local, provincial, and central governments as permanent land records. The new landowners could not sell their land for fifteen years, and after they sold their land they were not eligible to apply for more land.

New landowners were entered in the Village Land Register and Village Tax Roll. They then paid taxes to their Village Administrative Committees to be used for local services and local projects like building schools, health clinics, roads and canals, and rural electrification. They would not pay back taxes or back rents or any new tax for the first year of land ownership. The initial rent and tax relief enabled farmers to jumpstart their status in life by immediately increasing their income by around 50 percent. This both enriched rural people and empowered their local popularly elected officials to promote democracy from the bottom up.

This program distributed some 2,500,000 acres of prime rice farmlands or secondary crop lands currently being tilled by tenants, or roughly one-third of all cultivated land in South Vietnam. Combined with the distribution of 330,000 acres (120,000 hectares) of communal land and 175,000 acres (70,000 hectares) of religious land, this made a total of almost 3,000,000 acres, equivalent to 60 percent of the prime rice-growing land, or 40 percent of the 7,500,000 total number of acres of cultivated land in the country. An estimated 800,000 families of tillers nationwide received land, thus affecting almost six million rural people, or more than one-third of South Vietnam's total population at that time.

The compensation processed for about fifty thousand landlords required paperwork that trailed all the way from the villages to the provinces and on to the capital in Saigon. There were many more landlords in the LTTTP than in the previous land reform program, because the LTTTP law affected the smaller landholdings in Central Vietnam that Diem's Ordinance 57 Land Reform Program did not touch.

We worked with a sense of urgency. The program called for the distribution of the non-communal and non-religious lands (2,500,000 acres) in three years. The program was launched in the second quarter of 1970 and half a million acres (200,000 hectares) were redistributed by the end of that year. Around one million (400,000 hectares) were redistributed during each of the two subsequent years, 1971 and 1972. This set a record for peacefully redistributing land. The USSR, PRC, and DRV redistributed land faster or on a bigger scale only by slaughtering a whole class of citizenry in the process.

Land reform in South Vietnam was accomplished without violence or bloodshed and with fair compensation to landowners. Not a single landowner lost his life or was maltreated in any way. The only people who died in this enormous undertaking were some of our Rural Development cadres, who were savagely assassinated by the Viet Cong while carrying out their government's land distribution procedures at the grassroots level. They were our true heroes, they gave up their lives so that their fellow compatriots had a chance to better their livelihood. They deserve our people's profound appreciation and everlasting gratitude because they played a big role in turning South Vietnam into a nation where the middle class landowners were in the majority.

While waiting for the General Assembly to pass the LTTTP law, which took eight months of complex negotiation from conception to promulgation, the government took some initial steps. President Thieu ordered that all residual lands expropriated but not yet distributed during the previous agrarian reform program that were still in government possession (some 270,000 acres, or 107,000 hectares), and all the rice lands that the French government bought back from its citizens and gave to our government in the 1950s (625,000 acres, or 250,000 hectares), be immediately distributed free of charge during the first half of 1970 as a dry run for the big task envisioned under the

LTTTP. Before the end of 1970, what was left of the First Republic's agrarian reform program, roughly 900,000 acres of rice lands, was completed.

President Thieu also ordered that official titles of land ownership be issued even to farmers "given" lands by the communists in the areas they controlled but newly pacified by our government. There would be no forceful eviction of current tillers of any land by any authority, as had been the case in the old days after we regained control of any territory previously lost to the enemy.

As is well known, communism recognizes no private land ownership because lands belong to the state. So, the Viet Cong (VC) did not issue official titles of land ownership for farmers to whom they gave land, and farmers generally understood that they had no legal title to any land given by the communists. In fact, the communists went around at night and tore up a lot of our land ownership titles that we gave to the farmers as incontestable proof of property ownership, which made the recipients angry, to say the least. Computers could easily reprint the titles. We had to work with the early IBM-360 computers, which were huge and took an army of IBM card punchers to operate, and there were only three of these units in the whole country. Our IBM card-punching workers (always young women) invaded the US Embassy basement every night to print land titles by the thousands. If this were done by hand calligraphy as in the old days, it would have taken decades.

Learning from the bad experience of the First Republic land reform program, the prime minister issued a decree freezing all land transactions and all changes of current land status to prevent noncompliance and evasion by unscrupulous and recalcitrant landowners. There was not much that devious landlords and their sharp lawyers could do to evade the LTTTP law. Of course, many still tried, all the way to the Supreme Court, but without success.

MLRAD developed a detailed implementation plan and reorganized the Directorate General of Land Affairs (DGLA) from the highest to the lowest echelons, from central to local levels along the paper trail in order to execute the plan smoothly and rapidly. We also created a regional office in the Mekong Delta, where 80 percent of the work would be carried out, to speed up the resolution of problems that could be solved by mid-level authorities instead of channeling those issues all the way to Saigon. We also created new organizations that would perform the inspection and investigation functions to make sure that the proper procedures and the right amount of work would be done according to the implementation plan laid out from central to regional to provincial to local levels. We prepared to handle the expected increased number of grievances and inquiries from all sides.

It was a stroke of genius to adopt aerial photography to help map and identify the land plots to be distributed with the provision that accurate official cadastral maps produced with surveying equipment would be done some time in the future to formalize and legalize the photo mapping. Otherwise, it would have taken decades to finish this gigantic program with conventional cadastral methods.

The program called for the extensive training of some fifty thousand government employees at all levels in technical, procedural, and administrative issues. The MLRAD people were trained in-house by the DGLA. The Rural Development cadres of the Ministry of Rural Reconstruction (renamed Ministry of Revolutionary Development in 1969) were trained in rural pacification and rural development at the sprawling Vung Tau Training Center, run by Colonel Nguyen Van Be, a Viet Cong returnee who was very good at training cadres in doing things to defuse, deflect, derail, dismantle, demolish, defeat, and destroy communist tactics and strategies in the countryside. The CIA supported his activities by building near Vung Tau a vast training complex for that purpose.

Minister Than once sent me to the Vung Tau center to give a pep talk to a graduating class of cadres whose members would be assigned to the MLRAD to help implement the LTTTP in the villages, an experience I will never forget. After spending the evening dining with Colonel Be and his advisers to discuss land reform matters, I was taken to the huge parade ground at 9:00 PM. It was pitch black, because there were no lights and no moon. I could not see a single word of my prepared speech, which I had placed on the podium to read. While I was fumbling around behind the mike to find what to do about this unexpected and unsettling situation, I heard a blood-curling and ear-splitting series of yells from what must have been a division of cadres whose faces I could not see, welcoming me to the parade ground. My heart almost jumped out of my chest. So, what I did was to give a non-prepared rambling harangue on the main points that I still remembered, using my informal Southern farmers' vernacular.

The key tactical decision that accounted for our success was the decentralized work done by these armed Rural Development cadres, who were young peasants. The Village Land Distribution Committee of the local Village Administrative Committee supervised these cadres, and our MLRAD's Provincial Land Affair Service (PLAS) closely monitored the work. The VLDC was a group of about half a dozen local people (the village chief, a representative from the village council, the village commissioner for agriculture, the hamlet chief of the hamlet involved, the village land registrar, and a non-voting person from the VAC who acted as secretary) who did nothing but land reform work in the village government. The VAC was a dozen officials, two of them elected by the villagers themselves, being the village chief and his deputy, who had all kinds of other daily governing functions to do at the grassroots level, such as security, pacification, development, and administration.

Learning from the land distribution experience of the First Republic, we were determined to avoid tying up the court system with litigation, so the LTTTP called for the establishment of a Special Land Court system to be created by the General Assembly outside of the normal judicial system to handle nothing but the more serious land dispute cases. Arbitration by the VAC was expected to settle minor land disputes and grievances stemming from the application of the law. Major cases could be given to four Special Land Courts created under Ordinance 57 that already existed in Dinh Tuong, An Giang, and Long An provinces, and in Saigon. Cases that could not be settled by these courts were to be referred to the Central Land Reform Council (CLRC), an instrument of the executive branch of government made up of representatives of the prime minister, high officials of six ministries, and the directorate general of planning. The CLRC decision was final and could not be appealed.

Meanwhile, thirty existing provincial Courts of First Instance that were part of the regular judicial branch assumed the function of Special Land Courts for major cases in their respective jurisdictions free of charge. But the problem with these courts was that they usually sided with landlords because they did not understand very well the revolutionary nature of the LTTTP law. That was why all cases taken by these provincial courts were carefully reviewed by the Central Agency for Land Courts (CAFLC) in the DGLA headquarters. The commissioner of the CAFLC would present recommendations to the NLRC for final judgment if there appeared to be an improper ruling.

During the previous attempt at land reform, rich and educated landowners could hire sharp lawyers to drag out lawsuits for years. But we had very few cases of such magnitude. Fewer than a thousand grievances and inquiries required arbitration at the central level. Most cases were settled by local government mediation, with fewer than 10 percent being reported to the central authorities. Local officials knew the local people and the local situation better than any other entity, and they were able to resolve the greatest majority of disputes and grievances. Callison's dissertation analyzed nearly one thousand cases that came up to the DGLA.[5] There were fewer than nine thousand cases of complaints, grievances, disputes, contests, and inquiries of all sizes and all types stemming from the LTTTP. The majority of the rulings were in favor of the tenants. This was a mercifully small amount of discord considering the massive scope of the program.

Of course, we needed military support from village and provincial governments to ensure safe implementation. We had plenty of that because President Thieu personally ordered the military commanders and the province chiefs, who were all colonels or lieutenant colonels in the army, to support MLFAD's local services in the implementation of his rural social revolution. At frequent regional gatherings with local authorities, he personally pushed his accelerated pacification efforts. Some of the province chiefs were very good, especially after President Thieu purged the bad apples out of his government. I remember there was an egregiously bad province chief in Binh Dinh Province who was tried for corruption and sentenced to death. I remember also Colonel Quach Huynh Ha (a relative of Mrs. Thieu) who was the province chief of Bac Lieu, a big rice producer of the Mekong Delta. We test ran our LTTTP implementation machinery down there first to tune up all the cogs and wheels. Colonel Ha and his staff supervised and monitored our efforts daily on the spot with excellent results.

The president distributed the first few hundred land titles to teary-eyed black-pajama-clad farmers, who received them with trembling hands because it was the first time in the lives of these poor people that they owned so much wealth. A hectare of rice land was worth between VN$150,000 and VN$200,000 at official rates. Delta farmers could receive as many as three hectares. So you could see the enormous wealth farmers received in a hurry. It was like winning the lottery jackpot, and it nullified communist propaganda.

Nevertheless, we faced serious obstacles, and security was absolutely the biggest problem. We endured constant enemy sabotage (assassination of our cadres, threats to farmers, incendiary propaganda to everyone). To this day I still think that letting the local government people at the hamlet and village levels carry out the program was the best decision Minister Than made, as you could not get urban officials brave enough, dedicated enough, and knowledgeable enough about local conditions and local people to venture into the countryside for this dangerous work. There was no way we could protect tens of thousands of unarmed land service officials if they had to do this work in the far-flung fields instead of our armed local Rural Development cadres with the help of our Popular Forces.

Another problem was the lack of official land records and cadastral maps due to successive wars over the years that destroyed most land records. Almost 50 percent of land records were non-existent in South Vietnam. This problem made crosschecking to

---

[5] Callison, *Land-to-the-the-Tiller in the Mekong Delta.*

find out whether landlords owned land in different places in the Delta, which was quite common, nearly impossible.

Lack of roads to remote areas was another great obstacle. Work was done in more than 2,100 villages, comprising some twelve thousand hamlets. Many places were not accessible by roads. One could get there only by sampan, which often took a long time even when motorized. It would have taken years to contact all the people concerned to do the necessary work if we did not use grassroots government officials who lived and worked in situ. Without telephones, telegraph, or mail service, everything had to be done face to face.

Only a handful of trained professional land surveyors were available in the whole country, and we lacked surveying and map-making equipment. We endeavored to overcome this difficulty with the use of military aerial photography, but this was not always satisfactory. Aerial photos taken by fast flying jets (USAF F-4 Phantom reconnaissance planes), high up in the sky in weather that was seldom ideal, were sometimes of quite poor quality. Clouds blocking clear views caused long waits before a retake could be done, producing delays. Everyone wished the pilots would fly below cloud cover for more detailed and clearer photos.

Lack of funding appeared to be the most limiting factor. According to our best estimate, the program would cost anywhere from US$450–750 million, mostly for landowners compensation and other implementation costs. But governments are notorious for cost overruns. We got ten million dollars from President Nixon when we ramped up the program and another forty million dollars of counterpart funds for later expenses, but none of this could be directly used for compensating landowners. It was used to import goods for resale to generate funds for our budget to ease inflationary pressure due to compensation money being printed.

Evasion of the law by landowners was expected to be an obstacle to the smooth implementation of the government program. Attempts to circumvent the law by unscrupulous or influential landlords, in connivance with corrupt or pliable officials, created some difficulties in a few provinces. The majority of the cases involved illegal designation of ancestral worship lands and prime lands that the landlords wanted to distribute to their relatives in order to retain them.

During the first attempt at land reform by President Ngo Dinh Diem, so many loopholes and exceptions, and ambiguous language in the implementation decrees, gutted the program and made it unworkable. But this time, all our leaders were determined to carry out this revolution successfully. Minister Than was a sharp lawyer and he made sure that there were few ambiguities in the law that could lead to problems. When the program was launched, Minister Than made it clear that the law would be applied uniformly to everyone regardless of their prominence in the government, including the president, the prime minister, cabinet officials, and their relatives. My absentee landlord relatives were upset that I did not protect them from the law. It was the same for the senior officials and for many of my other colleagues. President Thieu entrusted his important programs to men of humble origins to carry them out with vigor, speed, integrity, and expediency instead of relying on the landlords or the ruling class of professionals. People with humble backgrounds tended to empathize with the disenfranchised farmers. President Thieu, Minister Cao Van Than, and the minister's team were the main players in this rural revolution at its inception and all came from humble origins.

We enjoyed effective coordination among different ministries of our government and military authorities at different levels. I made a point to directly inquire of villagers about how things were and what our officials were doing to help them. I rarely announced beforehand my trips to villages for obvious security reasons. I reported to the minister any problem I discovered, rather than relying on official reports, which tended to be excessively rosy and slow. Our officials in the field really feared these fact-finding tours of mine because it could lead to losing one's job when a situation was egregiously bad.

My American advisers provided me with transportation in fixed wing aircraft and helicopters of Air America, the CIA airline, to go all over South Vietnam, even towards the end of the American military involvement when, due to budgetary constraints, these flights were quite limited. I must have logged more flight time than any other official in our government in my eight years as an implementer of government programs. My American advisors helped me in many other ways as well.

MLRAD needed vehicles, but we didn't have funds to procure them. My counterpart, Robert Sweet, a USAID/Saigon assistant director, took me to the vast Long Binh Army Logistic Base and showed me hundreds of discarded Ford sedans, the fleet car for American officials in Vietnam, waiting for disposal as junk. A lot of them could still be in good working order with minor repairs or with clever tinkering. Bob asked me if I could put to good use these vehicles and I promptly said why not. We went to see the general commanding the base and Bob told him that the MLRAD needed these sedans to implement the land reform program and, pronto, the following week we had our Directorate of Farm Mechanization tow dozens of these cars home to their shops and other garages to work on cannibalizing, fixing, and upgrading these Fords for our use. Consequently, we never had a transportation problem until the big oil squeeze hit us in 1973.

All of this effort was worth it, considering the remarkable results achieved that were at the heart of the Second Republic's spectacular rural social revolution. Despite the war and the constant concerted efforts by the communists to disrupt, dismantle, and defeat the program, impressive goals were achieved right on target. The program was practically completed by the first quarter of 1973, when more than 2,750,000 acres of rice land and secondary crop lands were distributed to some 900,000 families, thus exceeding the set targets of 2,500,000 acres and 800,000 families. There were no more tenant farmers in South Vietnam. We were done!

There were farm laborers working for hire for landowners who tilled their own fifteen hectares of rice field that they were allowed to keep, or the five hectares of ancestral worship land exempted from expropriation, or for some religious lands. Actually, if you take into consideration the number of people given residual lands from previous land reform still in government hands prior to the LTTTP implementation, the number of families benefiting from this social revolution was more than 1,200,000, and if you multiply this number by seven, the average size of the Vietnamese family, you can see that the South Vietnamese countryside was populated mainly by middle-class people. This was a massive, peaceful change of social status, unusual in human history. Land reform in Japan, Taiwan, and South Korea took years and the scale was much smaller. Yet land reform did wonders for these countries' economic development. Just think of the possibilities if South Vietnam had not been abandoned by its allies!

President Thieu solemnly and proudly declared that the LTTTP was successfully completed on the third Farmers' Day Celebration in Can Tho, in the heart of the

Mekong Delta, on March 26, 1973. I was literally crying for joy listening to that famous speech. So were a lot of other officials. I even saw US Ambassador Bunker's eyes well up. Good old Bunker, the best American friend South Vietnam ever had. Looking at the happy and smiling faces of the hundreds of peasants gathered there to receive their precious titles of land ownership from the president, I felt as happy and gratified as when I won the USAID Leadership Training Scholarship, when I received my DVM degree, when I got married, and when my first son was born—all lumped together. This impressive feat not only drastically changed the lives of nearly seven million rural people almost overnight, but also completely remade South Vietnam for years to come, something that even the brutal communist coercive, authoritarian, and oppressive machine could not unravel years later.

The LTTTP is the most important and lasting legacy that the Second Republic of Vietnam left its citizens. The first economic impact was an almost immediate increase in agricultural production. Concurrent with the land reform program, President Thieu also launched an ambitious agricultural development program that was aimed at rapidly making South Vietnam self-sufficient in food production as the basis for the country's overall economic development.

The self-sufficiency initiative centered on the Accelerated Miracle Rice Production Program that jumpstarted the Green Revolution in Asia. I was in charge of its crash implementation during the years 1972 and 1973, which saw high-yield rice shoot up to roughly 890,000 acres, accounting for 53 percent of the total 6,700,000 metric tons of rice paddy (*lua*); this 53 percent was equivalent to 4,400,000 metric tons of processed rice (*gao*) produced in the 1973–74 harvest season, enough to feed the entire South Vietnamese population at that time. Thus, rice sufficiency was achieved after ten years of deficiency, and even in the middle of a raging war. According to UN/FAO, South Vietnam, Laos, Burma, Cambodia, and Bangladesh were the countries that had the highest annual per capita consumption of processed rice in the world: 150 to 170 kilograms. At even the highest rate of consumption, the amount of rice we produced in that harvest season was adequate to feed more than twenty million people, even taking into consideration all the waste, loss, and damage in production, processing, transportation, storage, and distribution.

The second economic impact was improvement in rural income. Farmers no longer shared as much as half of the harvest with their landlords or paid as high as 60 percent interest to money lenders. Also, for the first year, as previously mentioned, new landowners did not have to pay any rent or tax, for the first time in their lives. All of a sudden they could enjoy the entire fruit of their labor. They now had a chunk of money they could use to build their new life and jumpstart their future. Thanks to this rent and tax relief alone, during the first year of land ownership new landowners had a 50 percent increase in their income immediately, even without planting a high-yield rice variety. With 2.5 acres of land properly cultivated with high-yield rice varieties, yielding three to four times native rice, a farmer could easily net VN$100,000 per harvest. Furthermore, he would earn two to four times as much if he could farm two to four crops a year as was possible in some areas with additional irrigation in the dry season and with new miracle rice varieties having short maturation, only 90 to 100 days as compared to 120 to 150 days for native rice strains.

Even more impressive is that with 7.5 acres, as the law allowed in the Mekong Delta, a farmer could theoretically earn three times more than this, or almost forty times the per capita income of South Vietnam. With the unofficial rate of exchange it would be half as much, but still it would be a sizeable amount of money to be able to acquire in such a short time. For poor farmers at the bottom of our societal scale, this amount of money was an enormous fortune to possess.

When I was the director general of agriculture, I frequently heard farmers say that they won the lottery jackpot because the only way for poor people to become a millionaire was to buy the weekly government Reconstruction Lottery and win the jackpot. That is why they called miracle rice "Honda rice," because now they could afford all kinds of Honda products: moped, water pump, tiller, generator, harvester, thresher, dryer, etc.

In 2005, I went back to Vietnam to see my dying mother for the last time and met two of my fortyish cousins on Cu Lao Ba Island, in the middle of the Hau Giang tributary of the Mekong River, in Chau Doc Province, where my mother was born and grew up. There I saw an example of rural prosperity based on the Second Republic's land reform that had survived failed efforts to communalize agriculture. Two single women were farming their ten hectares of high yield rice for export under the communist regime and growing fish on the side. Because their land had plenty of water, being on an island, they were able to grow three crops of broadcast high yield rice (*lua xa*) a year. They said they could grow four crops, but they wanted to relax three months each year. I did some quick calculations and was flabbergasted that they were making more money being commercial farmers than I was making in the United States with two small businesses. They asked me to find them American men who would marry them in order to immigrate to this country. I told them bluntly to stay put to make a living because they would not make that much money over here.

The third economic impact was the influence of the landowners' vast amount of compensation money injected into the economy. There was genuine concern about the negative impact of inflationary pressure on South Vietnam's fragile economy. Some of this concern was answered by two studies made near the end of the program. One was conducted between August 1971 and September 1972, by Charles Callison, mentioned earlier, who studied four villages in four Delta provinces: Long An, Dinh Tuong, Phong Dinh, and An Giang. The other study was made between January and June 1972 in forty-four villages of nine Mekong delta provinces by Henry Bush of the Control Data Corporation for USAID and the Republic of Vietnam. Both studies showed that compensation money generated only a small economic impact. However, these studies were small in scale (fewer than a thousand landowners and tenant farmers in each study) and too close to the end of the program to measure the full impact.

Most big landlords lived in cities and in France. There were not many industries in which compensated landowners could invest their money. Anecdotal evidence suggests that a lot of them invested their money in some sort of business. In my family's Do clan, I witnessed the following businesses cropping up after the LTTTP: my great uncle Gaston Do Van Diem went into the seafood and fish sauce business, my great uncle Charles Do Van Kia built sixty units of condos for rent, my mother invested her money in a commercial chick hatchery, and other uncles, aunts, and cousins opened up all kinds of retail businesses, such as tailor shops, restaurants, bakeries, construction supplies, dime stores, clothing stores, groceries, rice and chicken merchants, and other retail outlets. Some relatives who did not farm before, but who found that with increased security in the countryside modern commercial rice farming was quite lucrative, decided to go into agriculture. And that was just one clan. Vietnamese are hardworking, resourceful, and enterprising people, as was demonstrated by refugees who came to this country. They would not sit on their money to let inflation sap its value nor would they squander it all in consumer goods. This was why we never had uncontrollable inflation even at the height of the war.

The social impact of the LTTTP was another important goal of the government. The peasants constituted the largest component of our society. They contributed more than their fair share to the nation's welfare and defense by producing most of its GDP and by earning the greatest debt of blood in defense of the nation, but they always received less than their due. So foremost in President Thieu's mind was his desire to redress this injustice with his social revolution.

Even before this revolutionary land reform program was completed, farmers no longer felt like slaves or indentured servants, or inferior to landlords. They would not have to spend their entire life in virtual bondage at the mercy of landlords and moneylenders from generation to generation anymore. They now owned a major piece of property, a means to drastically improve their livelihood. This property was worth at least VN$150,000–200,000 (US$1,300–1,700) per hectare as per the official evaluation for owner compensation, but worth a lot more on the open market. They could acquire larger and more modern houses with TV, radio, sewing machine, refrigerator, kitchen appliances, furniture, clothes, watches, Honda moped, electricity, etc. The most disenfranchised segment of our society now had concrete social justice as enshrined in Article 19 of their country's constitution, and upheld by their leader.

The most important impact of all was political. The LTTTP redressed social inequities in rural society. It decreased rural disaffection and the potential for insurgency fomented by external forces and a foreign ideology. The results convinced farmers that the government they elected actually helped them to acquire private property, served them instead of exploited them, and tended to their daily needs and requirements instead of exacting labor and wealth from them. Furthermore, peasants now believed that the social revolution that their leaders often promised was as real and life-changing as the land ownership title they held in their hands, unlike the empty promises and taxation without representation meted out by the communists. Peasants had something to fight for now and were less prone to yield to terror by the communists or to stay neutral in their country's struggle to remain free. They had a bigger stake in their community and were less susceptible to the propaganda of the enemy.

The LTTTP reduced the farmers' traditional skepticism and cynicism toward established authority. It created unity and mutual trust among farmers, local officials, and local military personnel, ingredients that promoted political stability and security. As Callison concluded in his PhD dissertation: "One of the ironies of the tragic conflict in Viet Nam is that by 1975 the RVN had apparently won the war of insurgency, considered the more intractable threat by their American ally, and then lost the conflict to a conventional invading army, due to reduced logistical support and a classic battlefield blunder."[6] But I did not need a learned and scientific study to come to the same conclusion. Instead, I simply relied on my firsthand knowledge of events in the countryside, encounters with farmers in the villages, conversations with province chiefs, and the reports of my local service chiefs.

---

[6] Callison, *Land-to-the-the-Tiller in the Mekong Delta*, p. 366.

The LTTTP was the most remarkable and lasting achievement by the Second Republic of Vietnam, all the more remarkable because it was carried out in the middle of the most vicious and protracted war of aggression. None of this could have been accomplished without the wisdom, the vision, the determination, and the courage that President Nguyen Van Thieu showed in his decision to favor the rural disfranchised peasants. Until the LTTTP, the loyalty and support of peasants for his government were still in doubt, even while the urban rich people's anticommunism and allegiance were never in question. President Thieu's vision of a rural social revolution positioned the nation towards rapid economic development, the likes of which had been seen in Taiwan, South Korea, and Japan after similar land reform programs. Unfortunately, this prospect was cut short by the loss of our wartime ally.

ACCELERATED MIRACLE RICE PRODUCTION PROGRAM

The Accelerated Miracle Rice Production Program (AMRPP) was the third major MLRAD program that I was directly involved in. Even though the MLRAD was implementing more than two dozen agricultural development programs in the nine agricultural sectors that it managed, this program was by far the most important of them all.

After the completion of the LTTTP, the next step in President Thieu's rural social revolution was focused on various agricultural production programs to improve the farmers' livelihood. It was obvious that in a time of diminished foreign assistance, a major endeavor towards food self-sufficiency was mandatory. Rice exports had been discontinued since 1964 because of the disruption of war. There was no way that South Vietnam could afford to import an average of 435,000 metric tons of rice (the equivalent of 900,000 metric tons of paddy) for its annual consumption, as had been done during the height of American military involvement. During the period from 1966 to 1972, South Vietnam had to import 2,600,000 metric tons of rice, mostly from the United States. President Thieu considered that it was a matter of foremost and greatest urgency for our country to achieve rice self-sufficiency.

In 1972, the MLRAD was tasked with drafting a Five-Year Agricultural Development Plan for President Thieu to take to his meeting with President Nixon in March 1973. President Thieu hoped to obtain President Nixon's assistance in launching his country's agriculture-based economic development plans after the success of the LTTTP. Roughly 65 percent of South Vietnamese, or eleven million people, still relied on agricultural livelihoods.

President Thieu, on the first anniversary of completing the LTTTP, proclaimed that his Five-Year Agricultural Development Plan centered on the following three urgent objectives: to satisfy demand for essential commodities, to increase the living standard of rural people, and to decrease imports and increase exports. In his speech that day, he stressed that economic development must be carried out in parallel with the realization of social justice and economic well-being for all citizens, and that self-sufficiency in food would enable development of light industries and eventually the industrialization and modernization of the country. Translating the president's vision into a concrete plan was no simple matter.

I recall that after Minister Cao Van Than ordered the drafting of the plan, the work languished in various bureaucratic offices. Minister Than brought in one of his fellow University of Pittsburgh economics classmates as assistant minister to help direct the effort for a while, but it was still slow going and very inadequate. This was understandable, since this was the first time something of this magnitude had been tackled at the MLRAD.

A deeper problem was a lack of cooperation caused by resentment among the veteran bureaucrats of the MLRAD. The former Ministry of Agriculture (MoA), the earlier version of the MILRAD, was one of the oldest portfolios of our government. The old French-trained agricultural technocratic clique had been running it. Minister Than was the first American-trained economist and lawyer, and thus non-agriculturist, who was put in charge of the portfolio, and President Thieu had chosen him to implement the LTTTP. Minister Than was one of the President's best and brightest individuals of the Specialists Group working in his inner circle at the palace. I was also a young American-trained veterinarian, brought in at the third-highest position as director of cabinet, bypassing quite a few people. As a result, a lot of leading rank and file officials in the ministry demonstrated resentment, reticence, lack of cooperation, and disinterest. So the work of formulating a plan was done perfunctorily and with constant delays.

In mid 1972, MLRAD Minister Cao Van Than appointed me to be Director General of Agriculture (DGA) with two important and urgent tasks: to finalize the drafting of the Five-Year Agricultural Development Plan and to speed up the implementation of the nascent Miracle Rice Production Program to achieve food self-sufficiency at the earliest time possible. As DGA, I was responsible for the biggest entity in our government with its nine directorates in Saigon and its local offices in the four military regions and in forty-four provinces up and down the whole country, employing some twenty thousand full-time people with variable numbers of temporary employees. The nine directorates were for Crop Production and Protection, Livestock Production and Protection, Fisheries, Forestry, Farm Mechanization, Irrigation, Farm Co-operatives and Farmers' Unions, Agricultural Extension, and Agricultural Research.

Our first task was to complete the drafting of a good, workable Five-Year Agricultural Development Plan in time for the president to take it with him to his meeting with President Nixon. The drafts prepared by the nine directorates were written by different people in different formats, but based on their work, and with the assistance of American advisors from USAID, a unified, detailed plan with English translation was completed in a couple of months. Thereafter, we gave our full attention to implementing the plan.

At that time, the South Vietnamese government tended to be fragmented with animosity between Southerners, Northerners, and Central Vietnamese—akin to the Yankees and Rebels in the United States a century before; also, there was resentment among French-trained, Anglo-American-trained, and locally trained technocrats. Furthermore, there was friction between old and young generations, suspicion between different religious backgrounds, and competition among people with different political allegiances. I was a thirty-four-year-old American-trained Buddhist Southerner with relatively little experience in the government bureaucracy. So I agreed to be the DGA chief if Nguyen Van An, who was a senior official of the ministry with thirty years of service and a Southerner agronomist trained in-country, would serve as my deputy. He enjoyed great respect and deference from the ministry's rank-and-file due to his age and length of service and was well-versed in the intricacies of our red-tape maze. It was a demotion for him, as my new appointment also was for me, but he finally agreed. He became a loyal deputy director general who dealt effectively with the labyrinthine red tape; knew where and how to pull strings to get results; kept subordinates in check, cooperative, and performing better than I had expected; and he protected my back and flank as I scurried around all over the provinces to push and inspect the implementation of our many programs.

I often overheard An telling slacking-off directors over the phone to shape up or he could not protect them from me giving them an early retirement in order to bring in my own people. I did not have to fire any senior administrators and the DGA performed efficiently with good results. I always publicly gave my managerial people the credit whether they deserved it or not, and I was willing to accept the blame for any screwup by my people. I did things that no one else had done in our culture. For example, it was customary for lower echelon people to give gifts to higher echelon officials during holidays. I did just the opposite. I gave my directors gifts during those times and any other times that I wanted to thank them for anything they did above and beyond the call of duty. My father was a very rich poultry farmer who also owned a sugar cane plantation, rural bank, and a feed mill, and I regularly drew a salary from him as a technical adviser, even though I had not done a whole lot of work for him as busy as I was. So, I could afford this. And if they or someone else gave me anything, I would divide it up among my entourage instead of keeping it for myself.

A lot of managerial people in our government had the annoying habit of coming to work late and going home early, and thus causing their employees to behave likewise, bringing disgust to people who worked hard. Efficiency and productivity of public service suffered as a result. I put an end to that habit by ordering DGA employees working in the sprawling compound to assemble at 8:00 AM sharp for the daily salute to the flag, complete with the national anthem playing. The entrance gate was locked afterwards and the gatekeeper on duty would record all latecomers and early leavers, to be used for year-end performance assessment.

The number-one program that I spent a lot of time and effort to push was the Accelerated Miracle Rice Production Program because rice was the main staple of our people and, prior to 1964, had been our main export. We just could not continue to import an average of 435,000 metric tons of rice a year, especially with the Americans pulling out. The program was already in full swing, thanks to the previous efforts of Ton That Trinh, who headed the former MoA. Minister Trinh, a well-known French-trained agronomist and former college dean, had contributed much to establish the AMRPP. When President Thieu brought Minister Cao Van Than in to carry out the LTTTP, the main focus was shifted to this social revolution effort for a couple of years, but the momentum of the AMRPP was not greatly affected because our government gave a lot of priority to reach rice self-sufficiency and to resume the export of rice as a source of foreign exchange.

There are two main ways of increasing rice production: increase the acreage of rice production or apply modern technology to rice farming. We chose the second approach, even though it was more expensive because it required costly inputs like fertilizers and insecticides, as well as farm machinery and credit, not to mention the difficult task of training farmers in modern farming technology. Increasing acreage was not feasible because it would require military intervention to pacify the countryside, a slow and difficult process at best, and because of a shortage of farm labor due to the military draft on both sides of the conflict. Also, we could not afford the expense and time necessary for extensive land reclamation and land clearing projects.

We needed to produce roughly six million metric tons of rice paddy as soon as possible to cover the demand for food of seventeen million people at that time. Once that was achieved, we could resume the export of rice. In the past, "Saigon rice" was preferred the world over due to its high quality. But these high-quality rice varieties were notoriously low yield: one to two metric tons per hectare. So our rice scientists were busy researching to create new and improved varieties of both high-yield and better eating quality rice.

South Vietnam was one of the first countries to launch the so-called Green Revolution in Asia. In mid-1967, there was a big flood following a typhoon in the Vo Dat District of Binh Tuy Province near Saigon that caused massive damage to the first rice crop. Since Vo Dat was tucked in a secluded area, the MoA agreed with USAID to try planting a newly created, high-yield, short-maturation rice variety called IR-8, without fearing some untoward consequences to the country's rice varieties should there be some unexpectedly adverse genetic or biological effect.

This new rice variety had been developed in the Philippines at the International Rice Research Institute (IRRI). The IRRI had been set up and financed by the Ford and Rockefeller Foundations. It took prolonged high-level negotiation between the United States and the Philippines before the Filipino government allowed six metric tons of IR-8 seeds to be sent to South Vietnam and planted in some 120 hectares (300 acres) of rice fields. Because of late planting and lack of water in the dry season, the forty hectares that were planted produced a disappointing average yield of two metric tons per hectare (1,760 pounds per acre), which was only half of the expected average yield of that high yield strain. So the entire eighty tons of harvested IR-8 seeds were bought back from farmers and distributed to thirty major rice-producing provinces to be planted in the 1968 rainy season (summer–fall crop). Thereafter, farmers were expected to multiply the seeds themselves once they realized the profit they could make from the high yield they got.

Meanwhile, the Rice Service of the MoA used the USAID-provided Revolving Fund to pay for IR-8 seeds to propagate in other rice-producing areas in the dry season (winter–spring crop) of 1969. As a result, the 1968–69 planting cycle saw an official 23,373 hectares (roughly 60,000 acres) of IR-8 (renamed in Vietnamese as "TN-8," or Than Nong 8; Than Nong was the traditional god of agriculture) planted, with an expected average yield of four metric tons per hectare (3,500 pounds per acre). I say "official" because we had no record as to how much TN-8 the farmers planted on their own outside of the government-sponsored program, but we knew it was substantial. This was the opening shot of the Green Revolution that would be heard throughout Asia.

With this initial success born out of a disaster, and with the valuable assistance of USAID, the MLRAD launched the AMRPP. The next growing season, 1969–70, saw 510,000 acres (204,000 hectares) of high yield rice varieties planted. This acreage more than doubled again the following season, 1970–71, with 1,130,000 acres (452,100 hectares) of TN-8 planted. Under my leadership, the acreage of miracle rice was successively brought to 1,687,000 acres (674,740 hectares) in the 1971–72 harvest and 2,087,000 acres (835,000 hectares) in the 1972–73 harvest, and finally to 2,225,000 acres (890,000 hectares) in the 1973–74 harvest. The 1974–75 harvesting season saw an estimated 2,385,000 acres (950,000 hectares) of miracle rice planted within the government program. There was no way of knowing the acreage of high yield rice planting outside the official program.

To achieve a rapid increase of high-yield rice production like that, the DGA channeled most of its human and material resources to the Mekong Delta, where nearly

65 percent of our people (roughly eleven million) lived at that time, and also around the few provinces near the capital for ease of transportation of the produced staple to this main center of consumption. The Mekong Delta at that time was the most secure region of our country, thanks to the success of the Accelerated Pacification Program, except for remote and sparsely populated areas in about one-third of the provinces. So a lot of agricultural development work could still be carried out.

I put all my best young NAI (National Agriculture Institute, formerly the Superior School of Agriculture, Forestry, and Animal Science) graduates there to run the local services, experiment stations, extension services, demonstration sites, and special projects. The great majority of these graduates were recruited and employed with special out-of-budget funding provided by USAID. I specifically fought for these young men's military deferment and our government realized that their service was more valuable in the civilian sector than in the armed forces, considering the investment our government spent in training them (all our public university training was free). The agricultural sector enjoyed this unique favor all through the war years. The graduates of draft age were drafted and trained as reserve officers, but the Ministry of Defense always transferred them back to our different organizations upon our ministry's request. Those who did not perform well would lose their military deferment.

The Mekong Delta received a lot of financial and material support in agricultural development from USAID. Many American field operators and experts in different agricultural fields were assigned there, especially in Can Tho City, the hub and heart of the Mekong Delta region. Most of the programs and projects of our Five-Year Agricultural Development Plan were found in abundance there for obvious reasons.

Rice growing has always been an arduous undertaking. Growing the new high-yield variety was even more demanding. But we were blessed by having farmers who were progressive, smart, patient, diligent, innovative, and adaptive. The preferred method of getting the farmers to switch to growing TN-8 rice was to set up demonstration plots to compare the yield of native rice and miracle rice side by side, preferably on farmers' lands, with work done by the cooperating farmers themselves, but with our technical assistance and inputs.

Once the farmers saw for themselves the spectacularly convincing results, we followed up with the Mini Rice Growing Kit, used successfully in the Philippines. It consisted of a box of TN-8 seeds, N-P-K fertilizer, and Diazinon systemic insecticide with detailed instruction to grow a small plot of land for seeds that they could use in the next growing season. Our cadres visited these participating farmers on a regular basis throughout the growing season to make sure that the first trial was successful. These demonstration plots were so well cared for that some of them produced an incredible ten to eleven metric tons per hectare (almost ten thousand pounds per acre). I saw some government experiment stations using optimal techniques under ideal conditions that were able to produce an astounding yield of fifteen metric tons per hectare (thirteen thousand pounds per acre). When farmers saw this kind of yield with their own eyes, nothing could prevent them from growing TN-8.

Farmers had a maxim about growing rice: "*Nhut nuoc, nhi phan, tam can, tu giong,*" meaning "First water, second fertilizer, third diligent labor, fourth seeds." This was true for traditional subsistence rice farming. For growing high-yield rice in a commercial setting we needed more than that. So I came up with four additional essential inputs for modern commercial farming with the following parallel verse to teach cadres and farmers: "*Ngu thuoc, luc tien, that co, bac thi,*" meaning "Fifth medicines [insecticides, fungicides, and herbicides], sixth money [credit], seventh machines [mechanized implements], eighth market [government rice trade policy]." The Mekong River system produces an abundance of water. The whole delta was created from silt deposited through eons, and the land is very fertile. Traditionally, there were two growing seasons in the South: the monsoon (wet or rainy) season, also called summer–fall harvest, from May to October, and the dry season, or winter–spring harvest, from November to April of the following year. However, with new short-maturing high-yield rice varieties that mature in only ninety to a hundred days, and with irrigation that makes water available all the time, the seasons blur, with year-round planting possible in many areas. The Mekong Delta is crisscrossed by a complex canal system comprising some four thousand miles of natural and man-made waterways, big and small. During the dry season, many farmers use irrigation from manually powered or mechanical pumps to bring river or canal or even well water into their fields. Our Directorate of Farm Irrigation was responsible for water management and conservation. Old canals had to be improved, new canals had to be dug, and water rights had to be established. The right kind of water pumps had to be used, and farmers had to be trained by our farm water management experts.

Traditional farming relied upon natural fertilizer, like the nutrients in the silt that the river deposits in flooded rice fields every year. It also relied upon human and animal waste or even algae and legumes. But this is inadequate for commercial farming with new nitrogen-responsive, high-yield varieties of rice. Chemical fertilizer, usually of a mixture containing nitrogen, phosphorus, and potassium (N-P-K) in various proportions depending on the soil analysis of where it is used, is mandatory for growing new high-yield varieties to achieve maximal production. Since one pound of N-P-K fertilizer is required to produce ten to fifteen pounds of rice, to bring about the full potential of high-yield varieties, it is recommended to use 250 kilograms of N-P-K fertilizer per hectare (220 pounds per acre). Most farmers could not afford that expense, especially at the beginning of the program. So they used lesser amounts. Also, there was the perennial question of availability and affordability. Chemical fertilizer was an imported input, making its price high unless it was subsidized. The government had to subsidize this commodity to increase rice production. Furthermore, its availability was a problem in areas far from cities, towns, or farm co-op sites.

The Ministry of Trade and Industry (MTI) devoted an important portion of government foreign exchange to the importation of fertilizer. More than 200,000 metric tons were imported in 1967, 230,000 metric tons in 1968, 483,000 metric tons in 1969, and 502,000 metric tons in 1970. More would be needed in succeeding years as the planting of miracle rice sharply increased. This was why the DGA of the MLRAD endeavored to develop agri-input depots by private-sector merchants, farm co-ops, and farmers' unions closer and closer to the end-users, which were miracle rice farmers. Learning from my past experience in successfully promoting private sector participation in our Accelerated Protein Production Program in 1967, I had numerous meetings with local private-sector investors and bankers, from rural banks to agricultural development banks and commercial banks, as well as farmers' co-ops and unions, in all the sixteen provinces in the Mekong Delta. I told my service chiefs to do likewise. Some officials were reluctant to deal with the private sector for fear of being accused of connivance or collusion, so I taught them how to do it right in an open and public manner. The distribution of fertilizer, as well as other vital agri-inputs, had to be turned over to the commercial private sector and farmers' organizations had to be more efficient, economical, and free of corruption. In 1967, the Tenant Farmers' Association distributed 30 percent of imported fertilizers to their members and more in subsequent years.

Rice farming is labor intensive and subject to many unpredictable vagaries of nature: flood, drought, typhoon, untimely rain, infestation by insects, infection by diseases, and ravage by pests (birds, rodents, land crabs, snails, fish). In wartime, damage could be wrought by churning military amphibious vehicles and wading troops. Farmers first rely on family labor during peak labor requirement times (land preparation, seedling planting, harvest time, insect control spraying, weeding). Some time-sensitive activities required hired labor or exchange labor with friends, neighbors, colleagues, and relatives. Well-off farmers might have draft animals like cattle (oxen or water-buffaloes) for land preparation and transportation.

Human labor was a limiting factor in wartime due to the military draft on both sides of the conflict. Americans always complained about the high desertion rate of our armed forces. But ours was mainly a peasant-based army. During peak labor time, our soldiers did come home to help their parents with urgent farming chores. Fighting and killing enemies, even sworn ones, had to wait. It was a matter of survival for the family. I saw this all the time in my travels about the countryside and a lot of our officers at all levels were empathetic to this need. I often saw whole platoons or companies of RF (Regional Forces) or PF (Popular Forces) team up to help farmers with harvest chores as their civic action in order to have everybody stick together as a unit in case of need. To alleviate this labor constraint, the government promoted mechanization of farming operations. High yield rice farming required labor-saving machines due to the double or triple, or even quadruple, yields.

South Vietnam had hundreds of good-quality rice varieties that were famous all over the world (commonly known overseas as "Saigon Rice"), but, as noted previously, yield was low and maturation was long. There were long grain, short grain, medium grain, slender grain, and round grain varieties. There were aromatic and non-aromatic strains. There were white, red, purple, and charcoal species. There were sticky and non-sticky types. There were short-stemmed rice varieties growing in high lands, and twelve-foot long-stemmed rice varieties floating in deeply flooded fields. There were salty-water kinds that grow in the proximity of estuaries, and acid-stagnant-water rice kinds that thrive in land-locked fields. There were some eight hundred different local varieties of rice with suggestive, descriptive, and weird names.

But the main effort of the MLRAD was to grow the high-yield varieties developed by IRRI scientists to stamp out hunger in the third world. The first high-yield rice variety, TN-8, was soon followed by TN-5 (more suitable for deep water fields due to its long stem), TN-20, TN-22 (better cooking and eating quality), TN73-1, and TN73-2 (more insect-resistant, shorter maturation).

TN-8 had many shortcomings: the amylose (crystallized starch) content is high (28 percent), making the cooked rice hard to swallow when cold. The plant stem is short, thus unsuitable for deeply flooded rice fields. And the grains are short and big, unlike the long, slender grains of expensive rice. Although TN-8 was poor for eating because it quickly hardened when cold, it was wonderful for making noodles that did not break off and get mushy in soup. And Vietnamese eat a lot of noodles. Our specialists constantly conducted research to understand how to optimize yields of the new varieties in actual growing conditions and were instrumental in determining which variety grew best in which locality and at what time of year.

The miracle rice plants were susceptible to insects. Our crop protection specialists at the Crop Protection Service under the DCPP were always on the lookout for signs of trouble. Insect infestation was more effectively dealt with by preventive measures and early control than when it was full-blown and widespread. We found that TN-8, unlike later varieties or our native rice, was very susceptible to insects. Moreover, the heavy use of chemical fertilizer also promoted the rapid growth of weeds in rice fields. This necessitated the use of herbicides. Hand weeding was ineffective due to the lack of labor.

We had to import very expensive, highly health-hazardous, environment-degrading insecticides and herbicides and other plant protection chemicals. Sometimes overzealous and ignorant farmers misused these chemicals, which resulted in severe problems, such as the destruction of fish and snails that were part of farm families' diet and other living creatures that were links in the food chain. This necessitated more training and regulatory work to minimize the adverse side effects to the environment and people's health. We made a significant step forward by helping the private sector set up the first in-country biodegradable nonsystemic insecticide (Diazinon) manufacturing plant in 1972. A second plant producing a similar but more toxic biodegradable systemic pesticide (Furadan) was built in 1973. Three domestic fertilizer blending plants were constructed, two in 1972 and one in 1973.

Since farming is a risky proposition at best due to the unpredictable and uncontrollable vagaries of nature, the normal sources of commercial credit, such as banks, are out of reach for many farmers. Yet we found from experience that farmers were good borrowers. Special governmental or quasi-governmental sources of credit had to be made available to farmers close to their villages, particularly during the start-up phase. Thus, national credit unions, agricultural development banks, and rural banks were born. The original National Credit Unions (*Quoc Gia Nong Tin Cuoc*), set up by the Diem Regime, were inadequate. So, with loans from the Asian Development Bank, our Agricultural Development Banks (ADB, *Ngan Hang Phat Trien Nong Nghiep*) were developed. Farm Cooperatives and Farmers' Unions also provided credit to their members according to their means.

The amounts loaned with ADB funds showed how fast the program was growing: 1968, VN$4.13 billion; 1969, VN$4.62 billion; 1970, VN$6 billion; 1971, VN$10.067 billion (to 170,611 farmers and fishermen); 1972, VN$18.924 billion (to 202,714 farmers and fishermen); 1973, VN$26.4 billion (projected); 1974: VN$28.7 billion (projected). Small, non-collateralized loans averaged VN$25,000 or less; medium loans went up to VN$50,000; large loans went up to VN$500,000. Forty percent of this low-interest credit was earmarked for rice production and three quarters of these loans were made to small farmers without collateral. By the end of the year, more than three-fourths of the outstanding loans were repaid in full.

There were also forty-eight rural banks, created following the Filipino model, in order to mobilize private funding. These were established in district towns close to farmers. The owners of these banks were usually people who did business with farmers or landowners who received large compensation money from the government and wanted to invest in another line of business. Under the new Rural Banking Law, investors did not have to pay any taxes, fees, or interest for five years. Even though half of the money of these private banks came from the ADB and the training was done by the ADB, these banks operated under the new banking law without interference from the government. The ADB supervised their operations to make sure they did business according to the law. These banks were responsive to the needs of farmers. Village Administrative Committees (*Hoi Dong Xa*) even played a role in processing the loan applications of farmers.

Modern commercial farming requires the mechanization of farm operations to reduce the cost of production, especially when production is high but labor is scarce. To encourage mechanization, the MTI made its scarce foreign exchange reserve available for the importation by the private sector of a large variety of farm machinery. I saw all sizes of tractors for dry field plowing and tilling of soil. Farmers also used small Japanese and Taiwanese tillers suitable for wet fields and even mechanical planters of seedlings. And for the first time, during harvest, one could see all kinds of mobile harvesters, transportable dryers, threshers, automatic millers, and baggers parked along the highways to harvest and process the paddy. But the machine that we most saw everywhere was the water pump. There were all types and all sizes of water pumps. We imported 40,000 water pumps of all sizes in 1967, 174,000 of these small gasoline engines in 1969, and 186,000 similar engines in 1970 and in 1971. These machines not only were used for irrigation and draining of rice fields, but they were used also to motorize sampans and other boats of all sizes with some clever tinkering, and motorized water transport was a great benefit in many remote areas without roads. In 1970, the Ministry of Economy (MoE) earmarked US$15,000,000 for the importation of farm machinery of all types, including large quantities of small implements like hand insecticide sprayers and herbicide applicators for the control of insects and weeds.

Our Directorate of Farm Mechanization trained local cadres, farm co-ops, and farmers' unions, in collaboration with foreign manufacturers, in the use, maintenance, and repair of new farm machinery. Our mechanical engineers invented quite a few simple machines themselves that could be duplicated easily in-country and that made farming less labor-intensive. They helped local manufacturers produce some of this farm machinery, and we started to see in-country manufacture and commercial sale of grain threshers, dryers, grinders, and irrigation pumps.

Some enterprising individuals with financial means, such as former landlords, bought on their own initiative with their compensation money large or medium farm tractors or wet field tillers to prepare the soil for farmers, harvesters or mobile threshers, or transportable dryers and portable millers to process paddy during harvest time at mutually agreed fees. They made a brisk and lucrative business during certain stages of the crop season. However, most of these essential activities were performed for farmers by their co-ops and unions or by the farmers themselves once they made enough money to buy their own equipment, which more and more of them did.

Our Directorate of Farm Co-operatives and Farmers' Unions was quite busy organizing farmers into self-governing co-ops and unions to pool their limited resources so that they could obtain loans for agri-inputs at more affordable costs. Farmers' co-ops and unions also strengthen the farmers' bargaining power during the marketing phase. We were able to organize thirty thousand farmers and fishermen into co-operatives in 1972.

It turned out that marketing was the weakest link of the AMRPP because our government tightly controlled the rice trade due to the wartime need to deny food to the enemy. This tended to stifle the market and to discourage production at a commercial level. Farmers invariably choose to revert to subsistence farming if there is an artificial or arbitrary price control of rice that makes rice growing a non-profitable enterprise. Countries that control rice prices tend to be rice importers. Under our wartime condition, we did not have enough time to solve this problem.

At that time our country was plagued with constant problems of supplying rice to rice-deficient areas, with corruption by unscrupulous officials in charge of controlling the movement of rice, and with speculation, hoarding, and black market profiteering by rice merchants. Corruption is inherent with any effort to control markets. It wrought havoc in urban life and on the fixed income segment of our society, such as soldiers and civil servants, and it seriously distracted the central government. Consequently, there were concerted efforts by the MTI in 1973 to implement a new rice marketing policy based on free trade and private sector involvement in all aspects of the business, and to get the government's tight control and stiff regulation out of this vitally important sector of our economy. I will discuss this effort in the last part of this narrative when I turn to the Rice Marketing Program for which I was personally responsible.

I want to mention the assistance of our allies in implementing the AMRPP. The Philippines provided the first six tons of IR-8 high-yield rice from IRRI to jumpstart our Green Revolution. The IRRI rice experts and other Filipino agriculturists helped us carry out our rice research and new rice varieties adaptation since they knew a lot more about them than our experts. The Nationalist Chinese Aid Mission helped us with post-rice-harvest horticulture to supplement farmers' income and to fully utilize land resources. The mission introduced a lot of new high-yield fast-growing strains of vegetables and taught us modern horticultural practices. Farmers gained extra income from these secondary crops. The Nationalist Chinese were also good at fresh-water fish farming, which was a big commercial enterprise for people living along the many tributaries of the Mekong River system.

American advisors were a constant source of assistance, although they sometimes created unnecessary problems for us. One intransigent American pest-control expert working in the Mekong Delta was adamant about killing rice-field rats. His thinking was that rats destroyed an enormous amount of rice paddy every year, rice that could be put to good use feeding people in the cities. He supported his contention with all kinds of studies, and we could not convince him that farmers trapped these well-fed rice-field rats to eat and to sell in urban markets. Rats are ugly to look at but are a rich source of protein, are very tasty, and they constitute an easy source of cash for rice farmers.

We were caught between the unwilling farmers and a well-meaning American friend. I advised our people to do everything the American taught them to do about training farmers in pest control, but when he was gone they should take the poison home and use it in offices and homes to kill mice and city sewer rats instead. Meanwhile, I invited the American pest control expert and our field people to a scrumptious five-course "baby rabbit" dinner. When the American said that this was the best meal of baby rabbit he had ever eaten, I explained to him what he had eaten and that rice-fed field rats were an appreciated source of nutrition for our people.

One thing we appreciated was that USAID helped with funding to set up thousands of demonstration plots all over the country, especially in the Mekong Delta. At harvest time we trucked farmers from afar to see the results for themselves. All this grassroots work required a lot of agricultural technocrats from all levels, from engineers to technicians and down to cadres who would work with farmers in the countryside. The intensive training of these technocrats to make them well-versed in the latest rice-growing technology was extremely important. We had a huge, world-class Rice Research and Training Station in the Delta staffed by our best foreign-trained scientists and educators. We trained people by the thousands and they would go back to their provinces and villages to train other people and the farmers in their localities.

In wartime, security was a constant concern, but thanks to the government pacification program after 1968, about 80 to 90 percent of our hamlets and villages became secure enough for us to be active. Most of our problems in implementing the MLRAD programs nevertheless came from our implacable enemy. For example, some American fisheries expert obtained for us a wonderful fish species from the Philippines called Tilapia that reproduced extremely fast. All the farmers had to do was to release a few baby fish in the flooded rice-fields at the beginning of the growing season and by the end of the wet season they could harvest thousands of them without having to do anything. This fish is an excellent source of easy, good, and cheap protein. However, at night the Viet Cong would parade an individual with an advanced case of leprosy through the villages and have him or her say that the affliction was caused by eating Tilapia. This rumor spread through the Mekong Delta and caused many farmers to stop eating that fish. To counteract this scheme, a lot of our local officials and I visited villages to have a lunch of fried Tilapia fish with village officials and invited skeptical farmers to join in. I also requested that local authorities take all lepers to the Bao Loc Leprosy Colony for treatment by the Catholic nuns there. Wherever I went I hauled with me soybean oil for deep-frying small Tilapia fish. After a short time this scare tactic was neutralized, and to this day Tilapia fish are still popular in the Delta.

The successful implementation of any government program depended to a large extent upon leaders and administrators at the province and district levels. You could not achieve much without the strong support and close cooperation of regional, provincial, and local authorities during those war years. I devoted much effort toward developing working relationships with these people. Localities that were predominantly Hoa Hao or Roman Catholic were the most efficient for establishing working relationships because the people there were strongly anticommunist and easily influenced by their leaders. The top two rice-producing areas of the country to this day are still An Giang (which is mainly Hoa Hao) and Kien Giang (where many North Vietnamese Roman Catholic farmers relocated in the 1950s).

As far as our government was concerned, South Vietnam had achieved self-sufficiency in rice when 7,150,000 metric tons of paddy was produced in the 1974–75 harvest, and this figure does not include the high-yield rice produced outside the DGA-sponsored program, which was substantial. A small amount of American rice was imported for the last time in 1974, not because it was needed for the food supply but rather to calm the unstable rice market. By late 1974, the National Food Administration (NFA), an autonomous agency under the MTI that I headed since late 1973, had a strategic stockpile of some 200,000 metric tons in Military Region (MR) I, MR II, and MR III, with more coming in the pipeline on a daily basis from the Mekong Delta, despite heavy fighting and emergency shipments for refugees. In 1974, the NFA shipped only two thousand metric tons to perennially rice-deficient Central Vietnam as compared to forty thousand metric tons in 1973.

Another proof that rice was not in short supply was that some provinces in traditionally rice-deficient Central South Vietnam, like Ninh Thuan and Phu Yen, did not need Southern rice for the first time in a decade. It was only in the northern provinces of MR I, where a lot of heavy fighting caused the abandonment of rice fields and a sharp increase of refugees, that rice stored in Da Nang government warehouses was needed on a regular basis. A more significant proof that the rice situation was no longer critical was that no future plans to import rice were contemplated. The shipment of American rice to South Vietnam in early 1974 to stabilize the rice market was hardly used and ended up being stockpiled for strategic reserve. Only native rice was used on the market because imported rice lost its appeal due to the new nonsubsidized price set at the world market level under our new trade policy, which was put into effect during the first days of 1974.

RICE MARKETING PROGRAM: THE NATIONAL FOOD ADMINISTRATION

I was working on exciting spin-off programs when the president appointed me vice-minister of agriculture, a cabinet rank, which led to something even more important that I was called upon to carry out. This was the first time that the agricultural sector had a vice-minister. In late December 1973, President Thieu appointed me to take over the old General Supply Agency (GSA), renamed the National Food Administration (NFA), with the task of setting up a strategic stockpile of rice to stabilize the rice market and to end speculation and hoarding. Despite our success in increasing the production of rice, South Vietnam was caught in the most serious food crisis in years due to inflation. The price of rice and other food commodities—sugar, milk, meat, fish, vegetables—shot up day after day, and hoarding or hiding by unscrupulous merchants and retailers caused artificial scarcity and unavailability. Speculation and black marketeering were rampant, and the government was unable to cope effectively with the dire situation, despite the fact that we had great success with our AMRPP. Newspapers were fueling popular discontent with incendiary and irresponsible reporting. The crisis was aggravated by the worldwide oil crisis of 1973, the serious refugee problem stemming from the 1972 North Vietnamese Offensive, and the farmers who stockpiled their rice as a hedge against inflation, among other things.

There was one thing about President Thieu that everyone who worked for him knew very well: he had the knack of picking out the right leaders, whether military or civilian, to do the important jobs and then completely trusting and supporting them in their tasks and never questioning their modus operandi. Neither the Independence Palace nor the prime minister's office ever called me or my boss, the Minister of Trade and Industry, about anything concerning the implementation of this vital program. I knew how to produce rice but did not know about marketing rice; I would have to learn fast.

The prime-ministerial decree establishing the NFA gave it sweeping power in the procurement, storage, and distribution of all kinds of food items, but no guideline on how to accomplish all that or specifically how to set up a strategic rice stockpile. I reported to Nguyen Duc Cuong, the newly appointed Minister of Trade and Industry (MTI), because the NFA fell under his jurisdiction. He advised me to simply focus on results and to establish a strategic rice reserve to stabilize the market as fast as possible.

To buy rice for stockpiling, we needed a lot of money and I soon understood that this was forthcoming. To begin with, the prime minister allocated VN$30 billion for NFA operations. No unit in the government except the Ministry of Defense handled that much money. Eventually, the NFA's rice operation would amount to some VN$70 billion, which, according to the Bunker Papers,[7] was equivalent to 10 percent of the government's annual budget.

I also requested a new salary structure for NFA employees. I proposed to the Board of Directors of the NFA, which Minister Cuong chaired, an outrageous salary and wage structure for our employees that was roughly equivalent to at least three times the current government employees' pay scale. When Minister Cuong objected to such an outrageous request, I replied that all NFA people would have to work double shifts and more to accomplish such an urgent task with the necessary speed. We would be expected to go out into the countryside at great personal risk to procure rice paddy from the farmers in direct competition with the VC; to ride shotgun on trucks, barges, and boats to safeguard the NFA rice or paddy to prevent pilferage; to live and work in warehouses and to take turns pulling armed guard duty day and night to protect and manage the NFA's stockpile. I argued that if the NFA was to be entrusted with tens of billions of piasters to buy rice for the government in order to stabilize our economy, it made no sense to treat NFA employees like any other group of civil servants.

In making such a bold request, I followed the advice of my deputy, Nguyen Thanh Qui, an old bureaucracy pro who told me that a usual ploy to get what you wanted in government circles was to ask for two or three times as much as you want and hope to get what you need after your proposal was scaled down by higher authority. I did not know how Minister Cuong was able to persuade the board of directors, but my request was approved in its entirety, which greatly surprised us.

Our people's performance was exemplary because I told them from the start that either they worked hard, efficiently, honestly, and beyond the call of duty for the NFA, and would be well compensated for that, or they would be transferred to the military, because I would not put up with any dereliction of duty or any semblance of transgression from normal behavior or any ethical violation. I had no time to babysit anyone or to look over everybody's shoulders. It was easy to manage personnel of draft age during a vicious war who were earning a salary three times higher than the current official pay scale. Consequently, the NFA incurred no major waste of funds or manpower considering the great number of people it hired. Furthermore, it incurred no serious damage of product stockpiled in all four military regions, considering the big volume it handled in such a massive undertaking.

There were NFA people who worked all night long, like those IBM card-punchers who operated the US Embassy's IBM-360 computers to benefit land reform. There were young people who carried, with trepidation, millions of piasters in attaché cases and followed provincial military operations for days on end to buy paddy, bargaining with farmers and middlemen and bringing rice safely back without a hitch. I was very proud of the NFA employees' performance. I still think that it was providential protection that allowed us to achieve such remarkable results in such a trying time. I would not have been able to do it without my trustworthy former students from the NAI that I trained into patriotic and dedicated employees.

The first thing I did when I began my duty in earnest at the NFA was to have a crash course on rice marketing by holding a staff meeting with the managerial folks of the old General Supply Agency (GSA), an arm of the old Ministry of Economy (MoE),

---

[7] Douglas Pike, ed., "The Bunker Papers: Reports to the President from Saigon, 1967–73," volumes 1, 2, and 3, Indochina Research Monograph, Institute of East Asian Studies, University of California–Berkeley and The Asian Foundation, 1990.

to find out how they procured rice for the government in the past. I learned that the GSA mainly handled the distribution of American aid PL-480 rice to our civil servants and our Quartermaster General at a subsidized price set roughly at 20 to 25 percent below the world market price. The GSA also handled the distribution of other American Food for Peace surplus items, like soybean oil and wheat flour. And it handled the distribution of other items that the MoE imported, like sugar, condensed milk, canned foods, French alcoholic beverages, Honda mopeds, and clothes, to stabilize the market and to help civil servants and soldiers' families survive inflationary pressure.

I found out that in early 1973 the GSA tried to procure native rice from the Mekong Delta at a price set too low for farmers to sell at a profit. It was an impossible policy despite all kinds of pressure from General Nguyen Vinh Nghi, the MR IV Commander, and the province chiefs down there. When farmers and merchants could not make a profit, they would neither sell their rice nor bring it to Saigon, especially with all the needed transport permits, the check points, and the harassment by authorities about storage limits. And that was the cause of our serious rice crisis that consumed so much of our government's attention, not to mention the great anxiety and hardship to the urban population that it caused.

The lack of an adequate strategic reserve of rice (equivalent to a two or three months' national supply) was the major cause of the 1973 rice-marketing crisis. Without this reserve, the MoE could neither intervene to control speculation nor calm the market by selling from its stock to satisfy demand, nor could it offer incentives for farmers to increase production, preferably through a previously announced attractive price for its purchase of rice to maintain the stockpile. I decided that the NFA would have to come up with its own new modus operandi to accomplish the mission given to it by President Thieu.

I needed to learn the best way to deal with this crisis, so I turned to the American experts with USAID. The South Vietnamese government did not have anybody who knew what to do, else we would not have had this kind of crisis to begin with. Most South Vietnamese officials were reluctant about asking American experts for advice for fear of showing their shortcomings, their ignorance, or their dependence on foreigners, or for fear of foreign interference in our affairs. I never had such an inferiority complex vis-à-vis the Americans because I remembered President Park Chung Hee's words given to our delegation years before about how he built an impressive country in a short time with American assistance. Of course, he was lucky that American armed forces remained stationed in his country to prevent a communist takeover, which, unfortunately, was not the case for us.

Nevertheless, we were fortunate to have the advice of Bill Bolton, an agricultural economist from Louisiana State University, who taught us to take the government out of the rice business and let the private sector in. Farmers were producing plenty of rice, but were reluctant to sell because the fixed price was too low and middlemen could not put up with all the problems caused by government controls that impeded the free movement of rice. Without the possibility of making a profit, farmers would go back to subsistence farming, and all our past efforts to promote miracle rice would come to naught. Open market competition would encourage efficiency and innovation with lower costs; bureaucrats are inefficient, ineffective, wasteful, and insensitive to consumers' needs. He recommended that we set up a strategic reserve as fast as possible, to allow a profit-driven private rice sector to develop in the economy, and to encourage the modernization of this sector with up-to-date processing and storage facilities. With Bolton's advice, it took us less than a month to ramp up our program to implement the policy of decontrol and deregulation of the rice trade that Minister Cuong promulgated in the first days of 1974.

Minister Cuong drew a lot of fire from the press for setting the price of rice 20 percent higher than the previous subsidized rice price to bring it into line with the world market price. This made it easy for us to stock the strategic reserve with local rice bought at prices between the new price of imported rice and the old fixed price on a supply-and-demand basis. Hardly anybody wanted expensive imported American rice anymore. So, the last shipment of imported American PL-480 rice from USAID was mostly stockpiled for strategic reserve. The North Vietnamese communists consumed most of that rice when their troops invaded and took over South Vietnam in 1975; you could rightly say that North Vietnam thereby received its first American aid.

After a few months, I knew at exactly what prices of paddy the farmers were willing to sell, what prices of rice the consumers were able to afford, and what margins of mark-up the middlemen and the retailers needed to operate profitably. The NFA made a VN$3.4 billion profit during the first year of operation on a VN$30 billion volume of business, which was unheard of in governmental circles.

To simplify and optimize our operations with a view to develop the private sector, we phased out our risky direct purchasing activities from farmers and their co-ops or associations and relied more and more on middlemen and private commercial banks through big contracts worth tens, scores, and even hundreds of millions of piasters each. Once rice was no longer subsidized and native rice was readily available, demands for the NFA's rice from retailers and consumers' organizations were on the decrease. Even the military wanted to buy native rice on the free market for its use. I encouraged that decision because that would grow the private sector, encourage competition, and, above all, lessen the NFA's burden, although a careless pricing policy could allow middle merchants to squeeze the farmers and adversely affect production, and procurement following established government procedures was wasteful and subject to corruption in comparison with the pricing policy of an agency like the NFA.

The rice supply situation was pretty much under control after a couple of months. I knew that our efforts were bearing fruit when the NFA began to run out of storage space toward the end of 1974, an indication that more rice was coming in to our warehouses than was leaving. That's when I was ordered by the MTI to conduct a study of the infrastructure needed for the coming resumption of rice exports, which had ended back in 1964 due to the disruption of rice production brought on by the intensifying war. It is instructive to note that South Vietnam got out of the "nanny statehood" condition, even under the stress and strain of a raging war, when our government stopped subsidizing rice and other food items.

The food crisis was not resolved to everybody's satisfaction. But it was nevertheless fundamentally resolved because Minister Nguyen Duc Cuong dared to promulgate the right rice trade policy. The NFA marketed probably less than half a million metric tons of processed rice in a country that annually produced more than 7 million metric tons. If we had not lost the war, the next few years would have seen an even more diminished role and decreasing activities for the NFA. The private sector would carry the heavy load once it became stronger and the government role became smaller.

All through the escalating war years, food supply had been a perennial problem that so often wrought havoc in urban life, especially among the fixed income segment of our population. But in 1973, it was really serious because it was compounded by a number of issues: tight government control of the rice trade; speculative hoarding by wholesalers and retailers; the world oil crisis; a delay in the importation of American PL-480 rice due to the tight world market; a higher rice consumption quota given to civil servants and soldiers as a subsidy to alleviate the burden of inflation on their fixed income; a higher consumption of government rice by large numbers of refugees after the 1972 North Vietnamese offensive; the harassment of farmers and rice merchants by the enemy in the form of heavy taxation and the restriction of trade; the hoarding of paddy by farmers as a hedge against inflation; a wait-and-see attitude by rice merchants in face of rumors about impending changes in government rice marketing policy; and the lack of an adequate government rice reserve.

One must understand that the policy of tight control and heavy regulation of the rice trade was born out of the ostensible need to deny food to our enemy. Yet, in reality, there were at best roughly fifty thousand guerillas in the vast Mekong Delta who consumed at most eight thousand metric tons of paddy a year at the high average per capita consumption of 160 kilograms of processed rice (an equivalent of 260 kilograms of paddy) a year. The communists controlled some 10 to 15 percent of the farmers living in remote areas, who kept up to fifty thousand metric tons of paddy from the rice trade, if even that. Usually, farmers could not keep rice for long due to lack of storage facilities and the need to pay high taxes to the communists. As such, there was no effective way for us to prevent the communists who lived with or close to the people they controlled or intimidated from getting all the rice they needed.

We were lucky at that time because the military and political situations occupied all our leaders' attention. So we, the civilians in charge of the economic realm, were pretty much left alone to do what we saw fit. For example, when I assumed my job at the NFA, the first operation I faced was the unloading and stockpiling of three emergency shiploads of American rice that were diverted to South Vietnam from other Southeast Asian countries. Out of curiosity, I went to the dock area to see how things were done. What I saw appalled me. I saw that workers from the powerful CVT (Confederation Vietnamienne de Travail, Confederation of Vietnamese Workers), the unionized dockworkers unloading the rice bags, caused a lot of breakage and waste on the barge so that they could pilfer that precious spilled rice later on. I also witnessed hordes of kids swarming around the loaded trucks with hollow pointed sticks commonly used to sample the contents of bagged grainy merchandise for testing and checking. The kids would stick the bags on the periphery to drain out a few pounds of rice from each bag into their own burlap bags.

I called the contractor doing the work there and threatened him with being blacklisted from doing business with the NFA. There was some improvement, but kids still chased the trucks and stuck the bags at every red light. And at the docks the union workers still stole bags of rice by throwing them to sampans swarming around the barges, or by sticking the bags to siphon off a few pounds from each bag.

So, I put my old high school mate, an Army Ranger captain named Do Quang Bieu, who had been discharged after being severely wounded in battle, in charge of unloading at the docks with orders to shoot if necessary to prevent pilfering by the laborers unloading the ships. I had one of my colonels in charge of our office defense force organize an NFA security detail armed with loaded M-30 carbines to ride shotgun on top of each truck from the dock all the way to the warehouse. I also had my six-man bodyguard detail ride their motorcycles and jeep in convoy with the trucks to deter pilferers. As a result, our 3 percent demurrage was close to zero and we gained almost an extra thousand metric tons of rice, something unheard of in rice shipping. In other words, the supplier gave us an extra three kilograms for each one hundred kilograms of rice they shipped to make up for unavoidable losses from their warehouses to our warehouses. We had almost no loss. And the NFA had a windfall of $30,000,000 extra piasters from which I rewarded the men who guarded against pilferage.

Our policies were intended to achieve the following results: by increasing the subsidized price of imported American rice to be in line with the world market price, we made American rice less attractive than local rice to consumers. By ending price controls on domestic rice, rice prices would follow supply and demand. By abolishing provincial restraints on the movement of rice, such as transport permits and inspection check points, rice moved expeditiously from producer to consumer. By ending limits on how much rice could be stored by farmers and merchants, we put a stop to irrational searches and seizures of warehouses. By having the NFA procure rice at competitive prices, we enhanced the benefits of market forces. In addition, after facilitating the creation a of stable market-driven rice sector, the NFA could begin to concentrate on plans to export rice on the world market.

Some of the important elements of our policy implementation were:
- Reorganizing the old GFA to handle the new functions of the NFA, in particular the establishing of a strategic rice reserve.
- Procuring Mekong Delta rice from farmers and their self-governing co-ops and unions, transporting it to our warehouses located close to points of consumption, and dispatching it to rice-deficient areas in Central Vietnam or distributing it to retail outlets or government entities that needed it.
- Decentralizing operations and delegating authority to regional and provincial offices to avoid wasting time doing everything through Saigon.
- Having committees of several persons make important decisions to promote transparency.
- Putting in place state-of-the-art management procedures for accounting, computerized inventories, procurement contracts, and distribution documentation.
- Creating strong inspection and investigation units for the early detection of potential problems.

Naturally, security for our activities in wartime was a constant concern. The Viet Cong threatened farmers against cooperating with us, but farmers would wait for our provincial or district military operations to sell us their paddy because later they could tell the Viet Cong that we had forced them to sell their rice to us. Our greatest initial challenge was to figure out how to do something our government had never done before, that is, to procure rice in an open market. Our purchasing agents learned how to do their jobs through trial and error. Initially, they bought rice directly from farmers, took it to the nearest commercial rice mills for processing, and then transported the final products (various kinds of rice and bran) to our warehouses. After gaining more experience, they made contracts with wholesalers, commercial banks, and farmers' organizations like co-ops and unions.

There were scores of young ag-school graduates each carrying millions of piasters into the countryside to find farmers or merchants, and then bargaining with them to come to a mutually agreed price. They then had to stick with that acquisition every step of the way, day and night, to ensure that nothing happened to it until its final destination. They then started another acquisition somewhere else and the whole process began anew. These young people were idealistic, dedicated, and patriotic.

I was fortunate to be able to assemble a staff of experienced, dedicated, and honest officials. Ngo Van Quyen served as chief of the Crop Protection Service; he had experience in the insecticide private sector and became my second deputy administrator general in charge of logistics. Nguyen Tram Thach, an agronomist working at the Bureau of Agricultural Statistics, became my director of rice procurement. Bui Dien Tho, another agronomist and the deputy director of farm co-operatives and farmers' unions, became my chief of inspection. Nguyen Xuan Dao, an agricultural economist and one of my best students at NAI, became the NFA director for MR III.

Nguyen Thanh Qui became my deputy administrator general in charge of administration and finance; he had vast administrative experience, having worked in government since the days of President Ngo Dinh Diem and having navigated our Land to the Tiller Program through the red tape maze. I asked him to bring in several top graduates from the National Institute of Administration to help us set up new administrative and financial procedures. Qui was made nervous by how the young "reformists" and I made our own rules and procedures, not following the existing bureaucratic formalities. For example, we did not go through any time-consuming bidding procedures to procure rice or to contract with service providers (transportation, rice milling, warehousing) as other government institutions would do. But I believe that I did it the right way because it solved a spiraling-out-of-control problem in a short time and it repositioned our country on a course of positive economic development. President Thieu nodded his head in appreciation of the swift results when he heard my report to the Council of Ministers of "Mission Accomplished." Price-Waterhouse validated the way we conducted our business as well.

In late 1974, I was the target of a vicious campaign of character assassination by our free but irresponsible press. In South Vietnam in those days, we had quite a few venal reporters who were good at smearing people in power to extort money from them. For several months a few of these hacks portrayed me under the worst imaginable light. Of course, I chose to ignore them because all the accusations were not only baseless but also ridiculous, and I suspected that their fabrications came from some of the former disgruntled employees of the old GSA that I had reorganized into the new NFA with my new people in managerial positions. At one point, the campaign was so distracting that it began to affect my performance and my family. I finally requested an audience with the prime minister to offer my resignation, but he told me to "learn how to play the democratic game" and not to worry about unfounded accusations, because if someone wants to distort the truth they always find some way to do it, as they also do to the president and his wife. He advised that we must learn to live with democracy and a free press and that I should stay put and carry on. As he walked me to the door, he offered this French saying, "*Si tu t'arretes chaque fois que tu entends un chien aboyer, tu n'arriveras jamais au bout de la route*," meaning, "If you stop every time you hear a dog bark, you will never get to the end of the road." And so I let the dogs bark and continued my journey until the military and political situations got so bad that nobody paid any attention to me or to the NFA anymore. But, it was disheartening and aggravating nevertheless.

One problem was substandard physical facilities and antiquated rice processing plants. To stockpile our strategic reserve, we needed a lot of warehouses. But our warehouses were old and substandard. They were easily infested with rodents and insects that caused unnecessary losses due to damage and waste. Also, most rice processing plants were small, inefficient, and antiquated, causing an unacceptably high level of broken rice—sometimes as high as 25 percent instead of the usual 6 percent. Granted that Vietnamese will eat broken rice in breakfast dishes and the price of broken rice is as high as processed rice itself. The usual level of acceptable broken grains in exported rice is 5 percent. Therefore, to export rice we had to build new modern facilities to process rice at higher grades.

On the other hand, in South Vietnam at that time, rice merchants made more money on the sale of rice-milling byproducts, which usually amounted to 25 percent of the weight of rice paddy, than they made selling rice itself. For example, one hundred kilograms of rice paddy on average produced seventy-five kilograms of processed rice (sold for $VN160–190 per kilogram), twelve kilograms of white bran (sold for VN$70–120 per kilogram), seven kilograms of brown bran (sold for VN$40–90), and six kilograms of broken rice (sold for VN$140-160). Rich rice merchants owning means of transportation such as motorized boats, barges, and trucks also made more since it cost on the average VN$900 per one hundred kilograms to move rice from the Delta to Saigon. So the business aspect of the rice market was embedded in the outdated infrastructure.

A problem we had in 1974 arose from a campaign for income tax recovery launched by a new, tough, incorruptible Director General of Taxation (DGT), who unexpectedly produced heavy income assessments on a lot of rice merchants. The estimated income tax originally was set at 1.5 percent of gross sales. Then, in July 1974, this was raised to 6 percent of gross sales. This wrought havoc in these businessmen's financial situations and severely disrupted their rice marketing operations. The NFA was caught in the middle of this unpredictable snafu that brought our rice procurement almost to a standstill until the matter was resolved between the taxpayers and the DGT through lengthy and difficult negotiations.

At the end 1974, there was another reshuffle of President Thieu's Administration. The NFA had two new bosses, the Minister of Trade and Supply (MTS, the renamed MTI) Nguyen Van Diep and the Vice-Prime Minister for Economy and Finance *cum* Minister of Agriculture Nguyen Van Hao. Both of these executives were educated in Europe and they did not know me at all. I had the impression that they did not think too highly of me. From their actions, I concluded that they had decided to curb my activities. Unlike my previous boss, Minister Nguyen Duc Cuong, this new economic team was very hands-on and the NFA was subjected to a lot of micro-management that made our operations slow and inefficient. They tolerated me only because I was President Thieu's appointee. This situation did not last very long because the political and military situations became chaotic at the end of our country's existence. Also, there were signs that the government was squeezing the private sector with a new credit and pricing policy that tended to make the merchants' profit margin a lot smaller. I sensed that the big powerful government squeeze was creeping back.

But not everything was difficult or bad. In fact, we were lucky to have a lot of good things that went our way. We were blessed with no shortage of funds. Furthermore, we profited from managing our business with great efficiency and relatively low waste or loss. The NFA did not lose any funds that the government entrusted to it. There were a couple of unscrupulous commercial banks that contracted with the NFA to buy rice but used that money to finance their more lucrative import business and could not deliver rice on time. We planned to pursue them in court to recover our money, but we had to be careful for fear of wrecking the banking system and destroying popular confidence. On the recommendation of banking authorities, the NFA was somewhat lenient with them about deadlines, but they were blacklisted and excluded from future business.

We developed good working relationships with most province chiefs in the Mekong Delta, where 80 percent of land redistribution had occurred and where most surplus rice was grown. I also had good relations with our Military Region Commanders, among whom General Nguyen Khoa Nam, commander of MR IV in the Mekong Delta, was especially important and helpful, because most of the NFA's operations were carried out in the Mekong Delta. General Nam was single and a devout Buddhist. At the end, he was one of our five general officers who took their own lives rather than suffer incarceration in the communist gulag by surrendering to the enemy.

At a meeting in the Presidential Palace when I was invited to report about the rice situation in the different Military Regions, I noticed something that spoke volumes about President Thieu's leadership. After my report that the rice situation was stabilized for any eventuality that might arise until the next harvest, the quartermaster general voiced his complaint about the nonsubsidized price of rice that caused undue hardship for soldiers and their families and he suggested that the NFA go back to the low subsidized price of the old days. When asked for my opinion, of course, with my past experience in land reform and agricultural development, the answer was unequivocal that we must find some other way to assist our deserving troops or we could risk the possibility that the farmers would go back to subsistence farming, and then not only our troops and their families, but all of us would be in a world of trouble.

He asked the opinion of the commanding general of MR IV, from where all the surplus rice was coming. General Nam seconded my opinion, saying that farmers were happy and prosperous and the rice trade was flourishing. As more and more rice is produced, the rice price will come down sooner or later, he predicted. He recommended that the current policy be continued, although we needed to find some other way to help our troops and their families.

President Thieu agreed and ordered the Ministry of Defense to study the problem to come up with a solution that did not change the rice trade policy. President Thieu usually favored the poor farmers more than any other segment of our society. Probably this was due to the fact that he came from a humble origin himself. His background included farming, fishing, and trading. Later, the government twice readjusted upward the fixed income of civil servants and the military to alleviate their income problem.

We were lucky in 1973, 1974, and 1975, because our Accelerated Miracle Rice Production Program was blessed with clement weather and the absence of insect infestation or epidemic diseases: conditions were favorable for profitable rice farming. There were increasingly abundant successive harvests that, according to the Bunker Reports, brought South Vietnam to a virtual rice self-sufficiency level by late 1974 or early 1975.[8] Good rice harvests always led to increased freshwater fish, duck, pig, and chicken production, and plenty of affordable food for urban people.

---

[8] Pike, ed., "The Bunker Papers."

We were also fortunate in having USAID's timely and effective intervention to provide an emergency diversion of three shiploads of PL-480 rice initially destined for other Southeast Asian countries, which helped quell urban consumers' anxiety. I suspected that the funding the NFA received from the government came from the counterpart fund generated by this rice. USAID was helpful in other technical areas as well.

We managed to stabilize the rice market within two months, rapidly building up the strategic reserve. At the same time, rice moving to urban markets eased consumer worries and ended speculation and black marketeering. Prices stopped fluctuating wildly, as the NFA used its stocks to control the rice trade. Along with the benefits of the AMRPP, our opening the market enabled some chronically rice-deficient central provinces, such as Ninh Thuan and Phu Yen, to become self-sufficient. Shipments of government rice to deficit areas in Central Vietnam were reduced from 40,000 metric tons in 1973 to 2,000 metric tons in 1974. Within three months we had established strategic stockpiles of some 200,000 metric tons, constituting the last shipment of PL-480 American rice as well as locally procured rice. We intended to procure 300,000 metric tons of rice in 1975 and maintain a strategic rice reserve of that amount at all times. In 1974, the NFA made a profit of VN$3.4 billion from the distribution of 297,000 metric tons of domestic rice to consumer markets. We were even able to send 48,000 metric tons of rice to our Cambodian ally.

Our new rice pricing policy made miracle rice farming lucrative. This policy propelled the AMRPP into overdrive in 1974 and 1975 and enabled South Vietnam to achieve self-sufficiency after producing an estimated 7.1 million metric tons of paddy. By the end of 1974, the rice trade was once again a profitable business, as the NFA injected VN$70 billion (one tenth of the national budget, according to the Bunker Papers) into the rice trade and its spin-off industries. Retail networks were thriving again, and even the military wanted to buy local rice on the open market.

The NFA wholeheartedly favored and supported the Military Commissary, a non-governmental outfit, to secure rice for soldiers' families to stimulate private sector growth and promote competitiveness. However, the Military Quartermaster was different. It was our biggest client, but if it procured rice on the open market following routine government procedures, there would be a waste of public funds and opportunities for graft and corruption. We changed that.

Consumers no longer had to worry about where they could find rice for their families at a reasonable price. Although they had to learn to get used to fluctuating prices in a market-driven economy, they no longer had to put up with frequent shortages, speculation, and black marketeering.

At the end of the war, we were focusing our attention on building infrastructure for the future export of rice. Looking back, it is remarkable that our accomplishments in reorganizing the rural landholding system, increasing the production of rice, and rationalizing the rice market were realized at the climax of a prolonged war caused by invasion from the north. The Vietnam War was not all about killing and maiming, battles lost and won, and American and Vietnamese frustrations, as nearly always depicted in books and media. It was for us very much about building a nation and changing lives, about social revolution, rural reconstruction, agricultural development, economic improvement, and building a happy future for our children. These are the lasting and beneficial legacies that the Second Republic of Vietnam, under the leadership of President Nguyen Van Thieu, left to its long-suffering people. And we, the civilian players of this drama, were and are proud of our achievements and the contributions we made to the struggle against international communism. Although we lost the war due to lack of logistical support, it does not diminish or nullify our efforts.

CHAPTER FIVE

BUILDING A MARKET ECONOMY DURING WARTIME

Nguyen Duc Cuong

I was born and raised in Hanoi, North Vietnam, long before Hanoi became a household name in the United States and worldwide. The great famine of 1945 and the uprising in August of the same year occurred when I was four years old. My mother sent all of us children to the countryside to stay with grandmother in Hung Yen province. The countryside was relatively safe and there was enough food. We returned to Hanoi after about one year. The roads were not safe, so we went by sampan and saw dead bodies floating down the river as we went. My mother owned a small business in Hanoi and we were relatively well off; we lived in a French villa (13 Dang Dung Street), located in a good section of town. I attended the French school Albert Sarraut.

The division of the country in July 1954 created havoc for hundreds of thousands of families in North Vietnam. My family followed the movement south of almost one million people and relocated to Saigon. There we shared a house with another family, whose head of family, Bui Nam, turned out to be Bui Diem's uncle.

I was admitted to the French secondary school Jean-Jacque Rousseau in Saigon and graduated first in my class. I obtained the baccalaureate degree (first and second part) and applied for a scholarship to study in the United States. I was accepted into the leadership program of the US Agency for International Development (USAID) and departed for the United States in October 1959. I did not return until June 1965. I attended the University of New Hampshire and graduated summa cum laude with a bachelor of science in electrical engineering in 1963. I then pursued graduate study at the Massachusetts Institute of Technology and earned a master of science in electrical engineering and completed course requirements for a doctorate in 1965.

The USAID leadership program created a core group of young technocrats with good technical training who returned home motivated to serve their country. This core group consisted of, just to name a few, Hoang Duc Nha, Tran Quang Minh, Nguyen Dang Khoi, Tran Van Khoi, Le Trong Muu, Le Manh Hung, Phi Minh Tam, Ha Xuan Trung, Vu Khac Dung, and Nguyen Ha Hai. We eventually all moved up through the ranks and became leaders of various government institutions.

I returned to Vietnam in June 1965 and began my ten-year career with the government of South Vietnam. In 1975, I resettled in the United States and began a new career in finance with ExxonMobil Corporation, in New York. I attended night school and earned a master of business administration in international finance from New York University's Stern School of Business in 1981. I progressed through the ranks in the treasury function of Exxon Corporation (president of Exxon Financial Services for seven years; tax and treasury manager for Infineum, a chemical joint venture between ExxonMobil Corporation and Royal Dutch Shell, headquartered in England for five years; and cash operations manager in the treasurer's department in Dallas, Texas, for five years).

In 2003, I retired from ExxonMobil after almost thirty years of service and settled in San Jose, California. After several years of retirement, I rejoined the academic world as a part-time adjunct faculty member at Northwestern Polytechnic University in Fremont, California, teaching corporate finance and foreign trade for the MBA program of the School of Business and Information Technology. I am currently enrolled in its doctor of business administration program.

My ten-year career with the government of South Vietnam was full of significant changes, serious challenges, and high risks, packed with events that could occur only in a country locked in a life-and-death struggle for survival against an implacable enemy and formidable odds. Nevertheless, I feel proud and privileged to have played a significant role in transforming the economic landscape of my country of eighteen million people. First, I had to cope with the large inflow of money resulting from the massive buildup of the US presence, then the subsequent and just as fast reduction of the US presence, which resulted in a significant void in manpower and financial resources that needed to be replaced.

My first job upon returning to South Vietnam in the summer of 1965 was as project engineer with the Industrial Development Center (IDC), an autonomous government organization under the aegis of the Ministry of Economy, headed by Director General Khuong Huu Dieu. He earned a masters of science in mechanical engineering from MIT in 1956. My job was to review business applications to set up light industries, such as the assembly of radios and small electrical equipment using imported parts. Given that I once had a summer job in the United States working on antenna designs for telephone companies, this first job was not too far off from my experience in the United States. Although investors were not lining up with projects in hand waiting for approval, this job gave me the opportunity to get reacquainted with the society I had left six years before. Significant changes had taken place. The country had gone through several political upheavals. Furthermore, it was facing an increase in large-scale armed attacks, and the United States had begun its massive military buildup to cope with the situation.

I met friends and colleagues who had attended various US universities through the USAID Leadership Program. They were selected on the basis of merit, and, after receiving their education in the United States during four to six years, they returned home to assume positions of increasing responsibility in the government. They shared similar views and were motivated by a strong desire to serve the country. In hindsight, the USAID Leadership Program was a very successful program in the training of future leaders of the country.

After one year on the job with IDC, an opportunity came along. Khuong Huu Dieu became vice minister of economy for commerce. The minister was Au Truong Thanh, an economist with a doctorate degree in economics from a prestigious university in Paris. Dieu needed staff to assist him in his new job. He asked several of us to go with him, among them Hoang Duc Nha, Tran Van Khoi, and myself. For me, it was clear that I would have to say good-bye to "engineering" and hello to "economics," whatever that was.

The Ministry of Economy (MOE) was staffed mainly with bureaucrats and administrators trained in the French tradition of focusing on regulations, documentation, file processing, and policy implementation. The only person concerned about policy formulation and direction was the minister himself. However, he had no staff trained in economics to support him and he lasted only about ten months.

My first job at the MOE was not well defined, to say the least. It was, first of all, a so-called "gofer" job, which eventually evolved into learning about US foreign aid, the mechanics of how it worked, and the US Commercial Import Program (CIP and PL-480) that was then expanding fast. I needed to understand the US tariff code, equivalent of the Brussels Tariff Nomenclature (BTN), so that importers could figure out what they were buying from the US suppliers. The job required some common sense and a good command of the English language. I needed to work with officials from the US Embassy and USAID, who also needed to understand how the MOE was going to administer this newly expanded program. Inflation was getting out of control and we needed to import goods to absorb liquidity.

There were subsequently two new ministers from mid-1967 to the end of 1969, but I was left alone in my cubbyhole. I had made myself knowledgeable enough that they could use my service. They assigned me to be a specialist on the US CIP program. This was when I met with three people who eventually would have a special impact on my career.

Pham Kim Ngoc joined the military cabinet of Prime Minister Nguyen Cao Ky in June 1967 for about six months as a member of an economic committee. He needed to understand how the US Commercial Import Program worked, which was the biggest thing that was happening. At that time, there were two American advisors working with us, Charles A. Cooper from the US Embassy and Willard D. Sharpe from USAID. They eventually were promoted to positions of authority at the embassy and the USAID Mission, respectively. In the meanwhile, Pham Kim Ngoc rejoined the new government, which was installed in October 1969, as minister of economy.

In the summer of 1969, I was drafted into the military. In the Quang Trung Military Training Center, I became reacquainted with two friends who were working at the National Bank of Viet Nam as economists before they were drafted. When the new government was announced, to my surprise, these two friends were called to join the new government: Tran Cu Uong, as vice minister of commerce, working for Pham Kim Ngoc; and Ha Xuan Trung, as vice minister for finance, working for Minister of Finance Nguyen Bich Hue. This coincidence of events took me back to the MOE in October 1969, where I would stay and gradually move up to the position of minister in October 1973.

This essay focuses on the economic situation of the Second Republic, and the measures to address it during the period 1970–74, a most difficult and critical period in its fight for survival.[1] The United States began its disengagement at the end of 1969, and

---

[1] At the conclusion of this chapter there is an appendix that provides sources for and some additional information about my narrative and experiences.

ended its military involvement as the last US soldier left in March 1973, following the signing of the Paris Peace Agreement. I was vice minister for trade from mid-1970 to October 1973, minister of trade and industry from October 1973 to November 1974, and advisor to the governor of the national bank from December 1974 to April 1975.

I was fresh out of school in mid-1965, equipped with several electrical engineering degrees, but had read neither Adam Smith nor John Maynard Keynes, yet was fortunate to be given the opportunity to learn and apply on-the-job basic economic lessons, undaunted by the complexity of the situation and not always fully aware of the great odds against which I was working. Now, with the benefit of hindsight, the availability of certain data, and reports that were not available then, I believe I can look at events in wider contexts and analyze them more systematically and thoughtfully than was possible when they occurred.

We, the economic team, were problem solvers, dealing with issues as they arose, at times reacting to events, often relying on insufficient data and with limited means at our disposal. We were practical in our approach, but reasonably steadfast and consistent in our policies. The measures we adopted were based on the observation that the market mechanism, deregulation, and more reliance on the private sector would work better than any other approach that had been tried before in the severe situation we were in: total warfare, relentless attacks, widespread destruction.

We were able to keep the situation under reasonable control in some areas and make real progress in others despite strong resistance to changes from within and pressure from without created by the fast pace of events and the emergence of unexpected factors. We did not claim to have the answers to the innumerable problems facing our country, but we believed that we had put together a viable and workable set of policies and measures that could withstand the test of time.

We were inspired by the success of neighboring countries and allies, such as Taiwan, Singapore, and the Republic of Korea, and we attempted to emulate their achievements. We held high-level meetings with their government leaders, with whom we shared similar views of the market place and of the long-term objectives of economic development policies, but we also recognized that our current environment and historical legacy confronted us with particular challenges that would take time to overcome.

Vietnam was an obscure, poor, and underdeveloped country thrust into the limelight of the world stage in mid-1954 when the Geneva Accords partitioned the country between two governments, north and south. During the period from 1945 to 1955, it was one of those few countries with the distinction and misfortune of being almost simultaneously at the crossroads of interests of several major powers having conflicting objectives as well as divergent political philosophies that ranged from the extreme right to the extreme left. It is difficult to imagine a more complex and challenging situation than that in which the country found itself. France, the one-time all-powerful colonial power and ruler, was seriously weakened by the devastation of WW II and by political instability, yet sought to retain its hegemony. Japan had occupied the country with its seemingly invincible army for a few years, and then withdrew after its defeat in August 1945. The Nationalist Chinese were entrusted by the Western allies to disarm the Japanese army in the north, and the United Kingdom was assigned to do the same in the south. The end of the Chinese civil war in 1949 resulted in the intervention of the Chinese Communists. In 1954, the Soviet Union co-chaired the

Geneva Conference with the United Kingdom. Finally, the United States emerged, in our minds, with a clear sense of purpose and seemingly unlimited resources.

The situation was made more complicated as various Vietnamese political parties, most prominently the Viet Minh, the Dai Viet, and the Viet Nam Quoc Dan Dang, were fighting for influence and power under the banner of national liberation, independence, and unification. The people were not sure who their government leaders were and thus needed to decide whether to move from the city to the countryside or vice versa to avoid getting caught in the crossfire.

Partitioning of the country in mid-1954 triggered an exodus of close to one million people who wanted to move south to start a new life. My family was among those that moved south. We moved to Saigon in two stages. First, we took the train from Hanoi to Haiphong, where we stayed for a few months. My three sisters went to Saigon by ship. My mother and I flew from Haiphong to Saigon on a military DC-3 aircraft. A representative of the Refugee Resettlement Committee greeted us at the airport with a cash gift of 850 piasters (about US$25) for each evacuee to help us with resettlement costs.

South Vietnam, the half of the country below the seventeenth parallel, struggled at first. The government of Prime Minister Ngo Dinh Diem settled the refugees from the north, asserted authority over several armed factions, overthrew Emperor Bao Dai, and organized the election of a constituent assembly to write a new constitution. The First Republic was born and people began to enjoy some degree of stability, normalcy, and prosperity from 1956 to 1963. For many of us, the future US-trained technocrats of the Second Republic, the years 1956–60 were among the best of our lives—we were full of expectation and promise. Following high school graduation, we took a competitive exam to qualify for a scholarship to study in the United States, sponsored by USAID. Upon graduation from various US universities and colleges, we returned home in the mid-1960s to a country engaged in a life-and-death struggle. We were motivated by the desire to do something good for the country.

The change of regime in November 1963, followed by military coups and countercoups, set the country back by several years. In mid-1965, it resumed its movement toward political stability and constitutional government. A new constitution was promulgated in 1967 and the Second Republic was born. A constitutionally elected government was inaugurated on November 1, 1967. There was an executive branch headed by a president and a prime minister, a bicameral legislature, a judicial branch, a general inspectorate at the central level, and several layers of locally elected officials at the provincial, district, and village levels.

The population of South Vietnam was estimated at about eighteen million people in 1970, of which about two-thirds lived in the rural areas and the remaining one-third lived in the cities. The country was poor by any standard. Total GNP was estimated at about US$3.2 billion per year during the period 1971–73. Average income per capita was about US$175, placing it clearly among the ranks of underdeveloped countries in the world at the time.

One of my first jobs at the Ministry of Economy in mid-1966 was to get a handle on how economic aid flowed through the South Vietnam economy. In particular, I wanted to know how US foreign aid, mainly the Commercial Import Program and the Food for Peace program (known as PL-480), worked in practice: what procedures were being used, what controls existed, where the bottlenecks might be, and which items were eligible for financing so that we were in full compliance with US laws and regulations.

It was not a difficult job, but rather interesting in the sense that it gave me the opportunity to learn about US foreign aid processes; to meet and work with Pham Kim Ngoc, who was then deputy minister of economy (from June to November 1967) in the cabinet of Prime Minister Nguyen Cao Ky; and with two senior American advisors who eventually would play a significant role in this whole episode: Charles A. Cooper, who held a PhD in economics from MIT, and was formerly a US White House aide before he was sent to Vietnam as economic counselor to Ambassador Bunker; and Willard D. Sharpe, who also held a PhD in economics, from Harvard, and who was assistant director of USAID for the Saigon Mission.

During Pham Kim Ngoc's short tenure in the military cabinet, the concept of reliance on market mechanism, deregulation, and the private sector began taking shape after it became clear how cumbersome and ineffective the existing import licensing system, the coupon and permit system, and the inspection and price control mechanism were. The system was administered manually, and the decrees and regulations could date back to the French colonial days. There was no well-defined decision-making process. Quite often the in-box of the office of the minister would be full of thick files and reports, all handwritten, waiting for his decision. It could be a mind-boggling sight for a new minister.

In response to the unmistakable intent of the Hanoi government, supported by the Soviet Union and China, to take over South Vietnam by force, the United States conducted a major military buildup between 1965 and 1969. This left an indelible imprint on the economic, political, and social landscape of the country.

The first contingent of US combat troops, about three thousand, landed in Da Nang in March 1965. In about three years, US soldiers numbered over half a million. To accommodate this massive and sudden presence required a significant budget to build infrastructure, such as roads, bridges, seaports, airports, warehouses, and military camps. Those were immediate requirements to ensure the safety, mobility, and standards to which the US military was accustomed. These facilities would be built to high standards and could become very valuable when converted to civilian use in peacetime.

Total cumulative assistance from the United States, economic and military, from 1955 to 1964, amounted to US$3.3 billion. In the next eleven years, 1965 to 1975, this figure jumped to US$22 billion. At its peak in 1973, total assistance amounted to almost $4 billion for the year, or 125 percent of South Vietnam's GNP, estimated at that time to be about US$3.2 billion.[2]

The impact of these inflows of money and military personnel on the South Vietnamese economy was significant. Domestic resources, such as manpower, infrastructure, local raw material, government administrative machinery, and private sector organizations, were totally inadequate and unprepared to cope with this sudden and massive influx. A labor shortage developed as the Armed Forces of the Republic of Viet Nam (ARVN) expanded. Economic distortion followed, and income disparity became more obvious, as indicated by the widening gap between the city lifestyle and that of the countryside.

Life in Saigon was relatively good, marked by conspicuous consumption, traffic congestion, glittering new cars, tall buildings, busy nightlife, and villas with air

---

[2] Douglas C. Dacy, *Foreign Aid, War, and Economic Development: South Viet Nam 1955–1975* (Cambridge: Cambridge University Press, 1986), p. 200.

conditioning and TV sets, occasionally disrupted by deadly rocket attacks and terrorist activities. Then there was the unsightly display of tax-free luxury goods, imported for use by US troops, but which found their way, illegally, to the sidewalks of Saigon, where they fetched very high black-market prices.

To foreign observers, news reporters, US congressmen on fact-finding trips, and high US government officials, life in Saigon was what they saw when they first arrived. It gave them the impression of an artificial society, evidence of the corrupting US presence, and views of wasted US taxpayer money. It conjured up an image of a society enjoying the good life, while evading the draft and leaving the fighting to the American soldiers and letting the farmers deal with the guerillas in the countryside. This suggested a society detached from the reality of war with corruption at high levels. Clearly, this had become a serious political issue, always high on the discussion agenda each time officials from the two governments met.

Nevertheless, Americanization of the war continued, relentlessly, unabated, supported unequivocally by the highest levels of the two governments. They shared the same vision, the same goal, which was to build a noncommunist democratic system of government and to prevent North Vietnam from taking over South Vietnam. These leaders had held three summit meetings at which commitments were made: Honolulu, in February 1966; Manila, in October 1966; and Guam, in March 1967.

The US Congress was grudgingly footing all the bills. In hindsight, it should have become obvious to a more objective and astute observer that to maintain this level of commitment in resources and prestige would be unsustainable in the long run. Anti-war voices were meanwhile rising. At his confirmation hearing in April 1967, Ambassador Bunker pledged his efforts toward the goal of a strong, viable, and free Vietnam. Senator William Fulbright replied with the question of "whether the right of self-determination of fifteen million Vietnamese is worth the damage it is doing to our own country."[3] This type of question was to become louder and louder, time after time.

The 1968 Tet Offensive dramatically changed the political landscape in the United States, which in turn affected the landscape of South Vietnam. President Johnson announced that he would not seek reelection. The Paris peace talks began. Anti-war demonstrations raged in the streets of major US cities. Richard Nixon was elected US president in November 1968, thus ushering in a new administration and a new policy.

American disengagement, or Vietnamization of the war, was a difficult and painful transition, for it represented a 180-degree change of policy and direction. The original mission was not yet accomplished and goals were now ambiguous, even conflicting. A major readjustment of thinking on the part of South Vietnam was required. In the United States, meanwhile, the centers of power and authority were shifting; anti-war movements became more vocal and influential.

Disengagement started in earnest in late 1969, with the phased withdrawal of US troops and their replacement by the ARVN. US troop levels started to go down in 1969, falling to around 300,000 by the end of 1970, to 160,000 in 1971, and to nil by March 1973. The ARVN troop target was 900,000 or more by the end of the process, or about 4.7 percent of the total population. This percentage was higher if calculated on the basis of only the population under effective government control from which manpower was drawn.

---

[3] Willard D. Sharpe, "Memorandum Addressed to Nguyen Duc Cuong," USAID/Saigon, December 12, 1973, Introduction, p. xv.

Vietnamization created a significant and growing strain on the financial and human resources of the country. Deficit financing, already the norm during the years of Americanization of the war, grew larger each year, and began to create a dual problem: inflationary pressure due to declining US foreign aid coupled with depressed economic activity due to the loss of income. Local employees in the US sector were laid off, with available jobs falling from 160,000 to only 17,000, and American purchases of piasters declined from a peak of about US$400 million in 1970 to less than US$100 million in 1974. The effects of the income loss were compounded by over one million internally displaced people (IDP) in South Vietnam created by the battles that repelled the communist offensive of 1972.

Total expenditure in 1974 was estimated at about VN$720 billion, or 40 percent above the 1973 level in nominal terms.[4] More than 90 percent of the total budget was for "current" operations, leaving about 7 percent, very little, for development. Security (defense and police) accounted for VN$347 billion, or 48 percent of the total. Another 33 percent went for civil operations, mainly public servant salaries and cash transfers to internal refugees and veterans.

The total payroll for 1.4 million soldiers and civil servants accounted for 47 percent of total outlays, yet they were consistently underpaid, given the high inflation rate. In mid-June 1974, they received an increase of 23 percent in total compensation, but that still left real wages in 1974 about 5 percent below 1973.

The US Agency for International Development (USAID) office in Vietnam estimated that the South Vietnamese national budget expenditures averaged about one third of GNP during the period 1972–74.[5] On the revenue side, tax receipts accounted for VN$343 billion (see Table 1), or 48 percent of the total budget, an increase of 39 percent over 1973. Next, the most notable development was a sharp rise in the sales of Treasury bills to commercial banks, i.e., government borrowing from the public, which accounted for VN$90 billion, as compared to VN$18 billion in 1973. This feature did not exist in earlier years and was part of the government's financial policy to attract savings from the public, absorb excess liquidity, and reduce the money supply. United States counterpart transfers (which are explained later) accounted for VN$258 billion, or 36 percent of the budget. National Bank advances, i.e., the government printing press, closed the gap with an estimated VN$29 billion, or 4 percent of the budget.

There were two significant components in the balance of payment equation. First, South Vietnam derived substantial dollar earnings from the US presence, in particular from troop spending and piaster purchases. Those may have been as high as $400 million per year at their peak in 1971, then reduced to less than $100 million by 1974.[6] Those earnings contributed to South Vietnamese foreign exchange reserves, allowing South Vietnam to import goods and services that US foreign aid did not finance (listed under the heading Government of Viet Nam [GVN] Foreign Exchange). Second, US foreign aid provided the South Vietnamese economy with the

---

[4] Data in Tables 1 and 2 were extracted from a declassified US embassy cable dated January 1975; see Ellsworth Bunker, *The Bunker Papers, Reports to the President from Viet Nam, 1967–1973*, three volumes, ed. Douglas Pike (Berkeley, CA: Institute of East Asian Studies, University of California at Berkeley, 1990).

[5] Ibid.

[6] Dacy, "Foreign Aid," p. 199.

Table 1
Budget and Source of Funding, 1974

Items	VN$ Billion	Percentage	US$ million equivalence (@550 per US$)
Security	347	48	631
Civil operations	229	32	416
National Food Administration (rice stock and subsidy)	70	10	127
Others	74	10	135
Total	720	100	1,309
Tax revenues	343	48	624
National Bank	29	4	53
T-bill sales	90	12	163
US aid counterpart	258	36	469
Total	720	100	1,309

bulk of the required foreign exchange via two main programs: the Commercial Import Program (CIP) and the Food for Peace program, generally known as PL-480. The CIP program financed a pre-approved list of US-source goods and services, such as refined petroleum products, machinery, fertilizers, and freight costs on US ships. The list included a certain number of US-made goods, such as automobiles. The PL-480 program purchased surplus agricultural products, such as rice, wheat, cotton, and tobacco.

In 1974, total imports were US$855 million (see Table 2, on the next page), financed by US aid of US$636 million for such items as described above. South Vietnamese foreign exchange financed US$196 million of imports. Third-country aid amounted to US$23 million. Compared to 1973, the increase in 1974 was mainly due to a near quadrupling of crude oil prices in late 1973 and early 1974, and also the rising cost of fertilizer and rice.

The import of US-aid-financed goods generated local currency, which was deposited by the importers into an account called the counterpart fund, owned and controlled by the US government. These funds were used to pay for the cost of US operations in the country as well as a large part of the South Vietnamese budget in mutually agreed upon amounts and projects (identified as "US aid counterpart" in Table 1).

Table 2
Imports by Source of Funding (US$ million)

Items	1973	1974
US CIP	253	395
(POL)	-76	-135
(Fertilizer)	-50	-75
Others	-127	-185
PL-480	153	201
(Rice)	-87	-139
(Other)	-66	-62
GVN foreign exchange	281	196
AID freight	30	40
Third-country aid	0	23
Total	717	855

One example of a specific project financed by US foreign aid is the Land to the Tiller Program, which was started in March 1971 and completed two years later, with a total price tag of US$450 million.[7] Another example is the rice marketing program, designed to stabilize the rice market, which required a large amount of working capital to finance the rice strategic reserve. It was given a budget of US$150 million, second only to the defense budget, and the goal of stabilization was achieved after six months, with plans for rice self-sufficiency by 1974–75 and the export of rice thereafter.[8]

One more example is the Agency for the Development of Da Nang Area (ADDA), which was set up to create temporary public works jobs for the large number of internally displaced South Vietnamese who flocked into towns and cities as a result of enemy military activity. This program was eventually expanded to all three military regions as well as the Saigon area, generating in total about 32,000 jobs.[9] We viewed this

---

[7] See Tran Quang Minh, "A Decade of Public Service: Nation-building during the Interregnum and Second Republic (1964–75)," elsewhere in this volume.

[8] Ibid.

[9] United States Agency for International Development, "Terminal Report—United States Economic Assistance to South Vietnam, 1954–1976," Vol. 1, Washington, DC, 1976, p. 32.

public works program as a stopgap measure to deal with the urgent IDP problem in the Da Nang–Quang Tri region, which, being at the northern extremity of our country, was particularly vulnerable to enemy activity, infiltration, and subversion. The goal was to relieve unemployment by creating public works jobs for the internal refugees instead of simply giving the usual welfare handouts. This project in some ways was experimental, using private management expertise with government initiative and funding. Credit for the success of the program should be given to Trinh Vinh Dien, the first general manager, an executive on loan from Vietnam Shell Oil.

Questions were often raised about the impact of US economic aid. Did the funds encourage corruption? Did they promote long-term dependency and economic dislocation? Were there cultural and psychological effects? Was the aid effective as a foreign policy instrument? Did it achieve any long- or short-term objectives, indeed, ultimately, did it serve its very purpose? Those are all legitimate questions that a donor country and the recipient country should always ask at the highest level of policymaking. In reality, there was not much of a debate in the recipient country, whereas debate was intense in the donor country, as costs of the war—both financial and human—escalated. I will discuss the practical aspects of foreign aid from my perspective as a Vietnamese government official involved with its administration.

Foreign aid as an instrument of US foreign policy had several goals, and those goals changed with changing circumstances. The underlying and constant goal, however, was economic stability. Without foreign aid, the economic situation would have been untenable. American foreign aid played a significant role in the economy of South Vietnam since 1955. In fiscal year 1955, US economic assistance was US$322 million.[10] In contrast, this amount was about US$1 million the prior year. I never found any meaningful background information on how the amount of US$322 million for fiscal year 1955 was arrived at. In subsequent years, there was more exchange back and forth between the US Embassy in Saigon and the State Department regarding the appropriate level of foreign aid. During the next ten years, 1955–64, economic assistance averaged about US$210 million per year. From 1965 to 1974, average economic aid jumped to US$650 million per year, equivalent to as much as 30 percent of South Vietnam's GNP. However, in real terms, a study by USAID indicated that real imports in 1974 were at their lowest level since 1965. Per capita real imports in 1974 were barely above the level of 1964 imports, the year before large-scale US involvement.[11]

Foreign aid had its own set of regulations, controls, and restrictions imposed by the donor country, meaning the US Congress, the US White House, the US Auditor and Comptroller General, and the US Embassy. On the Vietnamese side, the Directorate of Commercial Aid in the Ministry of Economy administered the foreign aid program. This was quite a challenge for a staff trained in the French administrative tradition, with limited knowledge of the American system. Needless to say, the initial procedure that was developed was cumbersome, difficult to implement, and left room for abuse. As the program expanded, a USAID advisor was assigned to the MOE to ensure compliance with American regulations.

A new government was installed in October 1969. Pham Kim Ngoc was appointed minister of economy. Working under him were a vice minister for commerce and a vice

---

[10] Dacy, "Foreign Aid," p. 200.

[11] Bunker, "Bunker Papers," p. 6.

minister for industry. Ngoc served in this capacity for the next four years, the longest tenure for a minister of economy. In the mean time, I had begun my military duty at the Quang Trung Training Center in August 1969. Being there turned out to be a most opportune situation, personally. Among the draftees sharing the same barracks were two friends, Tran Cu Uong and Ha Xuan Trung. They had been working at the National Bank as staff to the governor when they were drafted. Tran Cu Uong was subsequently appointed vice minister for commerce, working under Pham Kim Ngoc. Ha Xuan Trung was appointed vice minister of finance, working under Nguyen Bich Hue, minister of finance. About a year and half later, in another round of government changes, Ha Xuan Trung took over as finance minister, at age 30. The new economic and finance team, dubbed by the press as "The Kim Ngoc–Bich Hue Duo," was market-oriented in philosophy. The team was willing to prescribe tough medicine for the economy. It was instrumental in initiating several structurally significant changes to the outdated financial system, the foreign exchange markets, domestic commerce, the tax collection system, and the import tariff code and tax. The new team obviously needed staff. I was discharged from the military and sent back to the ministry of economy as a specialist on foreign aid. A few more changes ensued, and, about eight months later, I was promoted to the position of vice minister for commerce, working with Pham Kim Ngoc during the next three and half years.

As explained in an earlier section, foreign aid closed the balance of payment shortfall that the South Vietnamese economy on its own could not achieve without a significant devaluation of its currency. Foreign aid generated local currency revenues, the bulk of which were used to reduce the government budget deficit in order to keep inflation under control. Without this source of funding, the deficit could have reached 40 percent or more of the budget, and we could have been looking at an inflation rate in excess of 100 percent and spiraling upward.

The question has been raised regarding whether we could have taken steps to save foreign exchange currency, when the dollar was plentiful, for later use when the dollar became scarce; or whether we could have taken steps to discourage consumerism and encourage the import of capital goods instead. We believed it would have been impractical to take those steps given the environment we were in. First, the level of foreign aid was essentially tied to the level of South Vietnam's foreign exchange reserves. It would be difficult, even close to impossible, for the US administration and US Congress to approve foreign aid as a means to bridge the foreign exchange gap when such a gap could be bridged by South Vietnam's own reserves. Second, there were no private investment projects of any significance that would require capital goods to absorb the excess liquidity. Government investment projects were out of the question. Consumer items generated more tax revenues than capital goods. In a market-driven economy, the consumption pattern could be changed only through pricing, meaning exchange rate mechanisms and import tariffs.

We believed that the most practical approach under the circumstances was to develop a set of long-term policy measures, within our prerogatives, to optimize the use of foreign aid by striking a balance between the short-term need for stabilization and the long–term strategy of weaning ourselves off foreign aid while foreign aid was still available, but in anticipation of the day when it would not be forthcoming. By and large we had achieved the objective of stabilization in 1970–71. As the Vietnamization phase got under way in earnest, we worked on a gradual shift from stabilization to development.

There were two key programs that dealt with the long-term issue of foreign aid. They eventually turned out to be important for the country, only decades later. First was the agricultural development policy, the backbone of which was the Land to the Tiller Program. When the time would come that peace was restored and military personnel released and redeployed in the countryside to work the land and on other agricultural projects, we were convinced that we could achieve a steady increase in agricultural production of 10 to 15 percent per year, given an appropriate environment and set of incentives. Improvement in rice yield alone could eliminate the need for PL-480 imports after one year and create a surplus of about 1 million tons of rice for export by the second year. This amount could increase to about 3 million tons a year after three to four years, which would generate about $500 million per year from rice exports alone. CIP import financing could be phased out in three or four years and replaced by this new source of foreign exchange earnings.

The communist government collectivized farming following the takeover of SVN in April 1975, with disastrous results. Farmers went back to subsistence farming and famine threatened the country. The government was forced to de-collectivize farming and gradually reinstate the pre-1975 system. In recent years total rice production has climbed up steadily. This has been due primarily to market pricing, to significant yield improvement, and to shorter maturation of the miracle rice variety introduced in the 1970s. The country was able to export as much as five million tons of rice per year and was poised to become the number one exporting country in 2012.

Second was the search for oil. We started looking for new sources of foreign exchange earnings other than foreign aid and the export of goods, and, consequently, pushed forward aggressively the offshore oil exploration program. The first round of auctions in August 1973 netted the government about US$17 million, the second round in 1974 brought US$30 million. Pham Kim Ngoc was instrumental in pushing forward the offshore oil exploration program. Transparency, persistency, consistency of approach, plus a bit of luck helped us. One would have thought that looking for oil was a straightforward proposition, but it was literally a minefield. We learned via various newspaper articles that in congressional hearings in 1971, questions were raised about our motives, as well as those of the US government. The anti-war people claimed that oil was the reason why the United States was there to start with and why the American soldiers were not coming home. They were needed to keep in power the lease-granting government. Bella Abzug, a congresswoman from New York and a well-known critic of the war, questioned Pham Kim Ngoc in a congressional hearing in 1971 on the very subject of US involvement in Viet Nam and any connection it might have with our search for oil. Pham Kim Ngoc, without hesitation, told the committee there was none. They could not believe or accept or expect that, in reality, there was none.

Through his personal contacts, Pham Kim Ngoc was able to obtain technical help from Iranian specialists of the National Iranian Oil Company (NIOC). One of Pham Kim Ngoc's school friends in England in the early 1950s was the economic minister of Iran. Through him, Pham Kim arranged in February 1971 for a South Vietnam delegation, led by Attorney Vuong Van Bac (who became foreign minister in a government reshuffle in October 1973), to meet with Prime Minister Hoveyda of Iran. The prime minister introduced Vuong Van Bac to the Iranian oil minister, Jamshid Amouzegar, who agreed to send three of his specialists to help out—a geologist, a lawyer, and an economist.[12] We had to provide only housing accommodations and per diem fees, and we had no budget to do even that. A few rounds of calls with the banker at Viet Nam Thuong Tin, the largest government-owned Vietnamese bank, where Ngoc once worked and was instrumental in setting up its department of Credit and Import when it had just opened for business in 1956, came up with two empty apartments reserved for guests of the bank and some money to pay for the Iranians' per diem.

The most significant contribution from the NIOC experts was to draft the Model Concession Agreement. The clauses were well balanced between South Vietnam's long-term interests and near-term incentives for the oil companies to proceed expeditiously with oil exploration and drilling. The prime minister signed the Concession Agreements on September 1, 1973. Working closely with Pham Kim Ngoc was Tran Van Khoi, general administrator of the National Petroleum and Mines Agency. Tran Van Khoi has written a book, *Dau Hoa Viet Nam 1970–1975, Nhung ngay con Nho*, about his work and experience.[13]

The near quadrupling of crude oil prices at the end of 1973 hurt SVN with the higher cost of oil imports, but, on the other hand, helped attract large oil companies with high bids to the next auction. The first discovery of oil was announced in August 1974, less than a year after the Concession Agreements were signed. We attributed this remarkable achievement to a combination of several factors:

- A well-drafted Concession Agreement based on a solid legal foundation provided by the National Petroleum and Minerals Law;
- Persistence and hard work on the part of Minister Pham Kim Ngoc, Tran Van Khoi, and their staff, as well as the National Petroleum and Minerals Board;
- Highly qualified technical help from an unexpected source, the National Iranian Oil Company specialists, to compensate for our lack of experience. Had we sought American expertise at the start, we might have run into political issues with the US Congress, which could have delayed the program; and
- The odds of finding oil on the first few test wells at a location where drilling had never been done before were generally low. It was our good luck that oil was found with the first few wells.

President Nguyen Van Thieu visited the oil platform *Glomar IV* that found the Bach Ho oil field in February 1975. This field would turn out to be a giant oilfield producing in excess of 200,000 barrels per day at its peak and still continues to contribute about 50 percent of annual production for the country. Cumulative production of the Bach Ho oilfield is estimated at 1.5 billion barrels. According to the *Oil and Gas Journal*, Vietnamese oil reserves are estimated at 4.5 billion barrels as of January 2012, third in size in Asia, after China and India.

History will record that the oil exploration initiative undertaken during the Second Republic turned out to be one of two most important economic legacies of the Second Republic (the other one being its agricultural development policies). It provided the country with a significant head start in a field notorious for its high risk, long lead time

---

[12] Tran Van Khoi, *Dau Hoa Viet Nam 1970–1975: Nhung Ngay Con Nho* [Viet Nam Oil 1970–75: Days to Remember] (Houston, TX: Liviko's Printing, 2002), p. 53.

[13] Ibid.

to production, and large up-front capital outlay. We reduced drastically the first two factors when oil was struck quickly, and our lease-auction approach generated revenues for the government. Oil production provided a much-needed source of foreign exchange some twelve years later when the country was facing economic collapse as foreign aid from the Soviet Union was cut off.[14]

Our overall long-term development plans suffered a serious setback by at least a year due to the invasion by North Vietnamese troops in 1972. Although we managed to turn back this invasion, it devastated parts of the country and inflicted severe human, material, and financial losses upon us.

Finally, there are two more aspects of foreign aid that should be kept in mind. One is the lead time required to achieve self-sufficiency. We began laying the foundation for self-sufficiency in 1971, after sixteen years of being a recipient of foreign aid. We believed it would take about five to seven years for SVN to achieve self-sufficiency, assuming manageable levels of military activities. Second is confidence-building. Foreign aid was undeniably a confidence builder, especially when there was no end in sight to military hostilities. Witness the case of South Korea. The economy there had seen inflation as high as 2,800 percent per year during the war. But, the Korean people persevered and survived this catastrophic situation, and they eventually prospered with continued US assistance.

The Second Republic, during the period 1970–74, experienced constant military activity that caused a significant drain on human and financial resources, as well as serious economic disruptions that threatened to cause hyperinflation and promote black markets. South Vietnam's economy was essentially agricultural (principally rice and poultry). Rice farming was the largest component of GNP, accounting for about one third. The government sector, which employed about 1.4 million people (military, police, and civil servants), accounted for another third of GNP. The remainder was divided up between the industrial and private service sector, probably half each.

Total annual rice production was about 6.5 million tons in 1974. Assuming a world price of $200 per ton, rice production was worth US$1.3 billion. There were more than one million families benefiting from the Land to the Tiller Program, owning about 2.6 million acres of rice fields, or about one-third of a total of 7.5 million acres of cultivated rice land. There were about two million other families that were tenant farmers, working for large absentee landowners who were living in the cities or overseas. For farmers who owned their own land, the acreage held was rather modest. The size of farms was less than five acres, and these were mainly located in Central Vietnam, where the soil is not as fertile nor the weather as favorable as in the Mekong delta.

Total rice production indicated a dismal under-utilization of our rice land assets. Rice farmers were mainly doing subsistence farming because there was little or no incentive to do otherwise. Prices were kept artificially low. Movement and storage of rice were severely restricted.

The industrial sector was concentrated in large cities (Saigon-Bien Hoa, Can Tho, and Danang), where industrial parks were built by the government to attract investors. There were some light manufacturing industries, assembly lines, and processors of agricultural products. Needless to say, the risk of losses due to the war was high, and the government assumed most of that risk through the construction of infrastructure in

---

[14] Personal communication with Le Manh Hung, San Jose, CA, October 12, 2012.

the industrial parks and via financing by the Industrial Development Bank, a government entity. There were a few government-owned enterprises, such as the Ha Tien Cement Factory, the An Hoa Nong Son Coal Complex, the Viet Nam Sugar Mill, and the utility companies.

The service sector in the cities was doing rather well during the buildup of American involvement, but suffered when the US presence was being reduced. The banking sector consisted of a central bank, three government-sponsored development banks, and thirty-three commercial banks. The National Bank of Viet Nam, the equivalent of a central bank, was set up in 1956 when the French government turned over the administration of monetary and foreign exchange matters to the government of South Vietnam. Of the thirty-three commercial banks, fourteen were foreign owned. The largest commercial bank, Viet Nam Thuong Tin Bank, set up in 1956, was government owned.

The major banks were owned and run by bankers trained in the French banking tradition—conservative, with no incentive to change. Their main business was the handling of documentary letters of credit, foreign exchange transactions, import financing, commercial loans, and construction loans to finance housing and office complexes to accommodate the needs of the large influx of US personnel. The bankers found it to their advantage that interest rates were below the inflation rate and the local currency was overvalued, thus favoring imports and penalizing exports. They could borrow from depositors at a low rate and lend to the importers at market rates, realizing a markup of five to six percent. Naturally, they wanted to maintain the status quo. However, eventually we were able to convince the Bankers Association that it would be in its interest to work with our program of deregulation and to help us implement the needed monetary reforms, such as the mechanism to float interest rates, the issuance of CDs, and the purchase of Treasury bills.

South Vietnam inherited from the French an administrative system based on market intervention and management, a somewhat paternalistic and *dirigisme* view of economic activity. The system consisted of myriad regulations on prices, inspections, permits, quotas, and licenses. These were prone to abuse, misinterpretation, and inconsistent application of the rules and regulations. Bureaucratic processes and untidy filing systems bogged everything down. As the economy expanded, this antiquated system proved its obsolescence. It had become unwieldy, and was constantly under pressure from various groups with vested interests. It required more staff to administer the ever-increasing number of regulations, and this was in the middle of an acute shortage of workers due to military service. Nevertheless, the antiquated system remained despite all of its shortcomings. We were outsiders, political appointees, so-called specialists, equipped with new knowledge and ideas, who came and left with each change of government. The bureaucrats had been there long before we arrived. They assumed they would still be there long after we had left. We rather left them alone while we looked for a satisfactory long-term solution, which eventually would phase out or eliminate the need for their service.

We were under constant pressure in the short term to address the issue of economic stability (i.e., price inflation and its negative impact on fixed-income groups, such as soldiers and civil servants, on whose support we all depended). The need to maintain price stability, in our opinion, could not be underestimated in the context of a young republic struggling for legitimacy as well as fighting for survival. Specifically, we needed to absorb excess liquidity created by perennial budget deficits. We also needed to address the issue of an artificial exchange rate that resulted in a thriving foreign-exchange black market. That duty free goods, reserved for the US military, were found for sale on the sidewalks of Saigon was an "open scandal," according to Ambassador Bunker in his report to the US president. Finally, we needed to ensure adequate supplies of basic commodities, such as rice, petroleum products, and politically sensitive items, for instance, newsprint and cement. As we developed economic policies and measures, we realized that we needed to be pragmatic, flexible, and adaptable. We shaped our thoughts around the observation that wartime conditions were here to stay while US foreign aid was uncertain and declining.

In the countryside, we had control of the most fertile areas. We could offer the people living there something the enemy could not compete with, i.e., a means to make a decent living for themselves and their families. For the city dwellers, we offered them some degree of security. They were enjoying a higher living standard than the people in the countryside, although their daily activities could be interrupted by rocket attacks. We needed to continuously review our requirements, evaluate our resources, assess the risk–reward associated with the various economic measures, measure our own ability to react to unexpected changing conditions, and develop our strategy based on the concept of total warfare. Furthermore, we needed to look beyond the somewhat dismal present and nurture hope for a brighter and achievable future. There were seven aspects to this.

Raise Revenues

First, we needed to raise revenues to fight the war and to raise salaries for soldiers, policemen, and civil servants. There were a total of 1.4 million people on the payroll out of a population of 18 million. Being on a fixed salary in times of inflation, they were the most disadvantaged segment of the population in economic terms. We needed their support in our fight for survival, and an important part of this was trying to keep inflation in the range of 30-40 percent per year. Runaway inflation of 100 percent or more would be catastrophic.

Energy Conservation

Second, we needed to factor in the inevitable destruction of wartime. We could only count on the military to protect those assets considered strategic, such as the power plants, a few government-owned enterprises, oil storage facilities, rice warehouses, and key roads and bridges. Protection costs had to be weighed against the economic and strategic value of the assets to be protection.

A relentless enemy constantly put our resolve to the test. For example, a barrage of rockets destroyed 50 percent of our oil storage facilities near the port of Saigon in December 1973. We needed to restore those storage facilities quickly and to immediately negotiate the diversion of oil shipments to Saigon. We could not afford to run out of petroleum products, especially those necessary for military operations. Thus, we needed to cut our civilian petroleum consumption by at least 25 percent, which we attempted by increasing the price of gasoline, kerosene, and diesel oil by 66 to 140 percent. This was barely two months after OPEC's decision to triple world oil prices in October 1973.

By December 1973, our gasoline was priced at the equivalent of US$1.62 per gallon, one of the highest levels in the world. Diesel was so expensive that the price had to be rolled back. However, in the end we did achieve our objective of a 25 percent reduction in consumption. Also, until further notice, government office hours were shortened to 7:00 AM to 2:00 PM Monday through Friday, and 7:00 AM to noon on Saturday. The traditional two and a half hour lunch break was abolished to reduce traffic congestion, gasoline consumption, and pollution. Furthermore, the use of air conditioning in government offices was suspended until further notice.

Focus on Agriculture

Third, notwithstanding the large budget deficit, we needed to push forward with the necessary funding of projects judged critical to our strategy for winning the war. Three prime examples of such projects were the Land to the Tiller Program, the rice market stabilization program, and the agricultural credit program.

The Land to the Tiller program, promulgated in March 1970, was designed to eliminate farm tenancy for almost one million farmers and to provide them with ownership of the very piece of land that their families had tilled for generations.[15] The estimated cost was US$450 million, equivalent to about 50 percent of our defense budget. This program was approved at the highest level of government and was to be implemented without delay. It reflected a bold vision requiring courageous initiatives and effective implementation that was successfully undertaken by the Second Republic. It was a wise use of money, an example of using financial leverage and of taking advantage of our natural and human resources. South Vietnam was endowed with good rice land. The total cultivated area was about 7.5 million acres, or 50 percent of total arable land. The soil was fertile and the climate was favorable for rice production. It required little or no additional capital investment to make the land more productive, just hard work. In economic terms, our agricultural assets could provide the highest return on investment and the shortest payback period, about 100 to 120 days. The risk was low, being spread out over 2.5 million acres of rice land, and the benefits extended to about one million farm families, at a total cost of about $450 per family. This investment turned out to be the best and longest lasting legacy of the Second Republic. The original landowners were fully and fairly compensated, with 20 percent cash up front and the balance, 80 percent, in the form of a ten-year bond. Many landowners were satisfied to find a buyer for their land during wartime.

The rice market stabilization program was also approved at the highest level of government and given a budget equivalent to about 20 percent of the defense budget. The National Food Administration (NFA), under the supervision of the Ministry of Trade and Industry, was entrusted with the implementation of the program by building up strategic rice reserves in the three military regions. Within three months, the rice market was stabilized.

The expansion of an agricultural credit program also yielded results. The Ministry of Trade and Industry provided the necessary foreign exchange to help farmers buy fertilizer, miracle rice seeds, and small farm machinery and equipment, such as the

---

[15] For example, see: Tran Quang Minh, "A Decade of Public Service," elsewhere in this volume.

popular "shrimp tail" engines widely used to propel small boats all over the Mekong delta.

Farm Labor

Fourth, we needed to mobilize agricultural labor in the countryside. Our skilled-labor resources were spread thin, being drafted in the military, but we had a large, underutilized pool of labor in the countryside not of draft age, highly skilled in the farming business, but farming at a subsistence level because there was no incentive to do otherwise. These people could be making a significant contribution to the economy with little additional investment if they were provided with a good set of incentives and allowed to work the farms without being harassed by inspectors. This was where the agricultural development programs of the Ministry of Land Reform and Agricultural Development became important. Equipped with incentives such as land ownership, miracle rice seeds, market prices for their products, ample credit, the availability of fertilizers, and freedom of movement, Mekong Delta farmers could comfortably produce an extra million tons of rice per year for export, over and above the 6.5 million tons they were producing for domestic consumption. The small scale farming approach optimized the use of labor in the countryside, reduced war risk, and stimulated the spirit of entrepreneurship in the farmers.

Seafood and Oil

Fifth, we are endowed with a very high ratio of coastline to land mass. Cam Ranh Bay is one of the best deep-water seaports in the world. The seafood industry had great potential. As it was shown years later, the seafood industry could be developed to three times larger than the rice economy.[16] Also, coastal tourism would have great potential when peace was eventually restored.

Sixth, exploration for oil under the seabed of the vast open ocean was in our plan for the future. The National Petroleum Law was promulgated in December 1970. We believed that we could attract large international oil companies if we had a solid legal framework in the form of a well-drafted Concession Agreement.

Austerity and Deregulation

Finally, we needed to maintain austerity measures in order to ensure economic stability. Specifically, we increased tariffs on certain categories of imported goods, we pursued an aggressive tax collection strategy to reduce disparity and to show that the high-income groups were paying their fair share of taxes, and we devalued the local currency to mop up excess liquidity with higher import costs and higher receipts for the US-controlled counterpart fund, which eventually would benefit the national budget. While the end results were always price increases, we did not lose sight of our long-term goals of restructuring fundamentally the country's economic landscape using monetary, financial, fiscal, and pricing mechanisms, and reshaping the mind set of the business community to understand our resolve to carry out deregulation, to trust the markets, and to reduce short-term benefits and rewards in favor of a longer-term

---

[16] Randolph Barker, "Viet Nam and the Global Rice Market," unpublished manuscript, 2002.

perspective. Our objective was to find the right balance between the political cost of pushing too hard on measures to extract resources to fight the war and the economic cost of not doing enough. We had no historical data to assess adequately the impact of our measures. To go slow and take gradual steps was our approach, but sometimes we might have gone overboard with our sense of urgency.

We had considered "shock therapy," meaning an immediate and significant devaluation of the currency, a large increase in interest rates, and higher prices on commodities, such as rice and petroleum products, to cool off speculation and reduce inflationary pressure. However, we discarded this approach because our democratic institutions were still young and fragile, the enemy continued to test our limits with campaigns of disinformation and outrageous claims, and it could have a negative effect on soldiers and civil servants with fixed salaries. The other sector of the population from which resources could be extracted under any austerity or stability measure would be the city dwellers, who were always most vocal with their criticisms of government measures.

We tried price controls and adopted regulations on trade and foreign exchange with no or unacceptable results. For example, in the case of the rice trade, we viewed rice as a strategic commodity and needed to prevent it from reaching the enemy. We imposed price controls, set up road checks to restrict the transport of rice, and inspected warehouses to look for hoarded rice. Speculators were threatened with the death penalty. Yet, the black market continued to thrive. Rice was diverted to the highest bidder no matter who, shifted to hidden warehouses and possibly to consumers across the border in Cambodia. Rice was simply looking for the highest price, which was set by imports at that time. World prices shot up by 60 to 80 percent in 1973–74, as compared to 1972. Rice disappeared from the market, triggering a crisis that threatened to degenerate into a politically explosive situation. There was also some talk of accomplishing large-scale rice farming through mechanization, resulting in increased productivity and efficiency. We discarded this idea as impractical at that time. We were capital poor and labor rich, and we needed to create jobs first.

We had come to the conclusion that a market-based economy would work best for SVN in our wartime environment. Private ownership and initiative with minimum government interference were the other two cornerstones of our approach. This was not a matter of ideology or theory. It was a matter of practical experience, of what could work and what did not. It could be argued that we were forced to adopt this position because we had no capital to squander, no manpower, and no acceptable way to interfere with the marketplace. Moreover, we had seen market-based economies work well in small Asian countries, such as Singapore, Taiwan, and Korea. Those countries were our models. We had annual conferences with our counterparts in those countries to learn from them, to emulate their leaders, and to be inspired by their achievements. Our policies in general needed to be gradual and flexible. We needed to move forward cautiously, in phases and in small steps, allowing adequate time for us to learn how the market would work, how to adjust to it, and how to operate in a wartime environment.

Our policies could be described with three key points: market-based pricing in an open economy with minimum regulations; relative reliance on the private sector for initiative and management; and relegating the role of the government to the macro policy level, i.e., protecting infrastructure, establishing essential institutions, and adopting a solid legal framework to attract investments, foreign and domestic. There were arguments against lifting price controls, against deregulation, and against letting the markets work, in particular with respect to commodities viewed as strategic, such as rice, petroleum products, and fertilizer. These arguments were stimulated by negative effects on low-income groups, especially soldiers and public servants; by the diversion of goods into the enemy's hands; by the constant destruction and disruption of supply lines, roads, and bridges; and by the deficiency of the private sector, which could affect the smooth flow of goods that we hoped to achieve.

Despite a dismal present and an uncertain near-term outlook, it was imperative that we take steps to show that we had good reasons to believe in a better future. We needed to build a foundation for long-term growth, with a vision, a sense of direction, institutional support, and concrete measures to show that we were moving ahead. We needed to provide the marketplace and the private sector with good reasons to switch from a short-term-gain perspective to a long-term frame of mind. The successful implementation of the Land to the Tiller Program, stabilization of the rice markets, and exploration for oil offshore—all done under less than ideal conditions—demonstrated our determination to pursue a long-term strategy despite wartime conditions. During a three-year period, we established or strengthened a dozen government institutions that aimed to build a stable economy. We moved step-by-step to deregulate the market place, and worked in close cooperation with private sector institutions, such as the Chamber of Commerce and the Association of Bankers, to get them involved with certain decision-making processes. In some cases, we invited industry leaders to join the board of directors of our various government institutions. Furthermore, we contacted international institutions such as the US EX–IM (Export–Import) Bank, the World Bank, the Asian Development Bank, and OPIC (Overseas Private Investment Corporation) to inform them about our development plans.

As for the implementation of our plans, we ran into issues such as: passive resistance from the entrenched bureaucracy, which could see that the need for its service was being reduced or would eventually be made redundant; non-cooperation from groups with vested interests that had to give up their authority, for example, the banks, which preferred to ration credit with their own administrative decisions rather than to let the market decide; weakness in the private sector, which was more accustomed to waiting for government guidance and decisions and was more focused on short-term gain, being unwilling to take long-term risks; and the general weakness or lack of government institutions. We nevertheless pushed forward our strategy on four major fronts: monetary policy, price controls, institution building, and law.

We were under constant pressure to close the gap between the official exchange rate and the black market exchange rate. We faced a dilemma. On the one hand, there was a need to determine a fair exchange rate to convert the dollars spent by US troops into the local currency. A realistic rate, meaning a devaluation of the currency, would reduce the incentive to trade in the black market, encourage exports, discourage imports, encourage the use of local raw material, increase invisible foreign exchange earnings, and increase counterpart receipts. All of these would ultimately benefit the national budget, but, in the short-term, there would be an increase in inflation due to the higher cost of imports. On the other hand, an artificially low rate would be deflationary, encourage black markets, reduce official foreign exchange earnings, and increase the demand for imports, especially luxury items that were in high demand. To discourage this situation, it would be necessary to impose high import taxes on those items, which in turn would open up the trade in contraband goods coming from the duty free category granted to the American PX (Post Exchange) military system.

This dilemma revealed a serious deficiency in our tax system, which was ill-equipped to deal with windfall profits created by the price differential between the high price of new imports that had not cleared customs and the low price of stock that had already cleared customs. In theory, this windfall profit should be dealt with by direct taxation. In practice, it fell upon the MOE to find a solution. We would ask for a declaration of existing stock, impose an equalizing tax on this stock, and let the importer sell freely on the market. It was not ideal in the sense that we had to rely on the declaration of the importers, but, nevertheless, politically it was somehow acceptable.

Our tax laws were by and large translated from French law prior to the overhaul of our domestic tax system beginning in 1972. By 1974, our domestic tax structure was nearly up to the standards of a modern tax system. Indicative of the new system's success was a 70 percent increase in 1973 revenues over those in 1972. Adjusted for inflation, the increase was 17 percent.[17] Another aspect of the situation was that the source of foreign exchange was mainly from US government spending, and a low exchange rate was, in effect, a hidden subsidy from the US government. This was always a sensitive subject of discussion among government officials.

We announced the first series of austerity measures in October 1969. They consisted primarily of higher taxes on imports with a higher exchange rate for certain imported goods, designed to generate VN$10 billion in revenues and to reduce inflationary pressure while dealing with the black market of foreign exchange as well as duty free military goods. Needless to say, these measures were tough and highly unpopular, although recognized as necessary. The new economic and finance team spent three days being grilled by the National Assembly (the equivalent of the US House of Representatives). That was our first lesson on rules and procedures under a constitutionally elected government.

The long overdue austerity measures enacted by the new government raised several important questions. The National Assembly was probably right when it questioned the legality of the 1961 decree under which the government acted. However, it was probably wrong when it contended that the Assembly could have enacted such unpopular measures. We recognized that the implementation of the measures left much to be desired, and we assumed a big share of the blame for the weak performance in publicly explaining the measures, both domestically and internationally. US Ambassador Bunker, in his report to the US president, characterized the measures as an act of high political courage but poor political implementation, and also as an act of faith because the measures were taken before agreement on stabilization was reached with the US government and the IMF. Eventually the National Assembly enacted the Program Law designed to give the executive near full authority in monetary and foreign exchange policy matters. The National Assembly preferred to not be involved with highly unpopular measures.

We resolved to adopt a floating exchange rate policy in 1971. A floating exchange rate system meant a series of frequent mini devaluations, which we felt was politically more acceptable than a large devaluation. The concept of a floating exchange rate system was fairly new, even revolutionary, in a world where fixed exchange systems

---

[17] United States Agency for International Development, "Viet Nam: Economic Background Data," report from the Joint Economic Office, Saigon, July 1974, p. 9.

were the norm. The US Treasury was in the process of getting out of the gold standard and letting the US dollar float against other world currencies in the summer of 1971.

We introduced a floating interest rate policy in 1970 in view of the persistently high inflation rate, which at times exceeded 50 percent per year. A plausible or real rate of interest was necessary to attract savings and reduce inflationary pressure, but there was little incentive for this on the part of the banks. They preferred to keep interest rates low to keep their cost of funds low, and to ration credit by administrative decisions rather than to let the market play its role. Eventually, we were able to convince the banks that real rates of interest were here to stay and to get them involved with the interest-setting mechanism.

We introduced new financial products such as negotiable CDs, anonymous bearer bonds, and the selling of Treasury bills to commercial banks to soak up excess liquidity. These were fairly advanced ideas at the time for a country in the middle of a vicious war that was conducted both on the battlefield and in the economic sphere.

We significantly expanded credit facilities for the Agricultural Development Bank to finance fertilizers, small-scale farm machinery, and rice inventory in conjunction with our land reform and rice marketing programs. The number of loans went up fivefold between 1970 and 1974, whereas their value went up almost tenfold, although this was essentially due to price inflation. The average value per loan was less than $50. The collection records were very good.[18]

We also got involved with a social stability program to deal with the hundreds of thousands of dislocated persons flocking to the cities to avoid military activity in the countryside. This situation was compounded by rising unemployment as a result of layoffs due to the dwindling US presence. We took a field trip to Da Nang with the US Embassy counselor and were shocked by the enormity of the problem. A decision was made right there that we must create paying jobs immediately rather than doling out welfare cash for the thousands of refugees and unemployed before the situation degenerated into a social and humanitarian nightmare. We started out with a modest public works program in Da Nang, called the Agency for Development of Da Nang Area (ADDA). Some 8,000 jobs were created there. Eventually, the program spread out to two more regions, and at the end created some 32,000 jobs. We recognized that these were stopgap measures, a drop in the bucket given the overall magnitude if the refugee problem. We never believed that we should be in the business of directly creating jobs in the long run.

An important event in our economic policy was the removal of price controls and other administrative impediments to let the market find its own level. We had applied price controls and movement restrictions on the rice trade with disastrous consequences; it led to the rice crisis of 1973, which provoked us to do a complete re-thinking of the rice trade at the highest level of government. We believed that lifting price controls and other restrictions on rice was a success that led us to the threshold of exporting rice for the harvest of 1975. Many existing institutions were strengthened. For example, the National Agricultural Credit Agency was elevated to the status of an Agricultural Development Bank in 1967. A system of private rural banks was set up in all provinces as a joint venture between the private sector and the Agricultural Development Bank. Construction was begun on a second industrial park in Can Tho

---

[18] Hai Nguyen Dang, *Get Up One More Time* (Ellicott City, MD: H & T Publishers, 2007), p. 166.

province. The General Supply Administration was reorganized to become the National Food Administration in October 1973 and given full power and the necessary funding to deal with all aspects of rice supply and marketing. The National Standards Institute replaced the old Vietnam Standard Institute by legislative enactment in 1972. The Export Development Center was upgraded to director general status in 1974. In 1972, The Industrial Development Center was restructured to become the Industrial Development Bank, a government-owned institution. In 1973, the privately owned SOFIDIV (Société pour le Financement de l'Industrie au Vietnam), a real estate financing company established in 1961, was restructured in scope and operations to become the Investment and Development Bank, known as IDEBANK.

New institutions were created. The National Economic Development Fund was set up in March 1972 to finance Intermediary Credit Institutions. In 1974, the Industrial Development Authority was set up to administer the new investment law, the Investment Service Center was set up to administer the "one-stop" policy, the National Petroleum and Mines Authority was set up to implement the new Petroleum Law, and the Export Processing Zone and the National Tourism Authority came into existence.

We gave much attention to adopting a new legal framework suitable for foreign investors. We needed to attract foreign capital and know-how. We had to move expeditiously, because we were competing with places like Singapore, Taiwan, Korea, and Thailand. Our advantage was that we had abundant natural resources, a skilled labor force, a high literacy rate, and, also, that we were starting from the bottom. We needed to work with international institutions like the US Export–Import Bank and the Overseas Private Investment Corporation. It was essential to have a new solid legal structure for investment within the framework of our constitution. A law governing the extraction of petroleum and natural resources was enacted in 1970. A new investment law was enacted in 1972. These would serve as our basic legal structure upon which to build our investment for the future.

As for government-owned enterprises, such as the coal mines of An Hoa Nong Son, the Ha Tien cement factory, and the Viet Nam Sugar Mill, our general observation was that they were inefficient due to outdated equipment and that they were handicapped by security costs. We would contemplate upgrading or expanding the facilities if we could attract foreign investment; otherwise, we would look into privatizing them in due course. For example, in the case of the Ha Tien facility, after several years of negotiations, agreements were reached with the French government, with several banks, and with Polisius, the equipment supplier, to finance a $40 million expansion. This would bring total production of the facility to 80 percent of the country's cement requirement.

In the case of our search for oil, we ruled out setting up a national oil company to explore for oil offshore. It would take years for it to become operational. It would require significant capital upfront, technical expertise that we lacked, and could be subject to pressure from vested interest groups from all directions. Rather than receiving US$47 million upfront in signature bonuses within the space of about a year, we would have spent that much trying to rent drilling rigs, deal with drilling contractors, and hire specialists. It would have been a great waste of time and money had we pursued that course.

As for achievements, I kept no record of our actions and results, so I provide below what I have found in archived documents for 1971, the year when Vietnamization was in full swing; and from 1974, the last full year of the Republic. These were official reports filed by the US ambassador and subsequently declassified.

A report dated January 26, 1972, from US Ambassador Bunker to the US President:

> ... Yet more encouraging was the improvement in the economic situation. 1971 was the least inflationary Vietnam has seen since 1964. Its major economic reforms begun in September–October 1970 and carried forward in 1971 have radically altered the economic picture. At the heart of the program was the step-by-step move to a more realistic and flexible rate system and the dismantling of a large number of controls. A complimentary move upward on interest rates helped generate savings and quell speculation ... They serve to prepare the ground for stabilization in 1972, and for additional investment, production, and exports ... In short, the essential policies and institutional foundations are being developed for the long run.[19]

I had resigned my post as minister of trade and industry in November 1974 and, consequently, did not provide the year-end report for 1974. The following are excerpts from US Ambassador Martin's cable to the secretary of state dated January 1975:

> While 1974 started badly, particularly with the threat posed by the rapid rise in petroleum prices, Vietnam's economy came through the year gratifyingly well, in large measure because the government took measures called for by the situation ... Inflation rate was 65 percent in 1973, 41 percent in 1974, down to single-digit annual rate of 9 percent in the last four months of 1974 ... The government continued the policy, in effect since 1971, of frequent, small adjustments in the rate. The piaster was devalued from 550 to the dollar at the outset of the year to 685 at year's end, an overall move of 24.5 percent ... The approximate tripling of world oil prices in late 1973 and early 1974 had a profound impact on the Vietnamese economy in 1974. Faced with the prospect of paying up to US$299 million in 1974 for the same amount of Petroleum Oil and Lubricants (POL) that had cost US$80 million in 1973, the GVN set as its goal a 25 percent reduction in consumption. POL prices, which had already been raised by 36 to 47 percent in November 1973, were raised another 66 to 140 percent on January 26, 1974. At that point gasoline was priced at the equivalent of US$1.62 per gallon, one of the highest levels in the world ... Almost alone among non-OPEC countries, Viet Nam's foreign exchange reserves rose during 1974 ... The Overseas Private Investment Corporation (OPIC) guarantees for American investors were reinstated on August 27, 1974. The Export–Import Bank revised past policy and agreed to consider financing proposals; and the government decreed establishment of Vietnam's first Export Processing Zone on May 29, 1974. Some six firms have applied for OPIC coverage ... The oil companies paid US$30 million to Viet Nam in exploration fees during 1974 ... Pecten Viet Nam, a joint venture of Shell Oil (United States) and Cities Service, discovered quantities of oil and gas in two test wells drilled in August and September.[20]

---

[19] Bunker, *Bunker Papers*, pp. 848, 895.

[20] Graham Martin, *1974 Year-End Economic Overview* (Saigon: United States Embassy, 1975).

Appendix

Below are excerpts from several articles published in various US newspapers about our search for oil, courtesy of Pham Kim Ngoc, who found them in the Library of Congress.

From the *Los Angeles Times*, June 11, 1971:

"Are the potentially rich oil leases off the coast of South Viet Nam responsible for the Nixon Administration's failure to get our sons out of Viet Nam?" asked Another Mother for Peace demanding a Senate investigation ... Senator Fulbright [chairman] ... asked the State Department about the situation and Senator Aiken [ranking Republican on the committee] also expressed concern ... State Secretary Rogers wrote to Fulbright that the US government "has not provided South Viet Nam any technical assistance relating to offshore exploration."

From the *Baltimore Sun*, June 11, 1971:

Michael Tanzer, former Harvard economist and now independent oil consultant, testified before the foreign relations committee ... "the danger of a continuing US military presence there is to keep the concession-granting government in power ..."

From the *New York Times*, June 11, 1971:

Last March the Commercial Attaché of the French Consulate ... proposed that a French committee screen all the bids ... in effect to oversee the entire operation for the South Vietnamese, who are considered inexperienced ... Deputy Ambassador to Viet Nam Berger let it be known to Saigon that the United States would be perturbed if ... it "favored the French ... "

Other documents consulted:

Comptroller General of the United States. "Report to the Congress of the United States Relating to Activities of Department of State, Agency for International Development, Department of Defense," Washington, DC: The Comptroller General of the United States, July 1966.

—. "Report to the Congress of the United States, Review of the Administration of Assistance for Financing Commercial Imports under the Economic and Technical Assistance Program for Viet Nam 1958–1962, Agency for International Development, Department of State," Washington, DC: The Comptroller General of the United States, July 1964.

Food and Agriculture Organization of the United Nations. "Rapid Growth of Selected Asian Economies: Lessons and Implications for Agriculture and Food Security— Republic of Korea, Thailand, and Viet Nam," Bangkok: Regional Office for Asia and the Pacific, Policy Assistance Series, 2006.

Peter R. Kahn, "Land of No Peace," *Wall Street Journal*, August 1974.

United States Agency for International Development. "Report to the US Ambassador," Saigon, AID [Agency for International Development], for the years 1970, 1971, and 1972.

—. "Terminal Report: United States Economic Assistance to South Vietnam 1954–1976," Washington, DC, AID, 1976.

United States Agency for International Development, Viet Nam. "Annual Statistical Bulletin no. 9: Data through 1965," Saigon, Joint Economic Division, September 1966, and including Supplement no. 2.

—. "Annual Statistical Bulletin no. 11: Data through 1968," Saigon, Office of Joint Economic Affairs, October 1968.

—. "Economic Background Data," Saigon, Joint Economic Office, July 1974.

CHAPTER SIX

FROM THE FIRST TO THE SECOND REPUBLIC: FROM SCYLLA TO CHARYBDIS

Phan Quang Tue

> When I shun Scylla your father,
> I fall into Charybdis your mother
> —Shakespeare, *Merchant of Venice*

In his 1982 book, *On Strategy*, an investigation and analysis of the US army's role in the Vietnam War,[1] Col. Harry G. Summers, Jr., observed that almost all of the literature and analysis of the war ended with the Tet Offensive of 1968. At that time, the story of the early years of the war was for many Americans the whole story of the war in Vietnam, which is not accurate. As a result, the popular opinion was that, in Vietnam, America had lost a counterinsurgency war, a people's war. Counterinsurgency, countering an insurgency war, recently resurfaced again in the context of a debate at the US Military Academy, over the strategy used in Iraq and Afghanistan.

The truth is that the war continued seven years after the Tet Offensive. According to former CIA director William Colby in his book *Lost Victory*, the United States had won the people's war.[2] Saigon did not fall to barefoot black-pajama clad guerillas, he wrote; instead, it fell to a 130,000-man, 18-division force supported by tanks and heavy artillery. An incomplete record of events often leads to half-truths, misinformation, and, most seriously, false conclusions.

Most studies on South Vietnam have for too long been limited to the First Republic under President Ngo Dinh Diem, 1954–63, and neglect several key developments occurring after 1963, in particular the 1965–75 period, which encompasses the Second Republic. This latter period includes American military intervention; the rise to power

---

[1] Harry G. Summers, *On Strategy: A Critical Analysis of the Vietnam War* (New York, NY: Presidio Press, 1982).

[2] William Colby, *Lost Victory: A Firsthand Account of America's Sixteen-Year Involvement in Vietnam* (Chicago, IL: Contemporary Books, 1989).

of the South Vietnamese military; the campaign and elections for the Constituent Assembly in September 1966; the promulgation of the second Constitution on April 1, 1967; the negotiations with Ha Noi; the withdrawal of American troops; and, finally, the surrender of South Vietnam.

While it is a commendable academic effort to collect individual testimonies from living witnesses who played prominent roles in the Second Republic, oral history nevertheless has inherent defects and is thus not always entirely reliable. Perhaps some of you remember *Rashomon,* a movie first shown at the 1951 Venice Film Festival about a crime drama set in twelfth-century Japan. A notorious bandit attacks a *samurai* and his wife. The bandit is arrested and put on trial. The film opens with a priest, a woodcutter, and a peasant taking refuge from a downpour beneath a ruined gate. They discuss the bandit's murder and rape trial, and when the case is investigated by governing authorities, even the dead are summoned to testify. The film is a brilliant exploration of truth and human weakness, a fascinating account of the effect of subjective perception on recollection by which observers of an event are able to produce substantially different but equally plausible accounts of an event.

When we who lived through and played roles in the events of the First and Second Vietnamese Republics present our accounts, it is for you to decide, or to speculate, who among us is the priest, the woodcutter, or the peasant—or the spirit of the murdered victim.

According to the 2002 *Civil War Desk Reference* of the US Library of Congress, the largest library collection on earth, at least 50,000 books and pamphlets (some other estimates go as high as 70,000) have been published on the American Civil War. There is no record of how many books have been written and published on the Second Republic of Vietnam. Whatever the reasons for the limited literary record of this period, there are nevertheless vivid and imaginative records in the memories of its survivors.

Every story has a beginning. My involvement and later interest in politics began with a small but unforgettable moment. My father, Phan Quang Dan, returned to Saigon in September 1955, after a long political journey overseas that took him to several capital cities around the world. I was then fourteen years old and my younger brother, Tuan, was ten years old. We were both very happy and excited to be reunited with our father after many years of separation. We both attended Taberd School in Saigon, a private Catholic school managed by the La Salle Christian Brothers.

More than a year before, in May 1954, the French had surrendered at Dien Bien Phu, and the Geneva Conference began. On June 16, 1954, at his chateau near Cannes, France, Emperor Bao Dai appointed Ngo Dinh Diem to be prime minister of Vietnam. On July 20, 1954, the Agreement to Cease Hostilities was signed, and, with it, the partition of Vietnam into zones assigned to two governments: the Democratic Republic of Vietnam in the north and the Republic of Vietnam in the south. On October 23, 1955, Diem replaced Bao Dai as head of state by an overwhelming 96 percent of the vote in a referendum. Three days later, on October 26, 1955, Diem announced the establishment of the First Republic of Vietnam and proclaimed himself president of the Republic of Vietnam. The elections for a National Assembly were set to take place on March 4, 1956.

After our father returned, Tuan and I enjoyed the best time of our childhood with him. We followed him wherever he went. I remember a visit with our father in Phnom Penh towards the end of 1955 on the occasion of an international trade fair, the first in Cambodia. This was the only time I visited the temples of Angkor Wat and Angkor Thom. I also remember that my brother and I were treated to a sumptuous meal when my father met with Pope Pham Cong Tac and General Nguyen Thanh Phuong of the Cao Dai religious sect at the colorful Cao Dai temple in the province of Tay Ninh.

It was not until an incident before the 1956 National Assembly elections that my father and I discovered that we were under police surveillance. My father was driving and I was riding in the passenger seat next to him late one afternoon in February 1956. The car windows were down. Bored out of my mind, I crafted a paper airplane and threw it outside of the car. Suddenly we heard sirens and saw lights flashing. Police stopped us. Several individuals surrounded our car. We were ordered to get out of the car so that the police could search it for anti-government propaganda materials. We were ordered back to our car and instructed to follow them to a police station. I was separated from my father. It was the police chief of the First District of Saigon who interrogated me. I learned later his name was Le Van Tu, nicknamed "Co Tu," who conducted this police operation and who was my interrogator. I was held by a policeman and struck once in the face by the police chief.

I am a movie aficionado and one of my favorites is *The Godfather*, which I enjoy watching. The scene in which the corrupt Irish police chief in New York City strikes Michael Corleone always reminds me of my own experience. But in my case, Co Tu's strike did not break my cheekbone and did not cause me a permanent sinus problem. I never have to hold a handkerchief in my hand like the young Corleone in exile in Sicily! Nor did I need to have plastic surgery to fix my nose.

My father decided to run for a seat in the National Assembly elections in 1959. This was the first parliamentary election after the first constitution was promulgated in October 1956. He selected the Saigon second district, which is where the Presidential Palace was located. I was then seventeen years old and in my last year at Jean-Jacques Rousseau, a French public high school in Saigon. I fully injected myself into the campaign. Sixteen candidates were running for one seat. Army troops were transported to the second district to cast their votes, presumably for the government candidate. The leaflets we distributed at the campaign stops were collected by the government agents as soon as we left. On the date of the election it was reported that two of our candidate's observers at the elementary school of Van Thinh, on Tran Hung Dao Street, were denied their forty piasters per diem allowed by the election rules.

My father scored an overwhelming victory with 35,000 votes against Pham Van Thung, the government candidate, who had 5,000 votes. I was again riding with my father on the opening day of the National Assembly to attend the first session. Not far from home, police stopped our car. We were told that the police received information of a communist bombing plot that morning and they needed to search all vehicles entering Saigon. My father asked the police chief who conducted the search to speed up his search since he did not want to be late for the inaugural session. But the police chief asked my father to follow him to the police station to have some tea. At the Gia Dinh police station, the police chief bluntly informed my father that he had received instructions from the Presidential Palace to keep my father under his watch until President Diem finished his speech at the inauguration of the asembly and had returned to the Presidential Palace.

My father's election was later declared fraudulent and thus invalid. The runner-up government candidate was declared elected and took my father's seat for the Saigon second district. This episode was an eye-opening experience for me. Creating a genuinely democratic society is an arduous task, whereby one must keep pressing relentlessly every step of the way.

Early in the morning of November 11, 1960, Saigon and its adjacent province Gia Dinh were awakened by gunfire. My father, a physician, opened his clinic as usual, then closed it around noon. He sent for information and received news that paratroopers had already taken control of many government agencies, including the Saigon radio station and some military posts, and were encircling the Presidential Palace. My father and his wife then headed to a friend's house in the center of Saigon, leaving my brother and me behind in the clinic, which was also the family home, in Ba Chieu, Gia Dinh. This was the last time I saw my father until the Diem regime was ousted by the military on November 1, 1963. The November 11 coup attempt was quickly aborted and its military plotters fled to Cambodia. My father was arrested on November 14, 1960, at the home of his long-time and loyal friend Dinh Xuan Quang, who himself, with his wife and two children, were also arrested. Their whereabouts remained unknown for several weeks, as Diem's minister of the interior stonewalled all information regarding their plight. It was the timely intervention of international organizations and individual personalities that forced the government to finally admit their detention and thus saved their lives. Among those individuals was Huynh Sanh Thong, a graduate of Cornell University in the 1950s and later a Yale University faculty member. Many years later, after immigrating to the United States in 1975, my father told me that he had never met Huynh Sanh Thong.

My brother and I hunkered down in our Ba Chieu family home and clinic during the days following the abortive coup. On the morning of November 14, 1960, we heard loud banging on the clinic's iron sliding door. A mob was massing in front of our home. They smashed and knocked down the sliding door. We fled out the back door with only the clothes on our backs. None of the neighbors alerted the police about our escape. The mob freely looted the clinic located downstairs, then ran upstairs and hauled away clothes, books, and family treasures. They piled up our furniture in front of our house in the middle of the market and set it on fire. This was in full daylight in plain view of the Gia Dinh Police Station and the office of the Gia Dinh province chief. My brother and I watched from afar, inside a neighbor's home. To this day, I keep in my mind the image of a rowdy mob chanting virulent slogans and demanding that my father be hanged. Among the belongings that were set on fire by the mob were memorabilia I cherished as treasures of my childhood: a stamp collection book; a book in French, *Les Grands Hommes*, with the poem *If,* by Rudyard Kipling, copied in the first page; and a boy-scout knife, all given to me as birthday presents from Helmi Maki, a Finnish friend of my father from the time they both attended the Harvard Public Health School in 1952–54.

The November 11 abortive coup was followed by my father's arrest, detention and torture, staged prosecution and trial, and imprisonment on Poulo Condor Island, and a campaign of character assassination perpetrated for many years by the supporters of Diem's regime. The coup also disrupted the lives of my brother and me. We became untouchables among certain circles in Saigon at the time. One man distinguished himself by his courage. Nguyen Dinh Quat, a millionaire contractor and later a presidential candidate against Diem, was not afraid to offer me a job as the tutor of his five children. His generosity sustained me financially throughout this difficult time. My education at the Saigon University School of Law was interrupted, however, for a year.

In February 1962, two Viet Nam Air Force pilots, Nguyen Van Cu and Pham Phu Quoc, bombarded the Presidential Palace. President Diem and his brother Ngo Dinh Nhu escaped unharmed. A series of arrests ensued, and I fell into the government security net. I was briefly arrested because of my contact with the brother of one of the two air force pilots. I was investigated by a Special Military Court prosecutor, then released.

I became involved actively in the Buddhist movement and participated in many student demonstrations against the government in August 1963. I was arrested on August 26, 1963, near the Saigon University Law School, along with several hundred other students. We were first transported by military trucks to the Quang Trung Military Training Center. Then we were screened and I was among a group that was transferred back to Saigon, where we were detained at the Vo Tanh National Police camp. There I was interrogated and beaten by the Doan Cong Tac Dac Biet Mien Trung (Central Region Special Work Group), a secret service operation under President Diem's brother Ngo Dinh Can and his agents. I was released along with all of the other students on November 4, 1963, following a military coup that resulted in the demise of the First Republic and the death of President Ngo Dinh Diem and his brother Ngo Dinh Nhu.

Learning from the failure of the November 11, 1960, coup, the generals had carefully planned, and, with a green light from the Americans, executed the operation to overthrow Diem's government. Judging from what followed, however, it is clear that there was no long-term political planning. A Revolutionary Military Council of Twelve Generals was formed to rule the country. A provisional cabinet was appointed. Two months later, General Nguyen Khanh toppled this council, replaced it with another Revolutionary Council, and formed his own cabinet with himself as prime minister. From January 1964 to June 1965 there were four military coups and counter-coups. From November 1963 to June 1965, there were five cabinets, the longest lasting eight months, the shortest three months. General Duong Van Minh, General Nguyen Khanh, and the civilian Phan Khac Suu took turns as chief of state.

The struggle for power among the generals lasted almost two years, until June 16, 1965, when the generals installed Nguyen Van Thieu as chairman of the National Leadership Committee and chief of state, and Air Marshal Nguyen Cao Ky was named to be the prime minister. Nguyen Cao Ky's official title was Chairman of the Central Executive Committee, and his cabinet, the War Cabinet, was sometimes described by his supporters in the local media as the Government of the Poor. People familiar with the history of the French Revolution believed that these appellations—as well as ideas such as a Council of Twelve, a Central Executive Committee, and a Revolutionary Tribunal—were all taken from the time of the Girondins and Jacobins in 1793 during the French Revolution and were suggested to the young General Ky by a small group of advisors and mahjong partners with whom he surrounded himself at the time.

In 1965, there were forty-four provincial councils and five municipal councils (including Saigon). Although they were elected by direct suffrage, these councils wielded no real power. The councilors were paid a nominal remuneration, their title was humble, and the government and media belittled their work. Against the advice of many, my father decided to run for a seat on the Gia Dinh Provincial Council. Newly graduated from Saigon University Law School, I worked part-time as a translator in the French Section at the Vietnam Press and was an attorney apprenticed to the Lambert law office, which was one of the two remaining French law firms in Saigon. Again, I actively participated in my father's campaign. To my knowledge, he was the only nationally and internationally known figure to contest a seat on a provincial council. I had, however, an idea where he was heading. On May 30, 1965, from a field of fifty-two candidates, he was elected with close to 80,000 votes. These were the first representative institutions popularly elected in the country since the end of the First Republic of South Vietnam. Ironically, the councilors were the only representatives elected in the country, unlike the chief of state, the prime minister, or the cabinet members, none of them being elected by the people. The Gia Dinh Provincial Council held its first meeting and unanimously chose my father as its chairman. On October 12, 1965, the provincial and municipal councilors, meeting in a national convention, approved a declaration urging the government to organize the election of a Constituent Assembly. Months passed without any action from the military to call elections. In March 1966, students started taking to the streets in increasingly large demonstrations against the government.

On April 11, 1966, General Thieu convened the National Political Congress with all of the chairmen of the provincial and municipal councils, as well as religious and political leaders. My father was elected chairman of that congress. After two days of debate, General Thieu signed an executive order for the election of a Constituent Assembly. September 11, 1966, was the election date. The campaign lasted four weeks, with 532 candidates contesting 117 seats. It is not very clear why the number 117 was chosen, or by whom, but the combined number of 117 (1+1+7) equals 9, which was believed to be a lucky number according to numerology. The Vietnamese local media often referred to this Constituent Assembly as the "Quoc hoi 9 nut" (National Assembly of 9 Points).

My father was elected with the largest vote total in the country; *Life* magazine featured him surrounded by his supporters in their issue of September 23, 1966. The newly elected assemblymen elected Phan Khac Suu to be speaker of the Constituent Assembly and undertook their task to draft a new constitution. There was a challenge to their work from the military, however. The military junta wanted to have the right to veto any portion of the constitution, a veto that could be overridden only with a two-thirds vote of the assembly. Assemblyman Tran Van Van opposed that provision. He was assassinated on December 7, 1966. My father was another opponent, and he narrowly escaped death twenty days later when an explosive charge planted under his vehicle detonated as he opened the car door.

On April 1, 1967, the constitution was promulgated, marking the beginning of the Second Republic of South Vietnam. Guidelines from the Constitution of the United States for a system of checks and balances were adopted. A cabinet under a prime minister appointed by the president was accountable to a National Assembly composed of a Lower House and a Senate. There were 159 deputies elected for four years, and sixty senators elected on fifteen-candidate lists for six years. The president was elected to a four-year term for a maximum two terms; a third term of five years was added in a constitutional amendment passed in January 1974 to allow Thieu to run for a third term. A nine-justice Supreme Court was created with constitutional authority and administrative power over the judicial branch. The justices were chosen by the two legislative chambers from a list of thirty candidates representing the bench, prosecutors, and private bar attorneys. The justices served six-year terms. There was a Censorate with investigative authority over all high-ranking officials of the three branches of the government. There were three consultative councils: Ethnic Minorities Affairs, Economic Affairs, and Educational and Cultural Affairs.

South Vietnam had a population over 19,500,000 according to a 1973 census, covering an area of about 174,300 square kilometers, or 67,300 square miles. (By comparison, that's a bit smaller than the size of the State of Washington in the United

States, which has a population of over four million.) Administratively, it was divided into 44 provinces, 10 cities, 271 districts, 2,560 villages, and 12,919 hamlets. Militarily, the Republic of Vietnam under the Second Republic was divided into four corps or tactical zones (CTZ), renamed in 1970 as Military Regions (MR I to MR IV), each headed by a corps commander. MR I covered the northern part of the country, with five provinces and a population of 3,362,000. MR II covered twelve provinces in the central highlands region with a population of 3,429,000. MR III covered Saigon and eleven surrounding provinces with a population of 5,665,000. MR IV covered the Mekong Delta region with sixteen provinces and a population of 7,065,000. Each corps commander had under him the regular military forces assigned to his region as well as the whole network of province chiefs who, in turn, controlled the district chiefs and, under them, the villages and hamlets. Overall, at that time, the entire system was under the control of the military establishment.

September 3, 1967, was the date for the first presidential election since President Diem's First Republic ended in November 1963. A one-month campaign was to open on August 6, 1967. Both Thieu and Ky wanted to have their own tickets, as both wanted to become president. The military establishment, however, wanted to have only one military ticket so as to not split its supporters. Under pressure, Ky reluctantly accepted the second post in a ticket headed by Thieu. With their ticket now solidified, the generals had at their disposal the military and administrative network from the regional, provincial, district, village, and hamlet echelons. They also had the support of the police and army, and of radio, television, and print media through the system of censorship.

On the civilian side, ten tickets were formed. The election rules did not provide for a run-off election, no matter how low the percentage of votes secured by the winning ticket. Eighty-two percent of registered voters cast their ballots. The Thieu–Ky ticket won with 35 percent of the votes. A ticket headed by Truong Dinh Dzu, who ran on a peace-at-any-price platform, came in second, with 16 percent. The Phan Khac Suu–Phan Quang Dan ticket finished third, with 13 percent.

During the early hours of January 31, 1968, the first day of the Lunar New Year, the Year of the Monkey, North Vietnamese and Vietcong forces launched a wave of simultaneous attacks in major cities, towns, and military bases throughout South Vietnam. The attacks were in violation of a previously observed cease-fire agreement during Tet, a national holiday. It took the South Vietnamese and US forces by surprise and lasted several weeks, until the captured territories were reclaimed. The communists held the ancient imperial citadel of Hue until February 24; they executed thousands of civilians in Hue, an event subsequently known as the "Massacre of Hue."

The Tet offensive was a military turning point of the war. Although it was a military failure for the communists, it was a psychological and political victory for them, especially in the minds of Americans in the United States. President Thieu declared martial law throughout South Vietnam and ordered a full military mobilization. I received my own induction order to report for mandatory military service. After extended boot-camp exercises at Quang Trung Military Training Center, I was sent to the Infantry School of Thu Duc for reserve officers. After a nine-month course of training, Class 2/68 was commissioned. An attorney by training, I was assigned to Military Justice within the Department of Defense. In 1970, now promoted to the rank of first lieutenant, I was detailed to the Office of the Chief Justice of the

Supreme Court at Gia Long Palace, where I served as a staff attorney until the fall of Saigon in April 1975.

I am a native of Tam-Ky, the district seat of Quang Tin Province. Quang Tin was created from a part of Quang Nam province in 1962 under President Diem, but his administration ended with the military coup in November 1963, before Quang Tin had its own tribunal. For many years the Quang Tin people still had to go to Da Nang for their judicial duties and needs. I was sent to Tam-Ky to find a location for the construction of a building to be used for a tribunal. After the Tribunal of Quang Tin was established with an appointed judge and a fully staffed court, the first court session opened with the chief justice in attendance.

In 1971, I announced my decision to return to my hometown to run for a seat in the Lower House. With a loan of 200,000 piasters and a leave of absence from the Supreme Court, I headed back to Tam-Ky and started my campaign. Because of my limited financial resources, I stayed at the home of a supporter and at night slept on a balcony overlooking Phan Chu Trinh Street.

At the age of twenty-eight, I was the youngest of the thirteen candidates. I presented a two-point political platform. First, sex education should be included in the high school teaching curriculum. The first plank of my political platform was enthusiastically applauded by young voters, but opposed by local party leaders, who accused me of being immoral and depraved. Second, South Vietnam should enter into direct contact with the National Liberation Front (NLF) at all levels and without preconditions. My position was in direct opposition to President Thieu's "Four Nos": No negotiations with the communists, No communist political activities allowed in South Vietnam, No coalition government, and No territory cessation to the communists. My rational for advocating direct contacts at all levels and on all matters with the NLF was to project a peace-loving image of South Vietnam to counter the hawkish image of South Vietnam portrayed by the anti-war movement in the United States and in Europe at the time. While the "no political activities by communists" and the "no territory cessation" policy of President Thieu was rightly justified, I thought that his "no negotiations with the communists" was simply indefensible from a strategic as well as practical standpoint, because a nation at war with itself will close all doors to peace if it refuses to maintain channels of communication with itself.

In reality, Vietnam's main ally, the United States, was engaged in secret contacts and negotiations with North Vietnam since 1968. During US President Nixon's trip to China and meetings with Mao Zedong and Zhou Enlai in February 1972, Vietnam was already included as a trade-off in American negotiations with Beijing. To Nixon and US Secretary of State Henry Kissinger, Vietnam was an obstacle to a rapprochement between the United States and China. Why should South Vietnam then deprive itself of all contacts with the other side when Washington conducted secret negotiations over its head with Hanoi and Beijing? Direct contacts with the NLF would also sow and spread division between NLF rank and file members and North Vietnamese infiltration units.

Nguyen Vinh Lieu, commander of regional forces in Quang Tin, endorsed my platform. He sent his soldiers to escort me to meet his troops in their base at the Village of An Hai, near Tam-Ky. I met his troops on a memorable night under torch lights and a clear sky on the beach of An Hai. I was asked to clarify my position of direct, unconditional contact. I explained that village residents, regardless of which side they were part of, should not be prohibited from meeting to discuss all matters important to the daily lives of their families, from weddings to funerals, from the weather to the harvesting of crops, the raising and education of their children, the care of elderly parents. My speech was received with overwhelming support. However, I finished fourth in a field of thirteen candidates contesting three seats.

One morning in early April 1972, while I was in my office in the Gia Long Palace in Saigon, I received a call to fly to Da Nang to meet my father. From the airport we were driven to the base of Air Force Squadron 518. We were informed that Soviet missiles had shot down my brother, Captain Pilot Phan Quang Tuan, over Cam Lo in Quang Tri. It was April 6, 1972. Tuan was twenty-six years old. When this happened, our father was a deputy prime minister and minister of social welfare in the administration.

The court system in South Vietnam at the time had two Courts of Appeal—one in Saigon, the other in Hue. They had legal review jurisdiction over the Tribunals of First Instance in their respective jurisdictions. During the Tet Offensive in 1968, many court employees and their relatives were victims of the Massacre of Hue. Moreover, documents stored in the Hue Court of Appeal were destroyed during this time. It took many years to reconstruct those court files and replace the workers, causing long delays in the appeal process.

When the province of Ban Me Thuot fell in early 1975, followed by the retreat from Pleiku, I was on the staff of Chief Justice Tran Van Linh. I recommended to the Chief Justice that we should plan the rescue and evacuation of all personnel and files from Hue to Da Nang. I recommended that an ad hoc committee be formed to plan the evacuation and to temporarily assist the court personnel once they arrived in Da Nang or Saigon. Because of my familiarity with the region and local connections, which I developed during my 1971 election campaign, I volunteered for a mission to Da Nang and then to Hue to assess the situation and to report back to the chief justice. I left Saigon on March 22 and arrived in Da Nang the same day. At my request, Chief Judge Vo Nhat Minh of Quang Nam's Tribunal of First Instance called a meeting of all court personnel. Two clerks with families remaining in Hue agreed to accompany me to Hue, provided that they be allowed to take their families to Da Nang. At the Doc Lap Hotel, where I stayed, I ran into Prosecutor General Ha Xuan Te (the father of Finance Minister Ha Xuan Trung), who told me, "What are you doing out here in Da Nang? Everyone has been trying to go to Saigon and you, like a fool, are trying to get to Hue!"

With my two companions, I was able to reach the Court of Appeals in the ancient imperial citadel of Hue, remove the court files, and evacuate a number of court personnel. We returned to Da Nang, where I was able to secure a seat on one of Air Vietnam's last commercial flights back to Saigon on March 27. I immediately reported to the chief justice and urged him to take action and find a way to rescue court personnel and transport the court files to Saigon. He told me that he would have to convene a general meeting of the Supreme Court justices to discuss my proposal. That meeting never took place, for Da Nang fell on March 29.

On April 2, Prime Minister Khiem and his cabinet resigned. President Thieu resigned on April 21 and left for Taiwan four days later. On April 30, 1975, the Communists marched into Saigon, ending the Second Republic of Vietnam and, with it, South Vietnam.

In her book about Nixon's 1972 visit to China, *Nixon and Mao: The Week that Changed the World*, Margaret MacMillan notes that when Nixon met Zhou Enlai before being received by Mao Zedong in the Forbidden City, Nixon wanted Zhou to convey a very important message to Chairman Mao: "When I give my word—I don't give it very often—I want him to know that I will keep it."[3] Nixon did not keep his word to President Thieu or to South Vietnam.

The price paid by the South Vietnamese in their struggle to stay free as a noncommunist nation is staggering. It is estimated that 275,000 ARVN troops were killed in action, and as many as 250,000 people died in the post-war re-education camps. About one million took to the sea and became boat people; many of them lost their lives at sea. Another 465,000 civilians lost their lives during the war. Overall, 3.6 million Vietnamese on both sides lost their lives in the war.

The greatest loss to the Vietnamese people, however, was the chance to become a free and independent nation. In recent years, Vietnam has receded from the world stage into the sphere of Chinese influence. Because of the especially close relationship between the Vietnamese Communist Party and the Chinese Communist Party, Vietnam has again, as in centuries past, become deferential to China. In her memoir, *No Higher Honor*, former US Secretary of State Condoleezza Rice mentioned Vietnam only once—when recalling her participation in the Asia-Pacific Economic Cooperation (APEC) meeting held in Hanoi in October 2002.[4] In his memoir, *Interventions: A Life in War and Peace*, former UN Secretary-General Kofi Annan mentioned Vietnam only once, when referring to Vietnam's invasion of Cambodia in 1979.[5]

Vietnam has fallen back into the shadow of its northern neighbor. This is the price to be paid by those Vietnamese unborn when Saigon fell in 1975. They are the future generation of Vietnam.

---

[3] Margaret MacMillan, *Nixon and Mao: The Week that Changed the World* (New York, NY: Random House, 2007).

[4] Condoleezza Rice, *No Higher Honor: A Memoir of My Years in Washington* (New York, NY: Crown, 2011).

[5] Kofi Annan, *Interventions: A Life in War and Peace* (New York, NY: Penguin Press, 2012).

CHAPTER SEVEN

TESTIMONY OF A FORMER REPRESENTATIVE OF THE REPUBLIC OF SOUTH VIETNAM NATIONAL ASSEMBLY, 1971–75

Tran Van Son

EARLY YEARS

My ancestral clan originated in Son Tay Province, not far northwest of Hanoi. Family records reveal that in the 1530s it shifted to Thanh Hoa province to join Nguyen Kim against the Mac rulers, and in 1558 followed Nguyen Kim's son Nguyen Hoang into the south. My ancestors in that generation served in Nguyen Hoang's officer corps and were assigned land in Thanh Trung village, Quang Dien district. Thanh Trung was thereafter registered as our place of origin. By the nineteenth century my family had become peasants and lived on the soil in Quang Dien. In French colonial times, my grandfather was a tailor in Thanh Trung, which was about thirty kilometers from the royal capital of Hue.

In the 1910s, French authorities opened a school in Hue to train technicians for jobs in electrical power distribution, telephone and telegraph, railroads, and administration. My grandparents decided to send my father to this mid-level technical school. In Hue he met and married my mother. They built a house there on a piece of land given to them by my mother's parents. Her father was a descendant of Le Chat, one of the generals who helped Emperor Gia Long defeat his enemies and found the Nguyen dynasty at the beginning of the nineteenth century.

I was born on July 17, 1933, and am the youngest in my family; I have two brothers and two sisters. My father tried his best to send my brothers and me to school, but kept my two sisters at home in the traditional way to help my mother with housework. My sisters received no formal schooling, but they learned to read the Quoc Ngu alphabet.

My eldest brother, Tran Van Bach, died in 1946, at the age of eighteen, at Ben Cat; he was killed by the French army when it came back to reestablish French rule in Vietnam, which they had temporarily lost to the Japanese in 1945 prior to the Japanese capitulation to the United States.

My parents returned to Hue in early 1947 after having evacuated to the countryside for some months to avoid the turbulence of war. My mother went into commercial activities with my youngest sister. My eldest sister had married and was living with her own family in a nearby village. My father worked in a construction business. I attended Tran Quoc Toan elementary school in Hue.

In 1948 I was admitted to Hue's prestigious Khai Dinh High School. At that time the high school program lasted seven years. To graduate from high school and be eligible for university a student had to pass three exams: one after four years; one after an additional two years (Baccalaureate 1); and the last one a year later (Baccalaureate 2).

In 1950 my brother Tran Thanh Duong went to the maquis to join the resistance against the French, mostly in Binh Dinh province, Zone 5. He came back to Hue with his wife and children in 1954 when the Geneva Accords divided Vietnam into two parts at the seventeenth parallel. My eldest sister died of cancer in 1980. My surviving sister and brother are now each over eighty years old and living in Vietnam, my sister in Hue and my brother in Nha Trang.

In 1954–55, the French armed forces withdrew from the country as the United States became increasingly involved in supporting the government led by Ngo Dinh Diem. Diem faced immense difficulties in maintaining order. The Hoa Hao and Cao Dai religious sects and the French-trained generals Nguyen Van Hinh and Nguyen Vy tried to weaken Diem's authority and created chaos in Saigon. Diem nonetheless succeeded in consolidating his power and settling about one million refugees from the North, mostly Roman Catholics. Diem dismissed the official head of state, Bao Dai, through a referendum in 1955, and the Republic of Vietnam came into being.

After obtaining my Baccalaureate 1 in 1954, I applied for and was admitted to the School of Radio Electricity in Saigon. While at that school I prepared for and took the exam for my Baccalaureate 2 in June 1955, which completed my high school education.

At that time, all young people my age were subject to be drafted into the armed forces. That was why all of us, while attending universities, looked for an opening in military service that appealed to us. I took an exam organized by the Vietnamese Navy to go to the French Naval Academy in Brest, a French city on the Atlantic Ocean. It was the last class of a French training program held for officers in the South Vietnamese Navy. I took the course to become a naval engineer. The training was for three years. Two years were spent at the Naval Academy in Brest, attending classes and learning aboard ships; third-year students were to participate in a world tour aboard the frigate *Jeanne d'Arc*. The last year of my training (1957–58), however, was cut short at the end of August 1957 due to the deterioration of relations between France and Ngo Dinh Diem. By the end of 1957, the French navy departed Vietnam.

Returning to Vietnam, I was assigned to be chief engineer of the LSM (Landing Ship Medium) *Hat Giang* (HQ400). For some months, I was transferred to HQ03, the *Dong Da,* a coastal patrol ship. HQ03 was to leave Saigon for Subic Bay, in the Philippines, for an overhaul at a US ship-repair facility there.

In June 1958, while I was still in Subic Bay, I was reassigned to a training center in the coastal city of Nha Trang. The Nha Trang Naval Training Center was built in 1952 to train sailors for the new Vietnamese Navy, which was working alongside the French Navy. The Vietnamese Naval Academy was part of this training center, and by the time I arrived there, in October 1958, the academy was training fifty midshipmen in Class 8. The academy began using Vietnamese instead of French to teach naval subjects, which was a great challenge to me and to my fellow training officers. The Vietnamese language had replaced French as the official language at all high schools in the country in 1945. Hoang Xuan Han, a laureate from France, had edited a French–Vietnamese dictionary, entitled *Danh Tu Khoa Hoc* (Scientific Terms). This book helped us a lot, but was not sufficient for naval subjects. My fellow officers and I worked hard to create the necessary vocabulary terms.

I was in the navy for sixteen years, and I served at the Naval Training Center uninterruptedly for thirteen years with eight of the nine commanding officers during the life of the center. I came to the center as an ensign and left the navy in 1971 with the rank of commander (equivalent to lieutenant-colonel in the army and air forces). I resigned from the navy in 1971 when I was elected to the House of Representatives.

I married Nguyen Thi Phuong Thao in 1959, and by the time I resigned from the navy to serve in congress we had five children, two boys and three girls. All of them were born and grew up in Nha Trang, where I opened an office to serve my constituency.

IN THE NATIONAL ASSEMBLY[1]

Upon the promulgation of the constitution for the Second Republic on March 18, 1967, the election of a president and a National Assembly with a House of Representatives and a Senate was set for later in 1967. General Nguyen Van Thieu and Air Marshall Nguyen Cao Ky were elected on one ticket: Thieu as president and Ky as vice president. It was widely believed that Ky accepted the second position after securing a verbal concession from Thieu that he would have a free hand to run the National Assembly. Ky's intention was to use the National Assembly as leverage for power in the future, but after the elections, Thieu out-maneuvered him and curbed his power. By the end of Thieu's first term as president, in 1971, he controlled the executive and his political allies had the upper hand in the National Assembly.

Upon being elected to the National Assembly at the end of 1971, I chose to join the opposition to help balance the tendency of executive power to dominate the legislature, as we had seen during the first session of the National Assembly that was elected in 1967. I joined the opposition People's Socialist Bloc (Khoi Dan Toc Xa Hoi, hereafter PSB), which was composed of two political groups: Dan Toc, for "people," and Xa Hoi, for "socialism."

Xa Hoi emerged during the 1967–71 term, mostly comprising members of Viet Nam Quoc Dan Dang (Vietnamese Nationalist Party, VNP), led by Representative Phan Thiep, as well as some independent members with Buddhist connections from the provinces in the center of Vietnam and prominent members elected in the Saigon area, such as Ho Van Minh and Ho Ngoc Nhuan. Xa Hoi opposed the militaristic and dictatorial tendencies of President Thieu's government.

Dan Toc comprised representatives supported by the An Quang Buddhist Church, which had resisted military rule in 1964–65 and had boycotted the first election in 1967.

---

[1] To verify facts about my service in the National Assembly, I have consulted with the following former representatives: Tran Ngoc Chau (Woodland Hills, CA), Ho Ngoc Nhuan (Saigon), Phan Thiep (San Jose, CA), Ly Truong Tran (Garden Grove, CA), Dinh Xuan Dung (San Jose, CA), and Tran Cao De (Westminster, CA). I also consulted with Nguyen Van Ngan (Lakewood, CA), an advisor to President Thieu and with Tran Tu Huyen (San Francisco, CA), a lawyer, and with his son Tran Van Tuyen.

It participated in the 1971 election and successfully elected nineteen people, mostly from the center of Vietnam, of which I was one. The two most prominent members of this group were Le Dinh Duyen and Ly Truong Tran.

After the election, Dan Toc and Xa Hoi coalesced and formed PSB, with twenty-nine representatives. The nineteen representatives of Dan Toc formed the core. In addition to members of Xa Hoi, there were people who were followers of retired General Duong Van Minh, elected from the Saigon–Gia Dinh area. Some of the prominent people in PSB were Ho Ngoc Nhuan, Ho Van Minh, Nguyen Huu Chung, and Ly Quy Chung, and three influential independent representatives: Tran Van Tuyen, from Saigon; Dinh Xuan Dung, from Phan Thiep; and Tran Cao De, from Vung Tau.

At first the Buddhist Church considered Le Dinh Duyen to be the leader of PSB. Duyen was the son of Le Dinh Tham, the prominent Hue Buddhist who had rejuvenated Buddhism in the 1930s and made the ancient capital of Hue a bastion of Buddhism. The venerable Thich Tri Quang, Thich Thien Minh, and most of the well-known Buddhist leaders were products of Tham's influence.

But after consideration, the Buddhist leaders decided to support Tran Van Tuyen as leader of PSB. Tuyen was born in 1913 in the province of Tuyen Quang, some eighty miles northwest of Hanoi. He joined the VNP at the age of sixteen, got his law degree at the University of Hanoi, and was assigned as a district chief in Tuyen Quang. Thereafter he came back to Hanoi to teach at Thang Long private school, and became an acquaintance of Vo Nguyen Giap, who happened to be teaching history there. They followed different paths, ending up as adversaries for nearly half a century, until 1975. Tuyen was one of the signatories of the Caravelle Manifesto, issued in April 1960, calling on President Ngo Dinh Diem to institute reforms,[2] and Tuyen was subsequently imprisoned by Diem. After Diem was overthrown, Tuyen became the deputy prime minister under the government of Phan Huy Quat for four months (February–June 1965). When Quat could not deal with the situation and handed the government back to the generals, Tuyen returned to practicing law and served as a lawyer for the High Court of Saigon. He was eventually elected to be chairman of the Lawyers Association of South Vietnam, and was subsequently elected to the National Assembly to represent Districts 1 and 3 of Saigon–Gia Dinh.

The choice of Tuyen to lead the opposition proved to be a wise decision on the part of the Buddhist leaders. If not for Tuyen, PSB would not have survived four tumultuous years as a viable congressional opposition. PSB faced three antagonistic forces: President Thieu's reluctance to work with opposition politicians in the National Assembly, whom he tended to label as pro-communist; the communists, who endeavored to infiltrate the opposition and rally it into their camp; and US policy that aimed to end the war at our expense through negotiations with Hanoi.

During Thieu's first presidential term (1967–71) he marginalized Vice President Ky, his most serious rival. For his second term, he turned to Tran Van Huong as his vice

---

[2] The eighteen signers of the Caravelle Manifesto included people who had served in Saigon governments during the French war and also who later served in Saigon governments after the demise of the First Republic (1955-63): Tran Van Van, Phan Khac Suu, Tran Van Huong, Nguyen Luu Vien, Huynh Kim Huu, Phan Huy Quat, Tran Van Ly, Nguyen Tien Hy, Tran Van Do, Le Ngoc Chan, Le Quang Luat, Luong Trong Tuong, Nguyen Tang Nguyen, Pham Huu Chuong, Tran Van Tuyen, Ta Chuong Phung, Tran Le Chat, and Ho Van Vui.

president, a former high school teacher, former leader of the Vietnamese Red Cross, and former mayor of Saigon. Huong was widely respected and had many influential followers, called Lien Truong (Unified Schools Group). During the presidential election of 1971, Thieu ran unopposed after Nguyen Cao Ky and Duong Van Minh dropped out of the race. Although this diminished Thieu's political stature, American support encouraged his autocratic tendencies, which widened the gap between him and the opposition.

As for the negotiations in Paris, PSB was eager to see an agreement with the North that would provide a political solution based on the principle of self-determination for the people living in the South. However, for Tuyen, the situation was not so simple. He was suspicious of Nixon's and Kissinger's intentions. Former governor of California Ronald Reagan visited Tuyen during a trip to Saigon in 1972; Tuyen had visited him in Sacramento in 1965 when he was deputy prime minister. Tuyen reported to PSB that Governor Reagan asked for his opinion about how to end the war. We believed that the United States would reach an agreement unfavorable to South Vietnam. We, the opposition, had supported the position of President Thieu in opposing the signing of the Paris Agreement that did not require North Vietnamese troops to withdraw from our country simultaneously with the withdrawal of American and allied forces. However, Thieu finally had no choice but to yield to US pressure, and to rely on Nixon's promise to respond by force if the communists violated the agreement, which was signed on January 27, 1973.

On the eve of the lunar New Year on February 2, 1973 (a week after the signing of the agreement), Tuyen led PSB in a hunger strike in front of the National Assembly to denounce Thieu and the United States for signing the agreement. Tuyen warned about the impending collapse of South Vietnam. Thereafter he tried to persuade the two sides to implement the agreement. According to him, without American support, that was the only way to save South Vietnam from the grip of the Communists. We supported the formation of the Third Force between the Republic of Vietnam and the Communist side to participate in the three-part "National Council of Reconciliation and Concord" (Hoi Dong Hoa Hop Hoa Giai Dan Toc), which, according to the agreement, was to be responsible for organizing free and democratic elections. Unfortunately, the agreement was not honored by anyone and the National Council never materialized.

Tuyen had been a member of the Nationalist (i.e., opposed to the Communists) diplomatic team at Geneva in 1954. Since the signing of the Geneva Accords in 1954 that divided Vietnam into two parts, he had worked hard to preserve a free South Vietnam. His experience with the Communists taught him that Hanoi would not rest until the North took over the South. He knew the only way to achieve his dream was to build a strong South Vietnam, politically as well as economically.

He argued that if South Korea could survive, why not South Vietnam, especially because South Vietnam received more aid from the United States than did South Korea? But he knew that there were two important differences. The first was that the United States had a plan to leave South Vietnam. The second was that South Vietnam did not have a leader like General Park Chung Hee. President Thieu and his generals, most of them products of the French colonial regime, were not up to the job.

At this juncture, the three components of our bloc had different programs: the Buddhists opposed Thieu at any cost; the Vietnam Nationalist Party tried to rally people around itself; and the Duong Van Minh factions worked to bring Duong Van Minh back to power. Tuyen endeavored to keep those factions together in one bloc until the end. He also rallied with a component of the Roman Catholic Church, led by Reverend Tran Huu Thanh, to put pressure on President Thieu to fight corruption and ease the Press Law, but without any discernible result.

Tuyen knew that the situation was hopeless, but his instinct for survival pushed him to use his international contacts to seek a solution. After much thought, he came to believe that replacing Thieu with General Minh was probably a solution to end the war peacefully; and, considering the geopolitics of Asia and the Western Pacific at that time, there was a chance that South Vietnam might survive because there were plenty of indications that China would not be happy to see a unified Vietnam. China's concern about the presence of US troops on its southern border was abating, since all US soldiers had withdrawn from South Vietnam.

With this in mind, toward the last two years in the life of South Vietnam, Tuyen intended to place the full weight of the opposition behind General Minh. Unfortunately, this proved erroneous. After the signing of the Paris Agreement, the American strategy was to withdraw safely from South Vietnam without facing retribution from the South Vietnamese generals. The General Minh solution seemed to resonate with the appearance of a complicity of convenience between Hanoi and the US Embassy in Saigon.

This policy of supporting Minh explains the existence of a message in February 1975 originating from Saigon and wired to the US Congress, asking Congress not to appropriate US$300 million for military aid to South Vietnam. Rumors were that PSB was the author of the message. The truth was that President Gerald Ford had pressed the US Congress to appropriate the funds, and instead Congress decided to send a fact-finding group to Saigon to assess the situation. The group included Representatives Bella Abzug and Paul McCloskey, two of the most vocal opponents of the war and of support for South Vietnam. Upon arriving in Saigon, Abzug contacted Ho Ngoc Nhuan, an influential National Assembly member who was a National Liberation Front (NLF) sympathizer and a supporter of General Minh, and told him that the US Congress would not appropriate the funds in any case. Taking this as an occasion to pressure Thieu to compromise with General Minh, Nhuan drafted a message after a meeting of Minh supporters at Minh's residence and persuaded a handful of PSB representatives to sign it, then wired it to the US Congress. Looking back, an additional US$300 million worth of weapons at that late time would not have saved South Vietnam anyway. It might have lengthened the war, getting more Vietnamese on both sides killed. Morally, it would have been better if such a message had not been sent.

The North Vietnamese attacked across our northern border in 1972, taking part of Quang Tri province and threatening Hue. There were also major North Vietnamese offensives in the Central Highlands and toward Saigon. The North Vietnamese were defeated, but in that moment of emergency, Thieu obtained from the National Assembly legislation allowing him to govern by decree (*Luat Uy Quyen*, Power Delegation Law). In addition to allowing him to deal expeditiously with the military situation, it also expanded opportunities for him to neutralize the opposition.

In 1974, Thieu obtained an amendment to the constitution permitting him to run for a third term (1975–79). His argument was that "one does not change horses while crossing a river" (*khong ai thay ngua giua dong*). This was in the context of communist attacks intensifying all over the country, while the Americans cut aid to us below the level of "one-to-one replacement," as provided by the Paris Agreement. We in the opposition unsuccessfully opposed both the 1972 emergency legislation and the 1974 amendment. Public criticism of the amendment was muted because the Chinese invasion of the Paracel Islands in January 1974 put the issue into the shade.[3]

The circumstances of China's invasion and seizure of the Paracel Islands have not been well understood. The group of islands is located about 230 miles (379 kilometers) east of Da Nang, and was garrisoned only by a small unit of the South Vietnamese army. The National Assembly was not informed by President Thieu and representatives knew nothing about what happened out there until January 19, 1974, when international media broke the news that a Chinese naval unit had seized the islands after defeating a task force of the South Vietnamese Navy sent to defend the Paracels. The order to engage the Chinese invaders was given personally by President Thieu, and without consulting with the Americans. The opposition requested a congressional hearing about the loss of the Paracels, but the speaker of the House of Representatives turned a deaf ear to the request.

The event was embarrassing to the South Vietnamese because the US Seventh Fleet was nearby, but did not answer calls for help from Vietnamese Naval Headquarters to rescue crewmen from a sinking ship drifting on the open sea. It seemed that the United States knew about the Chinese plan to take over the Paracels, and thought that this was not a bad idea, because Hanoi would take over the South anyway, and it was better that the Paracels, at the entrance to the South China sea from the north, be in the hands of the Chinese rather than in the hands of the Russians, Hanoi's ally. It appears that US leaders intentionally looked the other way when the Chinese took possession of the Paracels.[4]

We in the opposition encountered another embarrassing situation when, on April 27, 1975, a joint session of the House and the Senate considered a resolution permitting President Tran Van Huong to transfer the presidency to General Minh. The resolution was in itself a violation of the constitution, but the situation dictated that we violate the constitution for peace. The Communists—with five divisions, including tanks and artillery, surrounding the capital—dropped the news that Minh was the only person they would talk to in order to form a coalition government to end the war peacefully. Before the vote, Representative Tran Cao De reminded Tuyen that the vote was a violation of the constitution, and Tuyen replied, "We are sacrificing the constitution to save the country." It seemed that the resolution was a dupe engineered by French Ambassador Merillon, with the collaboration of the media and the US Embassy, which wanted to buy time to evacuate the remnants of the American mission.

During the first session of the Second Republic's House of Representatives, 1967–71, there was no effective opposition. Representatives Phan Thiep and Tran Ngoc Chau led Xa Hoi. Chau was a rather prominent independent representative from Kien Hoa province, where he was twice a successful head of province, once under President Ngo Dinh Diem and once after Diem's downfall. Chau had been feuding with American advisors over the running of the Pacification Program, and ran for a seat in the National

---

[3] See Ho van Ky-Thoai, "Naval Battle of the Parcels," elsewhere in this volume.

[4] Regarding his visit to Beijing in late 1973, Henry Kissinger wrote: "Following the now well-established practice, the heart of the visit was a detailed review of the international situation by Zhou and me, together with our senior associates ... Our ties were cemented not by formal agreements but by a common assessment of the international situation ... Most of our conversations, as usual, traced our shared analysis of the world situation, though for equally obvious reason of Soviet sensitivities we could not announce that fact either."

Assembly in hopes that the new forum might help him to influence government policy. His political stand (not for Thieu, not for Ky) helped to get him elected general secretary of the House of Representatives, sponsored by Representative Nguyen Ba Luong, one of Ky's followers.

Chau, although a friend of President Thieu, worked closely with the US Embassy, giving rise to the perception that he was challenging Thieu's power. His big mistake was to contact his brother Tran Ngoc Hien, a high-ranking spy from Hanoi, without reporting it to Thieu, although he reported it to the Americans as a cover for his action. When the Americans refused to confirm that he had kept them informed of his contacts with his brother, Chau's fate was sealed because the contacts then fell into the definition of treason.

Thieu arrested Chau and, with a lukewarm nod from the US Embassy, tried him before a military court for high treason. By that time, Thieu had ousted most of Ky's people in the armed forces and in the civil administration. With Chau being discredited, he proceeded to neutralize Ky's followers in the National Assembly as well.

During the second session, 1971–75, President Thieu's backers in the National Assembly obtained a majority, but those elected from provinces in the center of Vietnam, from Quang Tri in the north to Phu Yen in the south, and from the capital of Saigon, were mostly opposed to Thieu or were independents. Nevertheless, an appearance of free elections was achieved. The opposition was then composed of representatives supported by the Buddhist Church, the Vietnamese Nationalist Party, and people supporting general Minh, with some Communist National Liberation Front sympathizers.

This gave the second session an appearance of a working democracy. The opposition, led by PSB, functioned as a genuine opposition. We could freely express our opinions before the general assembly on almost all subjects, criticizing President Thieu, his generals, and his administration at will. But we did not have the votes. The votes were for Thieu's agenda. Thieu was suspicious of the opposition, but at the same time he considered it to be irrelevant. He believed that the opposition was heavily infiltrated by pro-communist and anti-war elements, and had no strong leadership. He thought Tuyen was at best a mediator rather than a leader.

The voices of the opposition thus had little effect. This handicapped the contribution of the opposition to the building of democracy. At this juncture, the US Embassy had a strong influence on all aspects of South Vietnamese society, militarily as well as economically. Unfortunately, the United States did not pay attention to the opposition and did not have a concrete plan to help the opposition build a base for democracy in Vietnam. American embassy personnel were too occupied with preparations for ending the war, and the most they were willing to do was to keep afloat the opposition to counter the somewhat unjust American media accusations that Thieu was heading a dictatorship.

The US Embassy maintained contact with the opposition through Tuyen. He was on the list of guests to most social functions at the embassy, and an interlocutor with most of the high-ranking officials of the embassy. At weekly meetings of the People's Socialist Bloc, he rarely reported about his conversations at the embassy; probably there was not much worth mentioning. It seemed the US Embassy kept in contact with Tuyen, but the relationship did not work for the benefit of the country.

The most damaging factor in the failure of the opposition was that its members, as well as their opponents in the Thieu camp, did not have the tradition and experience of a working democracy. Up to that time, Vietnam had never been a democratic country. During the war against French domination led by the communists (1946–54), Vietnam, with Bao Dai as the head of government and with a French general commissioner at the top, did not know democracy. South Vietnam had a democratic constitution under Ngo Dinh Diem, but it was not functional. Opposition was repressed, and no voices antagonistic to Diem were heard in the National Assembly. The Constitution of 1967 was more democratic, but it was democratic in form more than in actual practice.

Looking back, it seems to me that Tuyen had enough information to know that the situation in South Vietnam was hopeless. The country had no viable economy. The armed forces—army, air force, and navy—of nearly a million troops were equipped and paid for by the United States. Through the CIA, the hands of the US Embassy in Saigon reached into all branches of government, the most evident being in the army and the least evident being in the National Assembly. At least twenty members of the National Assembly, from both houses, reported to the CIA. The agenda of the United States was to reach an agreement at any price with Hanoi in Paris in order to take back American prisoners, and to withdraw safely from the war.

Tuyen succeeded in preventing PSB from breaking up and tried his best to build a base for democracy in Vietnam. He believed that the war in Vietnam was not a civil war, but rather a proxy war between the United States and the China–Soviet alliance. Only with luck could South Vietnam be saved.

With his experience fighting the communists, Tuyen knew that there was no alternative to democracy, and he committed his whole life to promoting democracy. This explains why he went every extra mile to hold a divided opposition into one viable opposition, and also why he had opposed Diem, opposed Thieu, and, at the end, became suspicious of American policy.

Sometimes during our weekly meetings, Tuyen talked casually about his dream of an "International Alliance For Democracy." He said that during his many official visits to Africa, when he was deputy prime minister under Phan Huy Quat, he had raised the idea of an International Alliance For Democracy with North African leaders, such as Colonel Houari Boumedienne, then leader of the Revolutionary Council of Algeria; President Habib Bourguiba, of Tunisia; and president Gamal Abdel Nasser, of Egypt. All of them promised him that they would work toward that goal. Unfortunately, Quat's government was short-lived, and Tuyen went back to practicing law.

Toward the end, Tuyen maintained his dignity as a patriot, a committed politician, and a leader. He decided not to leave the country. On the eve of the communist entry into Saigon, Joe Bennett, a political counselor at the US Embassy, called Tuyen to offer him a lift out of the country, and he refused. It was said that after the collapse of South Vietnam he also declined the help offered by General Vo Nguyen Giap. Giap sent a field officer to let Tuyen know that he, Giap, could arrange with the military governor of Saigon to keep Tuyen from being sent to the concentration camps. Again, Tuyen refused. He wanted to share his compatriots' fate. This story was confirmed by Tran Tu Huyen, his son, now practicing law in California, and by the eyewitness account of Representative Ly Truong Tran, PSB secretary general, and Tuyen's closest assistant.

Tuyen was sent to Long Thanh concentration camp, not far from Saigon, together with three thousand other high-ranking officials from the government of South

Vietnam. After "nine lectures" given by cadres, the victors forced the prisoners to write autobiographies emphasizing self-guilt as "traitors of the people."

Instead, Tuyen wrote in his submission: "I did not commit any crime against the people. If you want, you may label me as a person who had opposed communism, imperialism, and dictatorship." By fall 1976, Tuyen was transferred to a concentration camp in Ha Tay, North Vietnam. On October 27, he died under suspicious circumstances. The victors might have decided his fate because of his rebuke of communism while in Long Thanh. Looking back, although Tuyen failed in his lifelong purpose of saving South Vietnam from the communists, he devoted his whole life to his country.

The long night of April 29, 1975, closed a chapter of American intervention and nation-building in Southeast Asia. It was a miserable failure. I think the US decision to help South Vietnam build a democratic country to counter the expansion of communism was strategically sound, but it failed because the war was conducted poorly, both militarily and politically.

Secretary of Defense Robert McNamara's conduct of the war by remote control and body counts was the wrong way to fight a guerrilla war. In addition to that, the United States had no clear military strategy because of its uncertainty about China's intentions. The United States was not willing to face China in a land war in Asia.

After the United States helped to overthrow Ngo Dinh Diem and committed US troops to Vietnam, the United States thought that American military muscle would break the will of Hanoi and restore peace in Vietnam. Unfortunately, the politicians in Washington bound the hands of their generals by refusing to deploy troops at the Vietnamese–Laotian border and expanding into Laos up to the Mekong River and the border with Thailand, to prevent Hanoi from sending men and materials south. Prime Minister Nguyen Cao Ky had proposed such a plan at the meeting with US President Johnson in Guam on March 20–21, 1967. If the plan had been adopted, South Vietnam might have had a chance to be pacified, and democracy might have had a chance to blossom. The neutralization of Laos by the Kennedy administration was a fatal legacy leading to ultimate defeat.

Another reason for failure, and maybe the most important, was a local one. South Vietnam, with no tradition of democracy, had weak non-government organizations (NGOs) and unqualified leaders. The opposition's anticommunist program focused on replacing Thieu, which was misdirected—it weakened Thieu's government instead of rallying the anticommunist components into one bloc. On the other hand, the communists were very successful in their infiltration into almost all the institutions of South Vietnam: the president's office (with Vu Ngoc Nha and Huynh Van Trong), the press (with Pham Ngoc An), the military (with Pham Ngoc Thao), and the National Assembly (with Ly Quy Chung and others).

THE END OF THE WAR

When the communists opened their spring campaign of 1975 in Ban Me Thuot, I was in Nha Trang. I felt that this would be the fatal blow for the existence of South Vietnam. The bad omen was a clause in the Paris Agreement, signed on January 27, 1973, permitting the North Vietnamese army to remain in the South, while all other foreign troops had to withdraw completely out of the country.

Five days before the communist army captured Nha Trang on April 1, I flew to Saigon and talked with retired General Duong Van Minh about the situation. He was optimistic about a political solution with Hanoi. I went back to Nha Trang puzzled by his cheerful mood. By this time, elements of North Vietnamese Division 10, under the command of General Vu Lang, had massed at Phuong Hoang Pass on National Route 21, from Ban Me Thuot to Ninh Hoa, which was the gateway from the highlands to Nha Trang.

An airborne brigade withdrawn from Da Nang was sent to defend Phuong Hoang Pass. But by the end of March the paratroopers were overwhelmed and the defense of Phuong Hoang collapsed. The communists reached National Highway 1 at Ninh Hoa District, and, taking a road built by the Korean army, they advanced to Cam Ranh while detaching a unit to Nha Trang to establish control there.

To avoid the turbulent situation in Nha Trang, my wife prepared for our family to leave for Saigon by Air Vietnam in late March. Two things happened that made me change the plan. First, the chaos at Nha Trang airport prevented orderly boarding. No one was in control of the situation, and people with weapons, mostly soldiers, shoved others aside and boarded. Holding a ticket did not mean a thing. Second, on the last day, many people in my constituency came to ask me about the defense of Nha Trang and its chances for survival. Their inquiries reminded me of my commitment to represent them, and I decided to stay in Nha Trang to share their fate, regardless of the consequences.

The first day of April was a day of chaos. Nha Trang was void of administration. Prisons, both civil and military, were opened, and criminals roamed the city. As South Vietnamese soldiers began to flee, some formed unruly and lawless mobs. I felt my safety threatened from both sides, especially by the coming communists, and I decided, together with two colleagues in the National Assembly, Tran Van Thung and Nguyen Cong Hoan, to rent a boat and take refuge on one of the islands in the bay of Nha Trang.

Tran Van Thung represented Khanh Hoa Province, and Nguyen Cong Hoan represented Phu Yen Province. Both were members of the People's Socialist Bloc in the National Assembly. After two days, I returned to Nha Trang and stayed low in the house, not knowing what to do or what fate awaited my family and me. The city was by then under communist military control, and very quiet. The communists reinforced their positions in the city and installed air-defense batteries against attacks by the Republic of Vietnam Air Force based at Phan Rang. The city streets were littered with trash, and the US Consulate was ransacked.

I learned about the advance of the communists by listening to BBC broadcasts in Vietnamese. The news was not heartening. By April 20, the divisions of General Van Tien Dung were at Long Khanh, trying to break Saigon's last line of defense, which was held by the Twenty-third Division, one of the best remaining divisions of South Vietnam, and commanded by Brigadier General Le Minh Dao. At the same time, US Ambassador Graham Martin worked hand-in-hand with US Secretary of State Henry Kissinger to try to find a political solution with the communists. Retired General Duong Van Minh and his neutralist supporters tried to have a role in the final solution. Afterwards, it was clear that all of this was just the wishful thinking of Ambassador Martin, or cover for his hidden agenda to safely withdraw remaining US personnel without recriminations from the Republic of Vietnam Army.

When the fighting finally stopped, I decided to follow the orders of the new authorities and registered myself at a subdistrict police station, after which I was ordered to go home and wait for further instructions. In mid-May, at midnight, the chief of the Nha Trang police, Captain Nguyen Van Linh, led a group of armed policemen and militiamen to my home at No. 2 Tran Van On to arrest me. They took me to the city police station on Tran Phu Boulevard. From there, I was transferred to the main interrogation center on the same street. Later on, I was moved to the army's old training center in Lam Son, in the district of Ninh Hoa, which had become a concentration camp for military officers, policemen, and high-ranking government officials of the late regime.

I came a little late to the camp, which had already been filled by about two thousand people assigned to live in houses identified by numbers. They put me in house #10 with the paratroopers, both officers and soldiers, who had been captured at Phuong Hoang Pass. The communists used Lam Son as a place to indoctrinate us, using lessons covering nine subjects to explain to us the strategy they used during the previous twenty years to win, and their policy of reconciliation and leniency toward us, the vanquished.

After two months in Lam Son, I was transferred to the civilian prison of Nha Trang, where the new administration kept regular criminals. The purpose of this was to assimilate us by association with the bad elements of society. After four weeks, I was transferred to Dong Gang concentration camp, deep in the forests of Khanh Hoa. Dong Gang was part of the virgin tropical forest in the Truong Son Mountains and had been used by the communists as a base to apply pressure to Nha Trang during the war. When I arrived, the camp did not have enough room to shelter the four hundred or so prisoners already there. A North Vietnamese police officer, Major Yet, commanded the camp, and was assisted by a policeman from the local National Liberation Front.

In Dong Gang, we built our own houses without walls. Bamboo beds each accommodated two prisoners. It was cold at night, and fog shrouded the camp into late morning. At night we were permitted to light a wood-fueled fire in the middle of the house for warmth. Plus, the firelight helped the guards to see us during the night when we slept. Food was scarce. We had rice and some vegetable soup with only water and salt. It was barely enough for our subsistence.

One fellow prisoner whom I never forgot was Ngo Viet Xiem, a South Vietnamese police captain and brother of the architect Ngo Viet Thu, the Rome laureate who helped build the army academy at Da Lat. Xiem was the chief mechanic of the camp and was appreciated by Major Yet and camp personnel because he helped to maintain their motor-bicycles in good condition. The communists had very limited technical knowledge to take care of their newly acquired means of transportation. Knowing that I was a naval engineer, Major Yet assigned me the job of opening shops to make necessary equipment for the camp. We prisoners did all kinds of things, from clothes alterations to ironworking. We even produced coke from coal and other materials that became a source of profit for the camp. The Republic of Vietnam Army's former officers were capable of many things. We even used spare electrical parts and small electric generators to build a modest power station. We generated enough electricity to light about fifty 100-watt bulbs and to power a loud speaker for Major Yet to address the prisoners or make public announcements. He was delighted with this new luxury.

On September 2, 1975, the camp prepared to celebrate Independence Day (commemorating September 2, 1945). We were ordered to make performances to celebrate the success of the communist revolution that had unified the country. Major Yet invited officials and his superiors in Nha Trang (thirty kilometers away) to attend the ceremony and to see his camp under electric lights. However, one hour before the show, the small gas-driven generator would not start. The usually soft-spoken Major Yet summoned me to his office and threatened to put me in iron shackles if I failed to provide electricity for the occasion. Shackling was the most severe punishment, reserved for recalcitrant prisoners. I had observed those released from the shackles. After a few days, the steel shackles could cut your flesh down to the bone, and the cramped position in the small cell could paralyze you, so that even after you were free, you could not move until hours later. I knew Major Yet was suspicious that I intended to sabotage the success of his show. I did not, but in my mind I did not exclude my own suspicions that the technical problems were caused intentionally by those helping me run the station. Anyway, we fixed the generator on time and thus averted the punishment, and the show was a success for Major Yet and also for the prisoners, who demonstrated their ability to make the show a success even under conditions of imprisonment and coercion.

On the recommendation of Ho Ngoc Nhuan in Saigon, Cao Dang Chiem, chief of police for the southern part of the country, asked the police of Nha Trang to send me to Saigon for a short course of indoctrination. Although Hanoi controlled the whole country, it maintained a temporary and separate administration in the South to give an appearance for the benefit of international observers that the people of the South, under the leadership of the National Liberation Front, had, in fact, supplanted the government of the Republic of Vietnam.

I came to Saigon at the end of November 1975. The indoctrination class was conducted at the headquarters of the defunct Vietnamese–American Association, on Mac Dinh Chi Street, and was given by well-known communists from the National Liberation Front, such as Nguyen Ho. More than a hundred participants were allowed to attend the indoctrination course. Once, Pham Hung, a Politbureau member, visited the class, and I still remember what he said to us. "If you have any questions, please don't hesitate to ask. Marxism–Leninism is the key to everything and can answer all your questions." Of course, we did not ask any questions. We all knew that asking questions would be interpreted as a challenge to the victors and might create problems for those who dared to do so.

After a month I was freed, and I came back to Nha Trang. I tried to rejoin society. I applied for a teaching position, without success. Later, I submitted a request for a job at the provincial Department of Construction. I was a naval engineer and had taught part-time at the School of Sciences in the University of Hue, as well as math and physics at many high schools in Nha Trang, such as Vo Tanh High School, now renamed Ly Tu Trong, a communist revolutionary.

LEAVING VIETNAM

In 1976, the leaders in Hanoi decided to bury the separate entity of the Provisional Government of South Vietnam and the National Liberation Front, its political arm. They organized an election for a unified National Assembly on April 25. At that time, they combined the two provinces of Phu Yen and Khanh Hoa into one province, called Phu Khanh. The authorities of Phu Khanh approached Nguyen Cong Hoan (former assembly member representing Phu Yen) and asked him to run as a representative for

Phu Khanh. Hoan knew the adverse feelings people in Phu Yen had toward the new regime; he did not want to join the communists, and he told me about this. I advised him that his "invitation" from the communists was tantamount to an order. Refusal would be considered as a sign of opposition and may threaten his safety.

Subsequently, Hoan became a representative of the new regime after the election. The new National Assembly was first convened on July 2, 1976, and passed a resolution declaring Vietnam unified, with the new name Cong Hoa Xa Hoi Chu Nghia Viet Nam (Socialist Republic of Vietnam, SRV). After his stay in Hanoi for the first session of the National Assembly, Hoan told me that there seemed to be some big ideas coming from the Vietnam Communist Party (VCP) leadership to build and control a big Southeast Asia entity in the mold of Japan's WWII-era Dai Dong A (Great East Asia). He said a map of Southeast Asia without lines of division between countries had been distributed to members of the National Assembly, and then in two days were unceremoniously collected without explanation. After the claimed success of defeating the United States, it was no surprise that Le Duan and his comrades in the Politbureau had irrational dreams. Hoan detected some comprehension of the situation among members of the National Liberation Front, especially Madame Nguyen Thi Binh, former representative of the Provisional Government of South Vietnam at the Paris negotiations; he found her to be silent and pensive most of the time.

In September 1976, Lieutenant Viktor Belenko of the Soviet Union Air Force defected to Japan with his MiG-25 Mikoyan-Gurevich, making big news around the world. I suggested to Hoan the idea of escaping from the country. At that time, no members of any National Assembly of a communist country had ever escaped to the Free World. If he escaped from Vietnam, it would create a media event like the one caused by the defection of Lieutenant Belenko and expose the disillusionment of Vietnamese people with the repressive regime.

According to our division of labor, Hoan prepared the escape boat. His father-in-law owned a small fleet of fishing boats and lived in Xom Con, a peninsula jutting out into Nha Trang harbor. Hoan made necessary contacts to provision the boat. His frequent presence at Xom Con did not attract the attention of the police due to his local and government status. I studied the route of escape using a map of Bien Dong (South China Sea) in the *Encyclopedia Americana* to plan a route. Two routes were available from Nha Trang: one northeast toward Manila, in the Philippines, and the other going southwest, to Singapore. I chose the second one for two reasons. It was a little bit shorter, and when navigating south we put ourselves in the middle of busy sea lanes for oil tankers from the Middle East headed to Japan, through the Strait of Malacca. The chance to be rescued at sea in case of trouble would be greater. I had no idea about when we would leave, or how many people could join the escape. Hoan was the one who took care of this, and we limited our contact to the minimum for the sake of secrecy. Hoan and I agreed on one thing, that Tran Van Thung, a former representative of Khanh Hoa and a colleague in the South Vietnamese National Assembly, living twelve kilometers from Nha Trang, in Thanh Minh, would be informed when the time came, and be invited to join us.

We set out to sea in the early morning of March 28, 1977, from Xom Con, on a small fishing boat with a total of thirty-four people. The police control of the harbor was light at that time of day, due to the number of fishing boats headed out to sea. The sea was calm for the first day, and we sailed east. On the second day, the sea was a little rough, and we turned southwest. As predicted, we soon found ourselves in the middle of many ships going north and south. At night they lit the sea with tiny lights, bringing us a sense of companionship and security. I doubted that our small boat could bring us safely all the way to Singapore, 1,300 kilometers away. Therefore, I took every occasion to attract the attention of large ships to our precarious situation. My hope was that one of them would pick us up. Before leaving, I knew from the BBC broadcasts that some skippers who picked up boat people in the open sea often had problems with their ship owners when giving assistance to boat people affected the ship's schedule and caused financial loss to the owners. Therefore, I was not surprised to find that the ships we navigated close to ignored our presence, even though this may have violated the international agreement about providing assistance on the open sea. Sometimes I acted foolishly by steering our small boat across the path of a large vessel to call its attention to us. Most of these simply changed direction to avoid a collision and continued on their way.

On the third day the engine stopped working. The mechanics aboard tried their best to fix it, without success. The wind picked up and the sea became rougher and rougher. The tiny boat shook violently, flattening nearly everyone aboard, among whom were five women and a two-year-old boy.

Late in the afternoon of the third day, the sky was gloomy and the sea became very rough. Fresh water was scarce and reserved for the women and the little boy. Food was limited to cooked dried rice that could be eaten after mixing with boiled water. The evening wore on and the situation became desperate. I did not know our exact position on the sea and could only guess that we were not far from the coast of Nha Trang. The hope of reaching Singapore vanished, and some people talked about returning to Nha Trang where the engine could be fixed. The mechanics told me that the engine had been broken beyond repair due to lack of lubricating oil. That night we used rags and debris to make a bonfire on the boat as an SOS signal.

At 6:00 PM on March 31, the fourth day, a Japanese ship going north sailed close to us. The skipper steered toward our boat for a better view. The huge ship stopped its engines and stayed about three hundred meters away from us, probably for fear that its waves could capsize our tiny boat. I did not know the skipper's intention, and there was no effective communication between us and the Japanese except for our waving vigorously with anything we had. At that point I made a life-or-death decision to jump into the sea and swim toward the steamship. I intended to let the skipper of the Japanese ship know that if he did not rescue us, thirty-four people would die. We had no water, no food, and our boat was disabled.

Approaching the steamship, I faced before me a huge wall of steel, later identified as the *Ryuko Maru*. This was one of the biggest ships carrying oil from the Middle East to Japan. This kind of ship had a huge main deck that could be transformed on short notice into a runway for military aircraft. That indicated the readiness of Japan to defend itself in case of war. Crew members dropped a long ladder made of rope to enable me to climb aboard. Reaching the main level, I was so cold and tired that I lay on the deck gasping. A crew member brought me a blanket and gave me time to rest.

A young officer, in the white uniform of the Japanese merchant fleet, came and talked to me. (Later I learned that he was the ship's executive officer.) After learning that we were refugees escaping the communist regime in Vietnam and in a desperate situation, he decided to send a team of technicians to the boat to fix the engine, replenish our vessel with water and food, and show us the best direction to safety. I stayed on the ship and watched the team of technicians go to the boat. After a while the team came back, and I waited to see what the crew would do. Later I learned that the team found the boat engine damaged beyond repair, so the skipper sent a message to the company headquarters in Tokyo for instructions. Rescuing and bringing the boat people aboard was the last resort.

The decision was made to rescue us, and the *Ryuko Maru* was instructed to take us all to the next stop, the harbor of Yokkaichi, six days away. A boat was sent out to pick up the refugees and a long wooden ladder was lowered alongside the ship for all to board the main deck. The crew supplied us with temporary beds and blankets. A meal was served, including a limited amount of Sapporo, a popular Japanese beer. We enjoyed the food, knowing that we had survived the first leg of our adventure and were now in good hands. Japan was a rich and democratic country, and Japanese are the most hospitable people in the world.

The following day the crew started to register our group members with name, profession, social status, and family to report to the UNHCR (United Nations High Commissioner for Refugees). Thung, Hoan, and I exchanged opinions about Hoan's status and what he should reveal. We knew that Japan had re-established diplomatic relations with the new regime in Vietnam, and we feared that they might return Hoan to Hanoi to avoid diplomatic embarrassment. The *Ryuko Maru* was still not far from Hai Phong harbor, and it would be easy to take him back. Out of precaution, therefore, Hoan registered under a different name and social status, and did not reveal his position as a representative of the Vietnamese National Assembly.

Five days later, once the *Ryuko Maru* anchored at Yokkaichi, south of Tokyo, and officials of UNHCR and the Japanese Immigration Service came aboard for paperwork, Hoan knew that it was time to tell them his true identity.

It seemed the officials did not believe their ears when they heard that a member of the Hanoi National Assembly was among us. Hoan's ID card, issued by the National Assembly and signed by Politburo member Truong Chinh, then the chairman of the National Assembly, was photographed and wired to the foreign ministry in Tokyo for verification.

The atmosphere around us changed from casual to secrecy after Hoan's identity was confirmed. The Japanese authorities considered that his presence on Japanese soil would cause diplomatic problems with Hanoi. Reporters were not admitted aboard, and from then we were separated from the media and the local population.

The harbor authorities arranged a route for our group that took us from our disembarkation point to a bus waiting to carry us to the refugee camp. The bus left the harbor late in the evening, escorted by a sedan with officials. Around midnight we arrived at a refugee camp in Kominato, Chiba Prefecture, about 110 kilometers from Tokyo. The camp was a private school belonging to the Rissho Kosei-Kai Church, a branch of Japanese Buddhism, hastily transformed into a refugee camp. At that time Japan took care of about three hundred refugees who had arrived before us under the auspices of the UNHCR. They were housed at several locations set up by Caritas, a Roman Catholic NGO. Rissho Kosei-Kai was a Buddhist branch in which the monks could marry and have families.

National law stipulates that Japan does not accept permanent refugees. Our status in Japan was considered to be "temporary transit," made possible by the leniency of the Japanese government. We were refugees under the jurisdiction of the UNHCR. The superior monk in charge of the camp had the responsibility to take care of our daily activities while waiting for the emigration process to unfold.

The news of Hoan's presence was embargoed, but students from the Free Viet Organization (Nguoi Viet Tu Do) who worked for the UNHCR as interpreters probably leaked it to the media, and we found that local journalists were present in the village. I still keep in contact with two of the students, Tran Van Thang and Huynh Luong Thien. Both eventually immigrated to the United States, and Thien became owner of the weekly Vietnamese magazine *Thang Mo San Francisco*.

By chance I got in contact with worldwide media. On the third day I was at Kominato I picked up a ringing telephone in the camp; it happened to be a call from a CBS reporter. In a short exchange I confirmed the presence of Hoan and that he was, in fact, a member of the Vietnamese National Assembly. At that point, Mr. Misei, a Japanese citizen representing the UNHCR in Tokyo, came to Kominato with a group of officials to speed up the process of emigration. It was around April 10, 1977, and the second anniversary of the collapse of South Vietnam was just twenty days away. We intended to organize a press conference to introduce Hoan and to tell the world about the repressed conditions in Vietnam under the communist regime.

There was no way to use the refugee camp to conduct the press conference; the church would not allow it. The Free Viet Organization rented a room at a nearby hotel and alerted the international press in Tokyo. Hoan, Thung, and I took care to prepare a text to be read at the conference. Hoan would preside over the press conference, and I would be his interpreter.

Weighing the consequences of the press conference against relations with Vietnam, however, the Japanese government decided to prevent the press conference from happening. Misei was asked to achieve that with his immense influence on us.

A week before the conference, Misei met me in the reception room of the church. He told me that a press conference would enrage the Japanese government and all of us could be sent back to Vietnam, not to mention that our relatives in Vietnam may face harsh reprisals from the government of Vietnam. I said that we were ready to accept any reprisals. As for sending us back to Vietnam, I told Misei that we would accept whatever the Japanese government decided. I knew that Japan, in any case, could not make this kind of decision without confronting adverse reaction from the international community.

Turning to the welfare of other boat people from Vietnam, Misei told me that if the press conference happened and we embarrassed the Japanese government by revealing the miserable conditions in Vietnam and by condemning Vietnam's policy of repression, in the future Japan may not allow Vietnamese refugees into the country. I thought the Japanese government could not do this, either, for it would consider world opinion to be more important than pressure from Hanoi. I said to Misei that the people in Vietnam would be happy with our decision to tell the world about their misery, and they would not complain about what the Japanese government might do to them in case they escaped from Vietnam.

Misei turned to his last weapon—he bribed us with the proposition that we tell the story of Vietnam under communism to the world, but from the United States rather than Japan. He said, "just tape" what you want to say; he talked about helping us produce one million audio cassettes, at a cost of one dollar each, that we could distribute once we arrived in the United States—and the Japanese government would foot the bill. It sounded like Misei, acting for the Japanese government, proposed to buy our silence for one million dollars. Our response to Misei's last proposition was that Vietnam was like a boiling kettle of water that could not wait.

At that time the preparations for the press conference were in full swing. At first we wanted to convene the conference in Tokyo, but Misei said that UNHCR would not let us go to the capital for the sake of our security. We, with the concurrence of Free Viet Organization, decided to relocate the conference in Kominato. Free Viet Organization paid the rent at a local hotel in Kominato, and sent out invitations to the press. The date chosen was April 30, 1977, the second anniversary of South Vietnam's fall.

On April 29, a local police officer asked me to sign an official request for the conference. I told him that in a free country people should not have to ask government permission to contact the press. The officer agreed, but said that he needed the request to arrange for the safety of the conference.

On April 30, many foreign reporters, European as well as American, were present, including Henry Kammp of the *New York Times*. The appearance of Hoan and his address to the media engendered great emotion. Kammp decided to meet us in private for more. He himself paid for a room in the same hotel. There, Hoan, Thung, myself, and Thien (student with Free Viet Organization) met with Kammp and his translator, a young girl of mixed race who was fluent in Vietnamese, French, English, and Japanese.

Media in the United States, including many small-town newspapers, carried news about the conference. This, then, was the first time the Americans heard about what they left behind when they rushed out of Vietnam during the dark days of April 1975.

Kammp wrote a report in the *New York Times* that featured news about the escape of Vietnamese people by sea. The *Times* persuaded US President Jimmy Carter to ask Congress for funds to help Vietnamese refugees. The US Congress wanted to hear more about Vietnam, and Le Thi Anh, a congressional lobbyist, contacted the US Embassy in Tokyo to arrange a trip for Hoan to testify at congressional hearings about the violation of human rights in Vietnam.

At the same time, I was moved to another refugee camp under the auspices of Rissho Kosei-Kai on the west coast of Japan to help organize newly arrived refugees. I stayed there for four months before moving to Tokyo, living with a member of Free Viet Organization and waiting for my departure to the United States. The UNHCR, working with NGOs in the United States, was looking for volunteers to sponsor us.

In October 1977, I received permission to immigrate to Boston, MA. My sponsor was Raymond Crombie, a government employee in southeastern Massachusetts. He was in Vietnam during the war, working in the psychological warfare section of the US Army. He spoke Vietnamese with an American accent, and at the time that he agreed to sponsor me he had about ten refugees under his sponsorship.

I stayed for a month in Massachusetts, and then I moved to Maryland with my high school classmate Nguyen Dinh Dieu and his family. Dieu was a naval officer in the South Vietnamese Navy who was attending a course in systems analysis at the US Naval Post Graduate School in Monterey, California, when South Vietnam collapsed. He was granted I-94 status and moved east to work as a systems analyst for the US Defense Department.

In Maryland I looked for work to support my wife and five children, ages seven to fifteen, still in Vietnam. In February 1978, Thai Doan Nga, another high school classmate of mine then in California, introduced me to his boss, who interviewed me and offered me an accounting job with CETA (Comprehensive Employment and Training Act), a federal on-the-job training program, in the office of accounting, which office was supervised by my friend Nga.

Nga bought me an airplane ticket and the following day I flew to Los Angeles, where I stayed with him and his family and started working two days later. I now had a job and a place to live, and some savings to send back to Vietnam to help my wife take care of our children.

I then went in pursuit of my reason for leaving the country, which was to find a way to liberate Vietnam from the Communists. Ten of my friends and I started to build a political party called the Vietnam Restoration Party (VNRP). The first meeting was convened in Los Angeles in December 1978. The second convention was held at the end of 1979, and thereafter every two years. I was made the founding chairman of VNRP, a position I kept until the seventh convention, in 1989. Thereafter, I went on to write political essays. My writings covered international affairs, but were mostly on subjects related to Vietnam and the efforts of overseas Vietnamese for regime change in Vietnam.[5]

The Vietnamese language programs of VOA (Voice of America), BBC, and RFA (Radio Free Asia) have broadcast interviews with me during the past twenty years. Nowadays I am concerned about the threat to Vietnam's security from China, particularly considering how China has been able to push its borders into Vietnamese territory.

I visited Vietnam two times, in March 1999 and in April 2001. After that my entrance visa applications have been denied. Vietnamese authorities mention a decree regarding national security as the reason for their denials of my applications.

THE AMERICAN "PIVOT" POLICY TO WESTERN PACIFIC

Both Vietnamese and Americans can learn lessons from the defunct Republic of Vietnam, especially now that the United States is returning to the Western Pacific. I am very concerned about the Bien Dong ("Eastern Sea"; the Chinese call it the South China Sea, and this term is used by the international community). For centuries the Bien Dong lay in the middle of international sea lanes from the Indian Ocean to the western Pacific Ocean. World powers did not pay much attention to it as long as the sea lanes could be used without infringement. But beginning in the 1950s, indications of oil and gas deposits were discovered under the seabed of Bien Dong, and international attention has become focused on the two groups of islands called Hoang Sa and Truong Sa (Paracel and Spratley).

When the United States was in the process of withdrawing from Vietnam after signing the Paris Agreement in 1973, for geopolitical reasons, it encouraged the Chinese to take over Hoang Sa in 1974. After 1975, regional dominance was contested between the Soviet Union and its Vietnamese ally on one side, and China along with the United States and Southeast Asian countries on the other.

---

[5] My essays are posted at the Vietnamese-language website www.tranbinhnam.com. As of August 2014, that site contained more than 475 articles dating from April 1998. Other selected essays have appeared in printed form in four volumes of "selected essays." See Tran Binh Nam, *Tuyen Tap Binh Luan Chinh Tri* (Selected Works of Political Commentary), 4 vols., vol. 1:1991-1994 (San Francisco: Mo Lang, 1995); vol. 2: 1995-96 (San Francisco, Mo Lang, 1997); vol. 3: 1997-99 (San Francisco, Mo Lang, 2000); vol. 4: 8.1999-6.2002 (Los Angeles: To Chuc Phuc Hung Viet Nam, 2002). From 2002 on, readers can find all my writings at my home page.

In the 1990s, with the collapse of the Soviet Union, Vietnam had nowhere to turn except China. Since then, China has pursued its ambition to replace the United States in the Pacific region and become a superpower in the twenty-first century. Vietnam, with its claims in the South China Sea, is an obvious obstacle to the unhindered expansion of Chinese power.

The United States may be a balancing force, but a very hesitant one, having been defeated in 1975, and its return to the Western Pacific Region will require difficult long-term strategic decisions. The Chinese increasingly compete with the Americans all over the world, and even the American economy is not immune from Chinese pressure. Hanoi leadership's loyalty may not be bought by Beijing as some people may think, but it has few options, and in the meantime waits for the United States while playing friendly with China.

CHAPTER EIGHT

THE TAN DAI VIET PARTY AND ITS CONTRIBUTION TO BUILDING DEMOCRACY IN THE SECOND REPUBLIC OF VIETNAM

Ma Xai

This paper describes the Tan Dai Viet Party (New Dai Viet Party), and its associated organization, the National Progressive Movement (Phong Trao Quoc Gia Cap Tien), as an opposition political party in the Second Republic of Vietnam (1967–75). The Tan Dai Viet Party was officially established on November 14, 1964, in Saigon. It was a spin-off from the Dai Viet Quoc Dan Dang Party (Dai Viet Nationalist Party), which was founded in Hanoi in 1939 by the prominent intellectual Truong Tu Anh.

Dai Viet (Great Viet) was the name given to the country by Vietnamese dynasties from the eleventh through the eighteenth centuries. Quoc Dan Dang is the Vietnamese pronunciation of Guomindang (the Chinese Nationalist Party) and means "national people's party." Often known simply as Dai Viet, the party was among the most active political and militant organizations in Vietnam during the twentieth century. Dai Viet promoted patriotism and fought for the country's independence from French domination and then against the expansion of communism. After independence in 1954, Dai Viet advocated for democratic reform and opposed authoritarian regimes backed by Westerners. Dai Viet objectives were to build an independent and strong Vietnam. Dai Viet had members throughout Vietnam, with three main regional chapters in the northern, central, and southern parts of the country.

In 1954, Ngo Dinh Diem returned from overseas and, together with his brothers, established the First Republic, which was characterized by dictatorship and nepotism. Dai Viet built many military zones in the central and southern provinces to fight against Diem's administration. These military zones failed, and many prominent members were either arrested (e.g., Ha Thuc Ky and Viet Huy) or exiled (Nguyen Ngoc Huy and Nguyen Ton Hoan). The rest remained in the country and secretly continued their struggle against the government.

When the Diem administration was overthrown in 1963, Nguyen Ngoc Huy returned from France determined to build a mature political party organization similar to those in the West. He believed that such an organization would contribute to the building of a democratic, free, and lawful society where the Vietnamese could enjoy a peaceful, prosperous, and happy life. In order to pursue his vision, Huy advocated changes in the Dai Viet Party. The party, according to Huy, should shift its strategy from a revolutionary party (using military means) to a purely civilian political party (using ballots in elections). The northern and central chapters of the Dai Viet, however, disagreed with Huy's idea for change. On November 14, 1964, the southern chapter, where Huy was most influential, decided to separate itself from Dai Viet and became a full-fledged party under the new name of Tan Dai Viet (New Dai Viet). One year later, Dai Viet's central chapter, led by Ha Thuc Ky, also separated itself from Dai Viet to become a new party, Dai Viet Cach Mang (Revolutionary Dai Viet Party). The northern chapter retained the name Dai Viet Quoc Dan Dang. Hence, twenty-six years after Truong Tu Anh founded the party in 1939, the original party had split into three independent parties, all of which continued to use the founding doctrine of "Dan Toc Sinh Ton" (Survival Nationalism) as their ideology.

Formally established after the fall of the First Republic, the Tan Dai Viet Party actively worked to build democracy during the Second Republic. In the period following the overthrow of Ngo Dinh Diem, successive military regimes failed to stabilize the political and social chaos in the country. Eventually, US Ambassador General Maxwell Taylor and South Vietnamese generals put an end to a series of coups. A war cabinet was formed on June 19, 1965. General Nguyen Cao Ky was the chairman of the Central Executive Committee. General Nguyen Van Thieu was appointed the chairman of the National Leadership Committee. Since then, June 19 became Armed Forces Day of the Republic of Vietnam. From 1965 on, with a military regime in place, US intervention rapidly accelerated.

The first two US marine battalions landed in Da Nang on March 8, 1965. This was the beginning of US involvement with combat troops in Vietnam. Although the war escalated, South Vietnam still pursued the building of a democratic system of government. Yielding to the demands of religious groups, political parties, and other activist organizations, the military government allowed a new Constituent Assembly to be established on September 11, 1966. The Tan Dai Viet Party occupied 12 percent of the seats in the assembly. In January 1967, a constitution was completed and served as the basis for the Second Republic. With this progressive constitution, the Republic of Vietnam was governed under a regime with the separation of powers in three branches: executive, legislative, and judicial.

The 1967 constitution was the work of 117 representatives in the Constituent Assembly. Among them were many Tan Dai Viet members who provided significant contributions, including Nguyen Ngoc Huy, who was involved in drafting the constitution. Tan Dai Viet also entered the presidential election of 1967 by supporting Truong Dinh Dzu, who finished in second place. Twelve other party members became congressmen in the House of Representatives in this election. The Tan Dai Viet Party also actively participated in the process of establishing the Supreme Court and the Supervision Court.

While the South Vietnamese government continued its efforts toward pacification and construction in the countryside, in 1968 North Vietnam launched the Tet Offensive. Although that strategy was a military defeat for the communists, it profoundly affected the US government and shocked the US public. It convinced many Americans that victory was impossible. A vocal and growing peace movement spread in the United States, and newly elected President Richard Nixon conducted peace negotiations in Paris, which further diminished the prospects for the survival of South Vietnam.

For South Vietnam, negotiations were not merely a discussion to end the war; they also signaled a tough political fight with Hanoi and the National Liberation Front. Professor Nguyen Ngoc Huy understood the seriousness of the situation and called for all political factions to unite to cope with the situation. Together with Professor Nguyen Van Bong (then dean of the National Institute of Administration), Huy reached out to many other political parties, religious leaders, and intellectuals to organize a mass movement to help protect the country from the communist threat. This mass movement was named National Progressive Movement (Phong Trao Quoc Gia Cap Tien). At its inception, the movement embraced the participation of the following political and religious groups: Tan Dai Viet Party of Nguyen Ngoc Huy; a large faction of the Viet Nam Quoc Dang Party, led by lawyer Nguyen Tuong Ba; part of the Viet Nam Phuc Quoc Hoi Cao Dai Party, led by General Truong Luong Thien; part of the Dan Xa Party, led by Colonel Truong Kim Cu; and the Protestant denomination, led by Pastor Ngo Minh Thanh.

Additionally, more than twenty senators and representatives and a large group of intellectuals, experts, and professionals also joined the movement. Bong was elected chairman and Huy was elected secretary general. With the support of many leaders, intellectuals, and scholars, as well as the middle class and young people, the movement soon spread out in both urban areas and the countryside, and it began to play an important role in South Vietnamese politics.

Officially launched in 1969, the movement exercised moderation in opposition to the government. It used only peaceful, legal, collective, and constructive means. The movement's aim for being in opposition to the government was to provide constructive input to improve the national budget, education, the economy, and government policies in other areas. The movement had a daily journal and a monthly magazine (*Nguyet San Cap Tien* and *Nhut Bao Cap Tien*, or "The Monthly Radical" and "The Daily Radical"), in which national and international issues were discussed. The movement performed so well in both its oppositional role and as a constructive force on the administration that President Nguyen Van Thieu invited it to appoint its members to participate in the Paris peace negotiations, and Huy was appointed to the South Vietnamese Delegation at the Paris peace talks.

Professor Nguyen Van Bong's political influence was also becoming recognized internationally. Henry Kissinger, national security advisor to President Nixon, met with Bong twice in Saigon during the Paris negotiations. It was rumored in Saigon political circles that Bong would soon be the prime minister in order to lead a new civilian cabinet. Some people thought that such a cabinet would be effective in dealing with North Vietnam and the National Liberation Front in light of the Paris talks. Bong's rising reputation, coupled with the reputation of the movement's and the Tan Dai Viet Party's supporters, earned favorable public opinion in and out of the country. Bong was perceived as a potential leader of South Vietnam at this stage of the war's culmination. He then became the target of North Vietnam. North Vietnam decided to eliminate a potential adversary by means of assassination, and a Viet Cong assassin killed Bong in Saigon in 1971.

Recovering from the loss of its leader, the movement continued to advocate for political freedom and anti-corruption measures. The political environment became much more intense in 1972 when President Thieu issued a new decree limiting the activities of political opposition groups. This action was followed by the creation of President Thieu's own party, the Democratic Party (Dang Dan Chu). With this new decree, the Democratic Party operated as the only legal political party.

Political struggle became more complex and difficult in 1973 as a result of the Paris Agreement. The volatile situation in South Vietnam created more obstacles to building democracy as the fight against communism continued and the United States and other allies withdrew from the country. Trusting in the promises of President Nixon to intervene if communist attacks occurred, President Thieu concentrated his efforts on strengthening his own followers among the generals, highly placed civilian officials, and police. He arranged for his own Democratic Party to hold the majority in both legislative houses, the Senate, and the House of Representatives. President Thieu placed his allies in the Supreme and Supervision courts. He furthermore arranged to have the constitution amended to allow him to run for a third term.

Tan Dai Viet leaders requested that President Thieu amend the 1972 law to allow all political parties to compete lawfully in a fair democratic environment. He refused, and his party continued to be the only party to dominate South Vietnam politics. He went even further by trying to eliminate other political parties. He ordered the dissolution of the Hoa Hao militiamen, a reliable anticommunist group in South Vietnam.

President Thieu's behavior originated from his overconfidence in American support for him. His authoritarian style of governing created resistance to his leadership during the last years of the Republic. The An Quang Buddhist group maintained its opposition to President Thieu by promoting the idea of a "third force" in the National Council of Reconciliation and Concord, as specified in the Paris Agreement. Catholic priest Tran Huu Thanh launched an anti-corruption campaign in 1974. The hostility and division among the political and religious groups clearly weakened the nation at a time when national unity was desperately needed to sustain the fight against the common communist enemy.

The situation in South Vietnam deteriorated after the signing of the Paris Agreement in 1973. The US Congress cut off all American aid to the Republic of Vietnam at the beginning of 1975. Convinced that the United States would not intervene and that the South Vietnamese armed forces were running out of ammunition and supplies, North Vietnam openly launched its offensive to take over the South. Under American pressure, President Thieu resigned on April 21, 1975, and his successor, according to the 1967 Constitution, Vice President Tran Van Huong, then also resigned. A resolution of the National Assembly then made General Duong Van Minh the president on April 28, 1975. Minh surrendered to the communist forces in the Presidential Palace on April 30, 1975.

The Tan Dai Viet Party and the National Progressive Movement promoted the building of a free and democratic Vietnam against the invasion of the dictatorial communists from Hanoi, who were backed by Moscow, Beijing, and others in the communist bloc. During the Second Republic, the party stood against President Thieu's government because it failed to unite the country in the struggle to preserve freedom in the South. During eight years in office, his administration failed to build South Vietnamese self-reliance or to create national unity. The hostility and division among the opposition groups and between the president and the opposition during the war against communism hindered national unity and strength.

During the war, the Armed Forces of the Republic of Vietnam fulfilled their duties to protect the country in a respectful manner. However, the political parties, the elites in the South, were not given the chance to engage adequately in political activity to mobilize the people to join in the fight against the communists. The two presidents of the Republic of Vietnam, both relying on their anticommunist stand, were slow to advance democracy and freedom for the people. The survival of the nation depends on its people.

The Tan Dai Viet Party highly appreciated the US Cold War strategy to prevent and fight against the expansion of communism in Southeast Asia. However, US intervention ignored the historic struggle for national independence in Vietnam. The United States interfered in South Vietnam's internal affairs by forcing its views through a leader whom it selected and then made fatal concessions in its peace settlement with Hanoi in 1973. This settlement allowed the North Vietnamese army to remain in the South while all US troops withdrew. North Vietnam continued to receive military and financial aid from its allied powers while the United States cut off military aid to South Vietnam. When US national interests required a strategic change, the United States imposed a solution and abandoned the Republic of Vietnam, a country previously considered by the United States as an anticommunist outpost in Southeast Asia.

CHAPTER NINE

NAVAL BATTLE OF THE PARACELS

Ho van Ky-Thoai

Ed. Note. Prior to the establishment of French Indochina in the late nineteenth century, the uninhabited islands, reefs, and rocks that comprise the Paracels were for centuries frequented by both Chinese and Vietnamese who came to harvest sea products, but the question of ownership or sovereignty did not arise. The French then claimed the islands as part of French Indochina. In the early 1940s, Japan gained control of the islands. In the late 1940s and early 1950s, France reclaimed and occupied the western group of the islands, known as the Crescent Group (Nhom Luoi Liem). In the late 1950s, control of this group passed to the Republic of Vietnam. At the same time, the eastern group of the islands, known as the Amphitrite Group (Nhom An Vinh), was claimed and occupied by, first, the Nationalist Chinese, and then by the People's Republic of China. Today, the archipelago, the island groups, and the various islands, reefs, and rocks all have both Chinese and Vietnamese names, as well as names used in English and other languages. In the account that follows, English names are used with Vietnamese names indicated in parentheses at first mention. The name Paracel or its variants appear on European maps as early as the sixteenth century, apparently derived from Portuguese nomenclature.

This is the story of a 1974 naval battle in which the People's Republic of China seized the Paracel (Hoang Sa) Islands from the Republic of Vietnam. The battle was barely noticed by the American press at that time.

The Paracel Islands are located approximately 190 miles east of the city of Da Nang, Vietnam, and a similar distance southeast of the island of Hainan, China. There are two groups of islands. In 1974, the Amphitrite Group (Nhom An Vinh), on the east side, was occupied by China, and the Crescent Group (Nhom Luoi Liem), on the west side, was occupied by Vietnam. The five main islands in the Crescent Group are Pattle (Dao Hoang Sa), Robert (Dao Huu Nhat), Money (Dao Quang Anh), Duncan (Dao Quang

Hoa), and Drummond (Dao Duy Mong). These islands were unfortified and had no permanent inhabitants, but Vietnamese military and administrative personnel resided there on a rotational basis.

Although at the time it was generally believed that the resource value of these islands was limited, their location has a particular strategic value because they can be used to control important shipping lanes navigated by merchant ships from countries such as Taiwan, Japan, Korea, the Philippines, India, Malaysia, Vietnam, and China.

In 1973, the United States agreed to withdraw all combat forces from Vietnam in exchange for North Vietnam's release of all US prisoners. This was a clear signal from the United States to the South Vietnamese government that it was on its own against North Vietnam, which continued to enjoy the backing of the Soviet Union and China. This was also the year that the Watergate scandal began to distract the American public's attention away from the communist threat to South Vietnam. With the United States out of the picture, China was free to make a move into the region.

On January 15, 1974, a South Vietnamese naval vessel, the WHEC (designation for a US Coast Guard High Endurance Cutter) HQ 16, on a regular mission to the Paracels, left Da Nang with a platoon of regional forces from the province of Quang Nam, a team of officers from the Army I Corps Headquarters in Da Nang, and one American from the US Defense Attaché Office (DAO) in Saigon. The presence of this officer, Gerald Kosh, on board the Vietnamese ship later became a subject of controversy and an embarrassment for the US government. When the ship arrived at the Paracels on the morning of January 16, the captain noted that some fishing trawlers with no flags were navigating around the islands and small flags were visible on Money Island.

Being in contact with the ship from the headquarters of CIC (Combat Information Center), I immediately ordered the WHEC's captain to identify the fishing trawlers, to request that they leave Vietnamese territorial waters, and to send a landing team to search the island. That same night, I Corps commander Lieutenant General Ngo Quang Truong was hosting a dinner for President Nguyen Van Thieu, who was touring the five northernmost provinces of South Vietnam. I attended that dinner, and my operations officer at the Da Nang Naval Headquarters phoned me there and reported that the fishing trawlers, as well as the flags on the island, were identified as Chinese. I immediately reported the situation to President Thieu.

Upon my return to naval headquarters later that evening, I dispatched the destroyer HQ 4, under the command of Commander Vu Huu San, to join the WHEC HQ 16 at the Paracels. The next morning, January 17, President Thieu arrived at the Da Nang First Naval Zone Headquarters and held a meeting that included Lieutenant General Le Nguyen Khang, deputy to the chief of the joint staff; Lieutenant General Ngo Quang Truong; Major General Hoang Van Lac, deputy commander of I Corps; Brigadier General Tran Dinh Tho, chief of J-3 (Joint General Staff); and me, as commander, First Naval Zone.

After listening to my presentation of the situation in the Paracels, as well as intelligence information about Chinese naval forces in the area and the Chinese navy overall, the president gave me detailed instructions that by all means, including the use of force, the Vietnamese Navy must request that the Chinese vessels leave Vietnamese territorial waters. He, himself, wrote two pages of notes that he asked me to read aloud to the group in the conference room. He also told me to ask him right then and there any questions I may have, to be clear that I understood his intention.

After the president left Naval Headquarters, I placed a call to Admiral Tran Van Chon, commander in chief of the navy, in Saigon, to report to him the president's instructions; I also told him of my plan to board the WHEC HQ 5, which was refueling at the Da Nang Naval Base, and to proceed to the Paracels. Admiral Chon instead ordered me to assign a senior captain from the ships operating in the First Naval Zone to be the officer in tactical command (OTC) of the ships at the islands, and he indicated that he was coming to Da Nang and that I should be ready to meet with him on January 19.

That evening, I met with Captain Ha Van Ngac, the patrol squadron commander who was visiting his ships on duty in the First Naval Zone. Ngac volunteered to be OTC and right after the meeting he boarded the WHEC HQ 5. I also ordered the PCE (Patrol Craft Escort) HQ 10 that was on patrol in the area to refuel and join the Task Group under the command of Captain Ngac. On January 18, the Paracels Task Group included WHEC HQ 16, Destroyer HQ 4, WHEC HQ 5, and PCE HQ 10 under the tactical command of Ngac.

It was reported to me that the Chinese fishing trawlers acted aggressively toward the Vietnamese ships, including activities such as cutting in front of the bow of our destroyer HQ 4 and pointing their guns, including handguns, in the direction of the Vietnamese ships. Early on the morning of January 19, Ngac landed sea commandos on Robert Island and Duncan Island. That operation failed, however, due to Chinese forces being already present on the islands and outnumbering ours. The result was the death of one officer and two commandos from the Vietnamese landing teams.

At 10:00 AM, Ngac reported to me that the provocative maneuvering of the Chinese ships endangered the Vietnamese ships, and the Chinese refusal to leave Vietnamese territorial waters showed that they were ready to engage in battle. Ngac asked for my authorization to fire when he felt that his ships were in danger. I did so authorize him, and at 10:25 AM I heard from the SSB (single side band) radio the first salvo of gunfire. Targets were assigned as follows: HQ WHEC 16 to target the Chinese ship MS 396; PCE HQ 10 to target MS 3989; Destroyer HQ 4 to target KS (Kronstadt) 271; and WHEC HQ 5 to target KS 274.

Advancing eastward, WHEC HQ 16 and PCE HQ 10 approached the Chinese MS 396 and MS 389 north of Duncan Island, while WHEC HQ 5 and Destroyer HQ 4 sailed towards KS 271 and KS 274 south of Duncan Island. The Chinese ship MS 389 was hit first on the port side and the ship circled around without firing and finally stood still, apparently grounded on the coral beach. PCE HQ 10 was hit badly, especially the bridge of the ship, where Captain Nguy Van Tha was standing; Tha was killed instantly. His second-in-command, Lieutenant Nguyen Thanh Tri, was also wounded, but managed to give the order to abandon ship and to supervise evacuation of the crew to the lifeboats. Tri died from his wounds hours later on a lifeboat. PCE HQ 10 drifted south and was sunk a few hours later by Chinese vessels, KS 281 and KS 282, that arrived on the scene after the battle was over. Besides PCE HQ 10 and MS 389, which were put out of action from the beginning, all remaining ships from both sides were damaged by naval gunfire. There were no signs that the Chinese were using rockets or air support during the battle. Two armed Chinese fishing trawlers, 402 and 407, did not participate in the battle. The gunfight lasted about thirty minutes.

Reefs /|/|||||/

Location of Chinese ships at start of battle ⊠

Route of Vietnamese ships into battle ⟶

Route of Chinese reinforcements — — →

Sites of battles \/\/\/\/\/\/\/\/

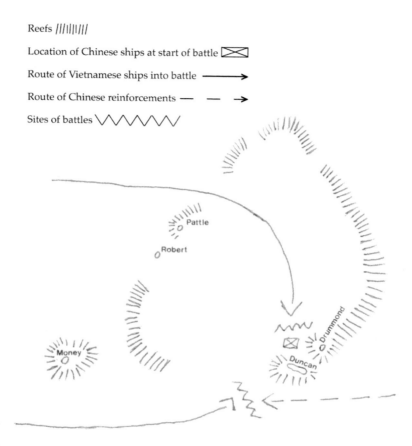

Battle of the Paracel Islands on January 19, 1974. Courtesy of Keith W. Taylor.

Shortly after the shooting stopped, Ngac reported to me the casualties on both sides. On our side, PCE HQ 10 was sinking, with sailors and debris spread around the ship near Duncan Island. Our other three ships were hit by Chinese gunfire, but without sustaining serious damage. On the Chinese side, MS 396 and MS 389 were put out of action, and MS 389 appeared to be aground on the coral beach north of Duncan Island. During the battle, two Chinese Hainan class ships, KS 281 and KS 282, approached from the east and finished off PCE HQ 10 with their guns.

I immediately called CIC of Navy Headquarters in Saigon to request rescue operations for the sailors adrift at the battle scene, hopefully from the US Seventh Fleet, which had ships close by. Meanwhile, I dispatched two more ships, WHEC HQ 6 and PCE HQ 11, to reinforce the Paracels Task Group. Admiral Chon landed at Da Nang airport shortly after the naval battle was over.

We did not receive any response from the Seventh Fleet to our request to help rescue our sailors. Instead, the First Naval Zone American advisor informed me that Chinese MiGs from Hainan would bomb the two Vietnamese reinforcing ships, WHEC HQ 6 and PCE HQ 11, if I did not order those ships to stay away from the Paracels. I then called General Nguyen Duc Khanh, commanding general of the First Air Division in Da Nang, to ask him if he could send F-5 jet fighters to engage the Chinese MiGs. Khanh, after meeting with his F-5 squadron chief, called me back to tell me that, because of the distance between the Paracels and Da Nang, the F-5s would not have enough fuel to engage the Chinese in air combat.

The First Naval Zone US Advisor also informed me that a Chinese formation of seventeen ships, including four submarines, was advancing toward the Paracels from the northeast. In view of the high threat to our forces, and after consulting with Admiral Chon, I ordered all Vietnamese ships out of the Paracels area and instructed the ships with personnel casualties to return to Da Nang.

The following day, at around 10:00 AM, the Chinese ships landed at least six companies (around five hundred men) on the four main islands (Pattle, Robert, Duncan, and Drummond) after first mounting a heavy shore bombardment by naval gunfire. Most of the troops disembarked from the same fishing trawlers that we had seen in the area during the previous days. With the superiority of the Chinese landing forces compared to but a single platoon of Vietnamese regional forces, some sea commandos, and some meteorological-station personnel, and with practically no fortification against an invasion by sea, the Vietnamese defenders of the islands surrendered to the Chinese. The Chinese captured all forty-eight men on Pattle Island, including the American Gerald Kosh. Kosh was released on January 31, 1974; the South Vietnamese sailors, soldiers, and government employees were released on February 15, and turned over to the Red Cross in Hong Kong.

Twenty-three sailors adrift on rubber rafts or floating debris were picked up by the Holland tanker *Kopionella,* and later returned to First Naval Zone patrol craft. Fourteen other sailors, on a rubber raft with no water or food, managed to survive almost ten days before they were rescued by a fishing boat near Qui Nhon, 200 miles southeast of the Paracels and 150 miles south of Da Nang.

On the Vietnamese side, HQ 10 was sunk and HQ 4, HQ 5, and HQ 16 were damaged. Seventy-four men were killed and forty-eight were captured. On the Chinese side, MS 389 was grounded; KS 271, KS 274, and MS 396 were damaged. The Chinese reported eighteen killed and sixty-four wounded.

Although the first shots came from the Vietnamese ships, the loss of crewmembers on the Vietnamese side was higher than on the Chinese side because the Vietnamese ships had a higher profile and were slower moving than the Chinese ships, which were smaller and lower in the water. Consequently, Vietnamese ships were good targets, while Chinese ships were hard to hit. Furthermore, the Chinese ships enjoyed higher speed and greater maneuverability.

Two days after the takeover of the Vietnamese islands by Chinese forces, the US Department of Defense spokesman, Jerry W. Friedman, said: "We have cautioned our forces (the US Seventh Fleet) not to get involved." Furthermore, the US Department of State public affairs officer, John F. King, reiterated the American position that the United States was not involved in the Paracels dispute, but did strongly desire a peaceful solution.[1] Chinese forces seized the western group of Paracel Islands with no objection from the United States. As a commander who was directly responsible for the defense of the Paracels, from the depths of my heart I wish that sovereignty over the islands be resolved peacefully in an International Court.

---

[1] "U.S. Cautioned 7th Fleet to Shun Paracels Clash," *New York Times,* January 22, 1974.

CHAPTER TEN

MILITARY AND SECURITY

Lan Lu

Four decades removed from the fall of Saigon, now is perhaps the right time to revisit the Vietnam conflict, for no longer pressing is the impulse to assign blame, discredit others, or find excuses. Akin to a card game where all players have finally revealed their hands, many wartime enigmas, rumors, theories, and assessments have been either debunked or buttressed through memoirs, interviews, and declassified materials from all sides. It is thus with this longer view of history that the following account and commentary on the military strategy and security under the Second Republic of South Vietnam are offered. This is based on the perspective of an 86-year-old retired officer of the Army of South Vietnam (ARVN) who was at the front line of the war from its inception to its bitter end twenty-five years later.

By all accounts, the birth of the Second Republic of Vietnam was a difficult one. It emerged only after four years of great chaos following the collapse of the First Republic. Most readers are no doubt familiar with the overthrow of President Ngo Dinh Diem in 1963. The prolonged period of political instability that ensued in the South emboldened Hanoi to go on the offensive, which it did in 1964, starting with a substantial infiltration of North Vietnamese troops. The military situation in the South quickly deteriorated with each failed attempt to form a government and with the accelerated disintegration of pacification programs in the countryside. United States installations were also attacked by the North Vietnamese, prompting retaliatory air strikes in return.

During this chaotic period, strategic hamlets, which had been put in place to protect the rural populace as part of a counterinsurgency strategy, suffered heavily from attacks or sabotage. Daily activities were frequently disrupted or paralyzed. The North Vietnamese propaganda machine, with the liberal US media as an unwitting accomplice, seized this opportunity to promote the view that strategic hamlets were nothing more than concentration camps holding peasants in confinement. To take further advantage of the situation, the Viet Cong ordered its Eastern Region's main forces to infiltrate the provinces and towns surrounding Saigon, resulting in numerous clashes, notably at Dong Xoai and Binh Gia. This brought about a general sense among the populace that security was lacking, and fostered a siege mentality that pervaded many localities, especially after nightfall. It was much to the credit of South Vietnamese local militia and regional forces that, instilled with anti-communist fervor and love of country, they stood ready to defend their villages and to restore order.

In June 1965, two veteran politicians, Phan Khac Suu and Phan Huy Quat, who were then the civilian head of state and prime minister, respectively, resigned and handed the helm of South Vietnam to the Supreme Military Council. That sudden event prompted the military leaders to appoint General Nguyen Van Thieu as chairman of the council. At the same time, Air Force General Nguyen Cao Ky and a group of politicians formed a new cabinet and forced Chairman Thieu to accept their administration. However, unrest and infighting among the different South Vietnamese political parties and religious affiliations soon resumed, and the call for a general election to establish a constitutional republic with three separate branches of government could no longer be ignored.

Faced with a worsening political and military situation, in 1965, US President Lyndon B. Johnson decided to commit a massive number of American ground troops to South Vietnam, most landing through the seaports of Da Nang, Cam Ranh, and Saigon. Armed with the latest fighting equipment and air transportation, US marine, airborne, and infantry units soon began their search and destroy operations against North Vietnamese regular units that had recently infiltrated into South Vietnam. Fighting soon broke out from Cua Viet to Khe Sanh in Military Region 1, and from Ia Drang to Duc Co in the Central Highlands. The North Vietnamese Army suffered heavy losses and was forced to disperse and fall back to secret bases in the Central Highlands, on the borders of Laos and Cambodia.

In February 1967, at a summit meeting in Guam, President Johnson met with Vietnamese government leaders to discuss a framework for coordinating the war effort with a "pacification" program centered on rural economic development. Johnson appointed Ambassador Ellsworth Bunker to replace then-ambassador Henry Cabot Lodge and directed the formation of CORDS (Civil Operations and Revolutionary Development Support). CORDS comprised all US agencies in South Vietnam dealing with pacification and was placed under American military command. This was an important shift of emphasis in the war effort.

On October 3, 1967, the era of the Second Republic of Vietnam was ushered in following a general election. South Vietnam elected an experienced and capable new leader as president, Nguyen Van Thieu, who managed to improve all aspects of government and to restore the morale of the populace and the armed forces.

With the formation of the young Republic of Vietnam in 1967, things improved considerably so that, despite the many mistakes and shortcomings that plagued our war effort, there was now hope that South Vietnam could win the war. This fact was reflected in statements by President Johnson and top officials in Vietnam indicating that there was light at the end of the tunnel. What came next, therefore, was a major shock to all. The Tet Offensive, as it came to be known, marked a milestone and a turning point in the war.

For Vietnamese, Tet, or the lunar New Year, is the most revered and significant traditional family celebration of all celebrations. There was usually a ceasefire for the occasion; there would be no fighting to allow troops from both sides to take leave and welcome the New Year with their families and friends. Therefore, it came as a surprise when, on the eve of Tet, January 31, 1968, the communists launched massive attacks on thirty-four provincial towns, sixty-four district towns, and all the autonomous cities, including Saigon, the capital.

For North Vietnam, the acknowledged purpose of this coordinated attack was to ripen the conditions for a general popular uprising. However, this planned "great uprising" never materialized. Instead, the South Vietnamese people and the armed forces at all levels resisted and fought back with courage and determination in support of their newly elected government. The Tet Offensive was a timely test of the fighting spirit of the ARVN, especially the regional forces and the popular forces, in both the cities and rural areas. It bears mentioning that, up until then, the communists had seldom fought any battle in daylight, or remained at any post previously captured. Everywhere in the fighting areas, while the South Vietnamese troops were actively involved in combat, civilians warily guarded their neighborhoods and reported any suspicious activities and communist hideouts. In many ways, the overall fighting spirit of the South Vietnamese people reflected their recognition of the legitimacy of their government in the fight against communism.

The fierce fighting during this period brought about heavy casualties on both sides. In the first month of the campaign alone, South Vietnam armed forces suffered around 3,500 dead and the United States lost more than 2,800 soldiers. During the next two months, five thousand more ARVN troops were lost in action and around fifteen thousand were wounded, while the foreign allies suffered more than four thousand killed and nineteen thousand wounded. On the North Vietnamese side, the losses numbered as high as 48,500 for the first two months. In addition, nine thousand North Vietnamese troops were captured. Civilian casualties were also very high, as many were caught in the line of fire: 14,300 dead and 24,000 wounded. Some 72,000 houses were destroyed and more than 627,000 people were left homeless.

The imperial city of Hue, in central Vietnam, was held captive by the communist troops for three weeks. During that time, they held so-called "people's courts" to execute those who were in any way associated with the "imperialist Americans." After the city was "liberated," an estimated six thousand bodies were discovered in mass graves; some individuals had been executed with their hands tied behind their back, others simply buried alive. Many were held captive and brought along when the communists withdrew from the city. A group of tourists recently visited the Imperial City of Hue and asked to visit the mass graves. The tour guide informed the group that, nowadays, Vietnamese children are taught in school that the mass murder of those innocent civilians during the 1968 Tet Offensive was the work of the US Marines. North Vietnam's blatant lies notwithstanding, in the collective memory of the South Vietnamese people, the atrocities committed during this period by the communists will always rank among the worst crimes against humanity.

As a military strategy, the Tet Offensive was a direct application of the guerrilla-warfare doctrine that Mao Zedong often preached. Mao said that when guerrilla warfare is developed to its full potential, it should not drag on indefinitely, but, rather, it should mature with the attrition of the enemy and the strengthening of self, and it should allow one to enter the conventional warfare phase in a position of strength. As the Tet Offensive was intended to be the last stage of guerrilla warfare, the communist units were not allowed to retreat as they had in earlier stages, but were required to win or to die fighting.

On the South Vietnamese side, the myth of the Viet Cong as "ghost soldiers" was no more. Until then, Viet Cong were often referred to as "ghost soldiers" because they were heard but rarely seen. One could easily hear the the Soviet-made, fully automatic AK-47s when fired, but the people who fired the shots were seldom seen or heard. Yet after Tet Offensive clashes, their bodies littered the streets. Finally, South Vietnamese soldiers could see the faces of their enemies, and had a chance to fight back when the North Vietnamese tried to hold a position. The fighting spirit of the Regional and Popular Forces, often referred to as Ruff Puff, were in particular higher than ever before.

On the American side, the Tet Offensive had a shattering and lasting impact on public opinion. The US media brought scenes of destruction and disaster home to Americans, which in many ways contradicted the idea posited by President Johnson that real progress was being made. Images of enemy troops entering the grounds of the US Embassy in Saigon were particularly shocking. In that sense, the Tet Offensive was a turning point in the war. One could say that while North Vietnam suffered a major disaster on the battlefield, it scored an equally decisive win with American public opinion. American confidence in US leaders' handling of the war plummeted, and the country's anti-war mood led to a subsequent shift in strategy.

For me, personally, 1968 was also an unforgettable year. Only a week into the Tet Offensive, on February 8, 1968, I was informed by the command center that I was to leave my post at Chief Central Training Command to assume command of II Corps, at Pleiku, in the Central Highlands. At my new post, my American advisor and counterpart was General William Peers, with whom I had a chance to get acquainted three years before in Ban Me Thuot Province. General Peers was working at the Pentagon at the time, and was sent to Vietnam to observe operations of the 23rd Division, which at the time was under my command. We met at a Pledge of Allegiance ceremony with local people in Darlac. He and I had a good working relationship during our two years of service in II Corps. One of our first projects was to visit all provinces in II Corps to be briefed on local conditions. This was in stark contrast with the experience I had with my first American adviser who, when I attempted to brief him about the tactics used by the communists, unceremoniously told me not to bother, as "American tactics and technology have prevailed in all types of battlefields in its 200-year history, from the jungles, to the deserts, to urban areas, and even in the Arctic."

In the aftermath of the Tet Offensive, with enemy forces weakened, the US and South Vietnamese shifted their focus to pacification, or taking away control of the countryside from the communists. It involved a new population-centric strategy in which clear-and-hold operations replaced search-and-destroy operations. Progress was measured by improved security in the villages and hamlets rather than by body counts following battles. A more effective structure was put in place to implement the new strategy. CORDS, the newly formed American civil–military organization, coordinated US contributions to Vietnamese programs for civil and military pacification. Signs of progress were soon noted in Washington. However, after the shock of Tet, official reporting from Saigon was viewed with mistrust.

At this stage in the war, General Abrams replaced General Westmoreland as MACV (Military Assistance Command, Vietnam) commander. Under Abrams, large-scale operations conducted primarily in the deep jungles gave way to large numbers of small-unit ambushes and roving sweeps to deny the enemy access to the population. The leadership team headed by Ambassador Bunker, General Abrams, and William Colby, who became the head of CORDS in 1969, operated as a "one mind" team on how the war should be conducted. Their strategy was described as "one war," in which combat operations, pacification, and improvements of Southern Vietnamese forces were of equal importance and received equal attention. Our monthly conferences in II Corps now included all senior commanders and high officials in the region.

An important development was the overthrow of Cambodia's Prince Sihanouk by General Lon Nol. The port of Sihanoukville, located in southern Cambodia, was then closed to enemy logistics and the communist forces were given an ultimatum to leave the country. With this new development, ARVN and US forces conducted a limited incursion into Cambodia. Up until then, Cambodia provided sanctuaries for Vietnamese communist forces. The allied operations were able to destroy communist bases along the Cambodia border and enemy stockpiles in the border region. The two-month operation achieved considerable success in clearing out base areas and setting back the enemy. Later in that year, more operations by the ARVN, acting alone this time, further disrupted the enemy's logistical activities and denied easy access to South Vietnam.

On a more personal note, I was gratified to have been able to rescue my Cambodian counterpart around that time. Upon being informed that the governor of the Ratanakiri region of Cambodia and his forces were almost encircled by communist forces, I swiftly dispatched two ARVN battalions to the border of Cambodia to escort them to Quy Nhon seaport, where Cambodian ships transported them back to safety in Sihanoukville.

The term "Vietnamization" first appeared in newspapers after Richard Nixon assumed the US presidency in 1969. However, as a matter of policy, the gradual transfer of security responsibility to the government and army of South Vietnam was already conceived under the Johnson administration when Robert McNamara was US secretary of defense. Ending the Vietnam War, either via an outright victory or a negotiated peace, had always been the ultimate goal of the United States, as it did not want to prolong the situation indefinitely. In the aftermath of the Tet Offensive, although Washington did not approve General Westmoreland's request for an additional 200,000 troops, it did increase the military aid budget to enable South Vietnam to train more combat units to replace the departing US troops.

There were three major tasks for General Abrams and Ambassador Bunker. First and foremost was the task of accelerating efforts to recruit, train, and make ARVN units comparably equipped to their American counterparts. The goal was to replace withdrawing US troops with newly trained ARVN units for day-to-day security operations. Second, all possible steps were taken to minimize US casualties. In practical terms, this was mainly accomplished by substituting the search-and-destroy strategy favored by General Westmoreland with the clear-and-hold strategy preferred by General Abrams. Third, efforts to pacify the rural areas were to be increased, with particular emphasis on destroying the enemy's infiltration infrastructure.

From the end of the Tet Offensive in 1968 until the Paris Agreement of January 1973 the Second Republic enjoyed its most prosperous years as American forces steadily withdrew and the ARVN made many institutilonal changes as it grew to more than a million members. Of special mention was the creation of the Inspector General Office (IG), for which I was the inaugural commander. The role of the inspector general was twofold. First, with inspections, we evaluated the performance of duty, the state of discipline, and the morale of our forces. Second, by investigations, we helped to eliminate inequities and corrupt practices within the military ranks. The long-range goal of the IG system was to improve the fighting ability of soldiers and to root out deficiencies by acting as the auto-critique mechanism for the armed forces. On average, the IG office conducted about 150 investigations every month. These investigations were initiated either by the normal IG inspection process, by complaints we received from members of the armed forces, or sometimes by stories in the press. About one quarter of these complaints involved some sort of corrupt practice, such as contract steering, and when the charges were substantiated, the individuals involved were usually punished and relieved of their positions. While there were unavoidable growing pains, as a whole this period saw the ARVN evolve into an efficient, professional army with proper oversight mechanisms in place.

While Vietnamization was pursued in the South, North Vietnam was also preparing for a transition of its own. Various intelligence sources at the time pointed to the North abandoning its insurgency tactics in favor of more conventional warfare using ground troops organized at the corps level, each composed of multiple infantry divisions supported by artillery, tank, air defense, and engineer regiments. To prepare for its eventual large-scale attacks, North Vietnam focused its efforts on upgrading its North–South supply lines and enlarging its rear-area bases located inside Laos and Cambodia.

The role of the Central Highlands in the Vietnam War cannot be overstated. As previously mentioned, shortly after the Tet Offensive in 1968, I was appointed Commander of II Corps and the 2nd Tactical Area, which included the Central Highlands. As the war escalated, this region was considered a strategically important area, partially because it included the Ho Chi Minh Trail, which was the supply line for North Vietnamese troops. In fact, according to many military analysts, General Vo Nguyen Giap, who was the most senior military commander in North Vietnam, often stated that control of the Central Highlands was the key to domination of the Indochina Peninsula. Whoever controls this area will gain the upper hand in any Indochina conflict. When North Vietnam launched its large-scale offensive in 1975 that led to the collapse of South Vietnam, the campaign started in Ban Me Thuot, a key city of the Central Highlands.

Geographically speaking, central Vietnam is in part characterized by the 1,100 kilometer-long Truong Son mountain range, which extends through Laos and Vietnam, and runs parallel to the eastern coastal region. To the west of the mountain range lies a series of plateaus bordering Laos, collectively known as the Central Highlands. The latter region is home to a large population of ethnic minorities divided into twelve ethnicities and twenty-four tribes, the largest ones being Bahnar, Jarai, Rhade, and Koho. Each ethnic group has its own language and customs. Most prefer to live in isolation and to shun contact with the outside world. Successive South Vietnamese governments enticed these minorities to join the fold, and the cabinet always included an indigenous person in charge of the Department of Minority Affairs, such as Secretary Paul Nur and Province Chief Yaba.

In the context of border surveillance and control of the Central Highlands, "special forces" was the general term used to denote units that were not attached to any particular military branch and that often operated outside the normal chain of command. Special forces filled their ranks with elite, adventure-minded volunteers from every military branch, all ready to undertake difficult and perilous missions at a moment's notice.

There were many special forces groups operating in Vietnam, among them the Fifth Special Force Group, the Seal Detachment, the Special Operations Wing, and the Air Commando Squadron. To this day, the very mention of these groups still conjures up images of spectacular military feats in no man's land, behind enemy lines, and sometimes right inside enemy bases.

The missions of the Allied special forces in Vietnam were to carry out interdiction, search and rescue, psychological warfare, long-range reconnaissance, and other unconventional warfare. However, it would be the successful establishment of the Civilian Irregular Defense Group (CIDG) program that came to define the contribution of the US special forces. With the advent of the CIDG, the development of paramilitary forces among the Central Highlands minority groups became the primary mission of the special forces in Vietnam. The purpose of the program was to extend government control into areas where it was lacking and to win the allegiance of the indigenous minorities lest they be swayed or forcibly recruited to become laborers or scouts for the communists. Over time, with each success, the posture of the special forces and the irregulars changed from one of securing area development centers to actively hunting and harassing communist infiltration routes and bases.

Throughout the war, the Ho Chi Minh trail served as the primary conduit for North Vietnamese troops and supplies into the South. Because it passed through Laotian and Cambodian territory, North Vietnam consistently denied its existence. Prime Minister Pham Van Dong in 1966 told journalist Stanley Karnow that allegations of North Vietnamese troops in the South were "a myth fabricated by the US imperialists to justify their war of aggression." After the war, he told Karnow that North Vietnamese combat forces had been sent down the trail by the tens of thousands.

Formally called "the Truong Son Strategic Supply Route" of the communists, the Ho Chi Minh Trail was put into operation in the middle of 1959, from starting points inside Quang Binh Province, just north of the 17th parallel. The trail was actually not a single route, but a network of crisscrossing truck routes and foot paths stretching from Vinh, the southernmost major city of North Vietnam, to Bu Gia Map, just inside the Vietnamese border with Cambodia, about 160 kilometers north of Saigon, via Mu Gia Pass and the plain of Attopeu along the eastern borders of Laos and Cambodia. In total, the trail was a web of tracks around ten thosand kilometers long, continually expanded and repaired over a fifteen-year period.

More remarkably, by 1969 the North Vietnamese Army's General Logistics Department constructed a parallel network of fuel pipelines running southwest from North Vietnam's Ha Tinh Province through Mu Gia Pass and reaching the Laotian city of Tchepone. By the end of 1973, the pipeline was extended to the outskirts of Phuoc Long, a short distance south of Bu Gia Map. To manage the flow of fuel, the pipeline was assisted by more than 110 pumping stations and numerous storage facilities.

At the height of the war, the Ho Chi Minh Trail was serviced and protected by more than 140,000 persons, with 100,000 being soldiers and the rest laborers or volunteers. Managed by a system of Binh Trams (the equivalent of a regimental logistical headquarters), the Ho Chi Minh Trail was placed under the responsibility of the 559th Group (re-designated Truong Son Command in 1973), a corps-level command reporting directly to the Military Affairs Party Committee and the General Staff. By the end of the war, the forces under its command included Anti-aircraft Division 377, Infantry Division 968, five division-level regional commands (470th, 471st, 472nd, 473rd, and 571st), and fourteen regiments of various specializations, such as signal, training, production, depot protection, and pipeline maintenance.

According to North Vietnam's published documents, about 1.4 million tons of supplies were transported along the trail, of which some 583,000 tons were delivered, with a loss of about 765,000 tons. Further breakdown shows that for every thousand tons delivered, the North Vietnamese Army suffered twenty-one deaths, fifty-seven wounded, and twenty-five trucks destroyed.

As the strategic supply line of men and materiel to the battlefields in South Vietnam, the Ho Chi Minh Trail was the target of extensive aerial bombing by the allies. From November 1968 to 1970, operation Commando Hunt dropped more than three million tons of bombs, most of which were concentrated on the route segments near the four trail checkpoints in Laos, namely Mu Gia Pass, Phu La Nhich, Ban Karai, and Ban Achoc. All the bombing proved to be of limited effectiveness, however, as the North Vietnamese Army either quickly repaired the trail or rerouted it. The air-defense systems used to protect the trail also got progressively better, to the point where the approach to the bombing run had to be made from farther away, thus reducing its efficacy.

The logistical system within the trail was also the object of various ground interdiction efforts, the largest being the Lam Son 719 campaign conducted in the southeastern portion of Laos along the road leading to Tchepone. At great cost to the ARVN, the campaign succeeded in delaying a large-scale invasion from the North by a year. After the Paris Agreement in 1973, the ARVN no longer had any means of interdiction, and the supplies flowing along the trail went unimpeded.

All these statistics should leave no doubt as to the enormous war resources provided by the Sino–Soviet bloc that were available to North Vietnam after the United States departed from the war effort. The result was a large imbalance of forces between North and South Vietnam. More eloquently and convincingly, it proves beyond any doubt that the Vietnam War was not a homegrown insurgency as described by the communist propaganda machine, but rather a long-term plan by North Vietnam to take over South Vietnam by force.

Long before "winning hearts and minds" became a cliché, it was apparent to both the United States and South Vietnam that military prowess alone would not vanquish the communist threat. In Vietnam, the goal of pacification as a strategic concept was to improve security and general living conditions in contested areas or in areas threatened by communist subversive activities. Beyond civic aspects such as improving education, medical, and social services, the pacification program also aimed at detecting and dismantling the enemy infiltration infrastructure.

Since its inception in 1956, the pacification operations pursued by the government of South Vietnam underwent successive refinements, each responding to the situation at hand, starting with Agrovilles, then Strategic Hamlets followed by the Accelerated Pacification Campaign, and ending with Rural Construction.

After a brief lull in 1964–65 during which the Strategic Hamlet program was being dismantled, pacification was again re-emphasized in 1966, with many new cadres being trained at national training centers. Pacification hit full stride in May 1967 with the formation of CORDS, which was significantly helped by the decimation of the communists during the Tet Offensive and thereafter produced substantial pacification gains throughout the country.

At the start of 1970, President Thieu implemented the "Land to the Tiller" reform, resulting in a million hectares of land being designated for distribution to some 500,000 families. The program was an instant success, as it allowed South Vietnam to quickly reestablish control over the countryside. Even the *New York Times* lauded it as "probably the most ambitious and progressive non-Communist land reform of the 20th

Century."[1] Most villages and hamlets conducted elections to choose their governing officials, a large number of which received training at national centers. Expansion and modernization of the Territorial Forces (Regional Forces and Popular Forces) continued, with these elements being made part of the regular forces, of which by then they constituted fully half.

Success during the 1968–72 period was due to the combined efforts of the new population-centric strategy and increased US support for South Vietnamese forces. By the time of the cease-fire in 1973, the southern "Viet Cong" insurgents were no longer capable of playing a major role in determining the outcome of the war. In 1975, it was not these insurgents but the regular army of North Vietnam, operating in division-size formations and supported by armor and artillery, that defeated the armed forces of South Vietnam, which had been crippled by drastic cuts in US funding and supplies. Whether we could have prevailed in a conventional war had the United States continued to provide air and logistic support is a "what if" question that cannot be answered.

With the clarity that comes with the passage of time, the lingering bitterness of feeling betrayed and abandoned harbored by many South Vietnamese should now give way to a sober look back at the historical reality. The truth is that Vietnam was a small and weak country facing an existential fight against the Sino–Soviet communist bloc. When South Vietnam's national interests overlapped with those of the United States, the lone superpower of the free world, close cooperation and assistance could be expected. However, once the United States had reached an understanding with the communist bloc, South Vietnam should have been prepared to fend for itself. Objectively speaking, after the Geneva Accords of 1954, except for the timely intervention of the United States, a free South Vietnam would not have seen the light of day. This was because, as a matter of common knowledge, much of the Vietnamese countryside was under the sway of the vast communist clandestine network. Under those conditions, all the UN observers in the world would not have been able to dispel the climate of intimidation and fear imposed by communist agents. It was thus with US assistance that the Republic of Vietnam enjoyed the subsequent twenty years as a thriving, free, and democratic country in Southeast Asia. Without the help of the United States, South Vietnam would have shared the fate of North Korea and Cuba from 1956 onwards. Judging from other communist regimes, this fate would have typically included bloody purges, deadly "re-education" camps, murderous forced labor, man-made famines, farcical show trials, outright mass murder, and genocide, such as the one perpetuated by the Khmer Rouge and re-enacted in the movie *The Killing Fields*. As it was, South Vietnam had a twenty-year respite, during which a remarkable experiment in building a democracy under wartime conditions was made, worthy of being remembered with pride.

Our cause was clear. It was a fight for freedom and human rights, against the communist ideology popularized among Vietnamese by Ho Chi Minh, who disguised himself as a nationalist in pursuit of national independence and unification. While he was able to deceive much of the world, his atrocities against his own countrymen proved that he was a worthy contemporary of Stalin and Mao. We should not forget

---

[1] For details about Land to the Tiller reforms, see, elsewhere in this volume, Tran Quang Minh, *A Decade of Public Service: Nation-building during the Interregnum and Second Republic (1964–75)*.

that Ho was a veteran communist leader who served the international communist movement being directed from Moscow with his activities in Europe and Asia for more than twenty years before his return to Vietnam. He also knew how to steer a middle course between Soviet leaders and Mao in order not to lose the support of either. In the end, Vietnam fell to communism, but no one can say that it is free from the influence of and intimidation by another superpower.

Throughout its history, Vietnam has found itself in the path of imperialism as well as the power struggles among the world's powerful nations. Today, with the geopolitics of Southeast Asia in a state of flux, there is much uncertainty about the direction of power politics in the region. The interplay of interests among the world's major powers makes the South China Sea an area of strategic importance, and Vietnam's location makes it a natural point of control for this part of the world. In the long term, a truly free and independent Vietnam depends on a strong alliance of nations that is committed to promoting and maintaining international law, security, and human rights for every country in Southeast Asia.

The outcome of a war has always been determined by more than just the military might of a superpower, or the mere determination of the people. History teaches us that in the face of human tragedy, the world has to have the courage and the will to stand up for universal values. What does the future hold for Vietnam? Will Vietnam find itself again just a pawn in the grand scheme of things? Will the conscience of mankind allow injustice to prevail? Only time will tell.

CONTRIBUTORS

EDITOR

Keith W. Taylor is professor of Sino-Vietnamese studies in the department of Asian Studies, Cornell University. He is the author of several books and articles about Vietnamese history and literature. His most recent publication is *A History of the Vietnamese* (Cambridge University Press, 2013).

CONTRIBUTORS

Bui Diem was born in Hanoi in 1923 and graduated with degrees in mathematics from the University of Hanoi in 1945. He was professor of mathematics in the Communist zone until 1950. He escaped from the Communist zone and subsequently held positions in the South Vietnamese government. He was a member of the South Vietnamese delegation to the 1954 Geneva Conference; minister at the Prime Minister Office (1965); Secretary of State for Foreign Affairs (1966); ambassador to the United States and special envoy at the Paris Peace Talks (1966–72); and ambassador at large (1973–75). He was a consultant at the Rand Corporation for the study "Why South Vietnam collapsed" (1977–79), a guest scholar at the Woodrow Wilson Center for International Scholars and at the American Enterprise Institute (1983–86), senior associate at the Indochina Institute at George Mason University (1986–92), and president and executive director of the Pacific Basin Research Institute (1993-2001). He is the author of *In the Jaws of History* (Indiana University Press, 1999), widely viewed as an important and illuminating book about the US experience in Vietnam.

Phan Cong Tam graduated from the South Vietnamese National Institute of Administration and was appointed to work at the Central Intelligence Organization (CIO) in 1962. Phan first came to the United States in 1966 to study at the University of Wisconsin/Madison, where he received his MA in political science in 1968. Upon his return to Vietnam, he resumed his work for the CIO until 1975. His last position with the agency was as director of the office of operation plans and assistant to the commissioner for special operations. After the Vietnam War ended in 1975, Phan returned to the University of Wisconsin/Madison and completed another MA in public policy and administration. He subsequently worked for the State of Wisconsin Division of Public Health for twenty-eight years until his retirement.

Nguyen Ngoc Bich was born in 1937 in Hanoi, was trained in Saigon, the United States (BA in political science, Princeton, 1958; doctoral candidate in Japanese literature, Columbia Graduate School, 1959–1965; and MA in bilingual education and historical linguistics, Georgetown University, 1985), Japan (graduate school, Kyoto University, 1962–63), besides short training courses in Austria (Vienna University), Germany

(Munich University), and Spain (Madrid University). Bich served as diplomat at the Embassy of Vietnam, 1967--71, in Washington, DC; director, National Press Center, 1972–73; department head for overseas information, Ministry of Information and Open Arms, 1973–75; and director general, Vietnam Presse, 1975. Since coming to the United States, he has taught at George Mason, Trinity, and Georgetown universities, and was appointed deputy director, then acting director, of OBEMLA (Office of Bilingual Education and Minority Languages Affairs, US Department of Education) under Secretary Lamar Alexander, 1991–93. Before his retirement in 2003, he was the first director of the Vietnamese Service at Radio Free Asia (1997–2003). Bich is the author of several books on Vietnamese literature, poetry, festivals, and art (architecture, ceramics and modern painting).

Tran Quang Minh (Dr. Gary Minh Tran) was born on July 18, 1938, in Chau Doc, South Vietnam, and was educated in the United States at Oklahoma State University College of Veterinary Medicine, under the USAID Leadership Training Program. In 1964, he was appointed assistant professor at the OSU College of Agriculture, Forestry, and Veterinary Science, and in 1967 was appointed associate professor and head of the department of veterinary science. Shortly after that he was on loan to South Vietnam's Ministry of Agriculture to implement the Accelerated Protein Production Program as director of the Tan Son Nhut Livestock Experiment Station. In 1969, he was appointed director of cabinet, the third-highest ranking official in the newly renamed Ministry of Land Reform and Agricultural Development, to assist the Land To The Tiller Land Reform Program. In 1972, he was appointed director general of agriculture to draft the Five-Year Agricultural Development Plan. He received a cabinet appointment as vice minister of agriculture in October 1973, and later that year he was appointed administrator general of the newly created National Food Administration, a job that he held until April 30, 1975.

Nguyen Duc Cuong served as vice minister for trade (1970–73) and minister of trade and industry (1973–74) in the Government of the Republic of Vietnam. He graduated Summa Cum Laude from the University of New Hampshire with a BSEE (electrical engineering) and went on to graduate studies at the Massachusetts Institute of Technology, where he earned a MSEE and the degree of electrical engineer. He attended New York University Stern School of Business, where he earned an MBA in international finance. He is currently an adjunct faculty member of Northwestern Polytechnic University, Fremont, California, where he teaches finance.

Phan Quang Tue retired on December 31, 2012, as judge in the San Francisco Immigration Court, where he served since his appointment in March 1995 by US Attorney General Janet Reno. Before that he was a trial attorney with the Immigration and Naturalization Service in San Francisco from 1988 to 1993, and he served two years as an administrative law judge, 1993 to 1995, with the California Unemployment Insurance Appeals Board in Sacramento, California. Before coming to the United States, he graduated from the French school Jean Jacques Rousseau, in Saigon, and the Saigon University School of Law, in 1965. After the Tet offensive, in 1968, he was drafted, commissioned, and assigned to the military court. He was deputy chief of staff of the Office of the Chief Justice of the Supreme Court in Saigon from 1970 to 1975. He and his wife and two small children entered the United States in April 1975 as refugees. He began his new life working as a teacher, dishwasher, shoe repairer, and machine operator in the Washington, DC, metropolitan area. He taught French at Georgetown Preparatory High School in Rockville, Maryland, while maintaining a part-time job as a dishwasher. He moved his family to Des Moines, Iowa, in 1979, where he returned to law school and graduated in 1985 from Drake University School of Law. He was administrative law judge at the Iowa Department of Job Service from 1985 to 1987 and assistant attorney general with the Iowa Department of Justice from 1987 to 1988. He moved his family to California in 1988. He has been a resident of Danville, California, since 1995 and maintains an active role in the Vietnamese community in the Bay area. He and his wife have seven grandchildren. Since his retirement, Judge Phan Quang Tue taught a course of immigration law at the Lincoln Law School, San Jose, California.

Tran Van Son (pen name, Tran Binh Nam) was born on July 17, 1933, in Hue, the former capital of the Nguyen Dynasty. He attended Quoc Hoc High School in Hue before he joined the Navy of the Republic of Vietnam in 1955. He was sent to the French Naval Academy to study naval engineering and graduated in 1957, after which he returned to Vietnam and was assigned to the Naval Training Center in Nha Trang as a professor. He holds a BS in mathematics from the University of Saigon. He served in the navy (mostly in Nha Trang) for sixteen years, until 1971, when he ran for and was elected to a four-year term representing the city of Nha Trang in the House of Representatives of the National Assembly. There he was a member of the Socio-Socialist Bloc of opposition (Khoi Dan Toc-Xa Hoi), led by lawyer Tran Van Tuyên. At times, he served as deputy leader of the opposition. When South Vietnam collapsed, he was sent to a concentration camp in Nha Trang, from which he escaped in 1977 by boat and was rescued by a Japanese ship on the high seas. He settled in Southern California in 1978 and enrolled in a government job-training program in accounting. He worked as an accountant for the Fair Housing Congress, a non-profit organization, for fifteen years and retired at the age of sixty-two. In 1978, he cofounded the Organization for the Restoration of Vietnam and served as its chairman for nine years. In 1987 he started writing political essays for various Vietnamese language newspapers overseas, and has published four volumes (1994, 1996, 1999, and 2002). All of his other articles (480 so far) have been posted on the Internet (http://www.tranbinhnam.com/binhluan/index.html). He decided to stop writing political essays when he reached his eightieth birthday, on July 17, 2013. His wife died in 2007. He has three daughters and two sons, all university graduates, married, and living in Southern California. He is currently living in Norwalk, California.

Ma Xai was born in Long Xuyen, South Vietnam. He earned his medical degree in 1964 and served as surgeon and ophthalmologist at Duy Tan General Hospital in Danang. He joined the Tan Dai Viet Party in 1965 and its associated organization, the National Progressive Movement (NPM), in 1968. (The primary objective of the party was to build a democratic rule of law and to cooperate with the government against the Hanoi communists. The NPM served as opposition to President Nguyen Van Thieu.) He was twice elected to the House of Representatives in the National Assembly and served two consecutive terms, 1967–71 and 1971–75. Dr. Ma was imprisoned following the collapse of the Republic of Vietnam. In 1981, he participated in the Alliance for Democracy in Vietnam. He later escaped by sea from Vietnam and, in 1982, became active in the Overseas Tan Dai Viet Party led by Nguyen Ngoc Huy. In 1983, he started to practice medicine in Florida. He was subsequently twice elected president of the Tan Dai Viet Party for two consecutive terms, 2009–13 and 2013–17.

Ho van Ky-Thoai graduated from the US Naval Postgraduate School, in Monterey, California, in 1954. He served the Vietnamese Navy from 1954 to 1975 in various duties—as ship's captain, patrol squadron commander, chief of naval personnel, commander of the Joint Sea Commando Forces operating behind enemy (North Vietnam) lines, commander of Naval Task Group 231.1, and commander of Naval Coastal Zone 1. He rose to the rank of rear admiral. He earned two US Bronze Star Medals with Combat V from the US Secretary of the Navy and one US Navy Commendation Medal for his commando unit. From 1976 to 2006, after resettling in the United States, he served in executive leadership roles in various educational nonprofit organizations, such as the Council for Advancement and Support of Education and the National Association of Independent Schools. He retired in 2006 to write the book *Can Truong tong Chien Bai* (Bravery in Defeat) published privately in 2007. In January 1974, while serving as commander of the First Naval Coastal Zone (the northernmost coastal part of South Vietnam) and of Task Group 231.1, he ordered the naval forces under his command to confront the Chinese naval forces that had attacked with intent to take over the South Vietnamese Paracel Islands. The result, described herein, was a deadly naval battle resulting in heavy casualties on both sides.

Lan Lu began his military career after graduating from the Vietnamese Military Academy in Dalat in 1951. Beginning as a company commander with the Vo Tanh regiment in 1951, he held a variety of command and staff positions, rising to the rank of general and becoming chief of staff of the Second Field Division in 1956. He then served as deputy chief of staff for operations and training for the RVNAF Joint General Staff (JGS) and as J-3 (operational command) for the JGS. He has commanded the Army of the Republic of Vietnam (ARVN) 25th, 23rd, and 10th divisions. He has also been commandant of the Command and General Staff College, chief of the Central Training Command, commandant of the National Defense College, and, before becoming inspector general in 1970, was the commanding general of II Corps and the 2nd Military Region. In addition to his training at the Vietnamese Military Academy, the general is a graduate of the Vietnamese Command and General Staff Course and the US Army's Command and General Staff College, at Fort Leavenworth, Kansas.